Shades of L.A.

Pictures from Ethnic Family Albums

Carolyn Kozo Cole and Kathy Kobayashi

The New Press, New York

In conjunction with the Photo Friends of the Los Angeles Public Library

To our husbands, our children, and our parents:

Raymond Cole, Chris and Justine Kozo, and June and Wilbur Jennings

Hal Barron, Maya Barron, and to the memories

of Ty and Martha Kobayashi

Library of Congress
Cataloging-in-Publication Data

Shades of L.A.: pictures from ethnic family albums / Carolyn Kozo Cole and Kathy Kobayashi.
p. cm
Largely photographs from the Los Angeles Public Library.
ISBN 1-56584-313-4 (pbK.)
1. Ethnology—California—Los Angeles—Pictorial works. 2. Los Angeles (Calif.)—Social life and customs—Pictorial works. 3. Family—California—Los Angeles—Pictorial works. 4. Photograph collections—California—Los Angeles.
I. Cole, Carolyn Kozo. II. Kobayashi, Kathy. III. Los Angeles Public Library.
F869. L89A1 1996 306.85' 0979494—dc20
96-696 CIP

Published in the United States by
The New Press, New York
Distributed by
W. W. Norton & Company, Inc., New York

All of the photographs in this book are part of the Shades of L.A. Archive and are reproduced with the permission of the Los Angeles Public Library.

A traveling exhibition entitled *Shades of L.A.* has been organized by the History Department of the Los Angeles Public Library. For more information on the exhibition, contact Carolyn Kozo Cole, History Department, Los Angeles Public Library, 630 West Fifth Street, Los Angeles, California 90071, tel. 213-228-7403.

Established in 1990 as a major alternative to the large, commercial publishing houses, The New Press is a full-scale nonprofit American book publisher outside of the university presses. The Press is operated editorially in the public interest, rather than for private gain; it is committed to publishing in innovative ways works of educational, cultural, and community value that, despite their intellectual merits, might not normally be commercially viable. The New Press's editorial offices are located at the City University of New York.

Interior book design by
Anthony McCall Associates, New York

Production management by Kim Waymer

Printed in the United States of America

9 8 7 6 5 4 3 2 1

Contents

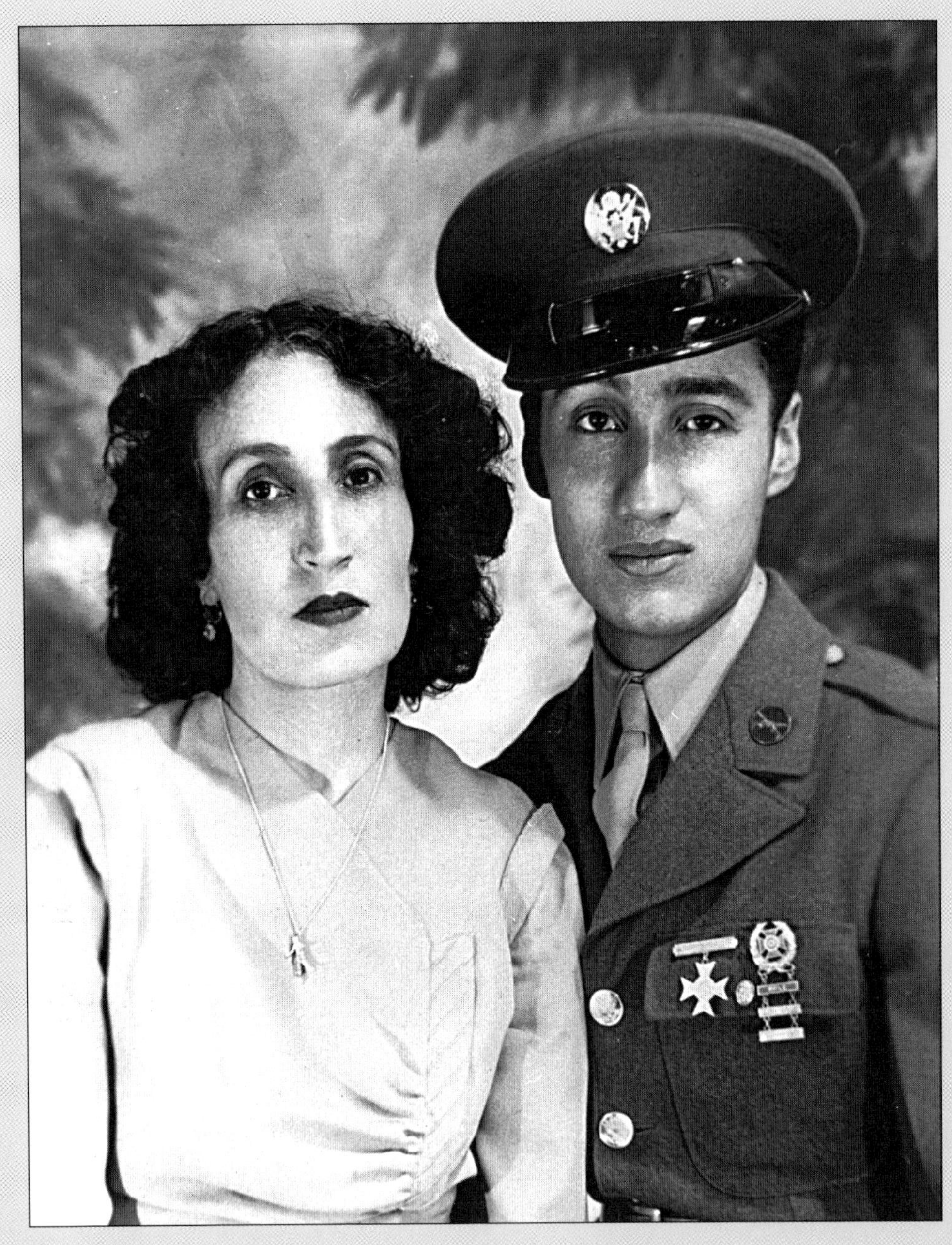

Maria de Jesus Banuelos and her son Adam,

photographed at a studio on North Broadway in Los Angeles, 1943.
Adam was on leave after U.S. Army boot camp,
before joining Allied forces in Africa.
(Mexican American)

Acknowledgments

This book grew out of the first phase of the project, "Shades of L.A.: A Search for Visual Ethnic History," which was made possible by the enthusiastic support of the Board of the Photo Friends of the Los Angeles Public Library. Our gratitude goes to: Carolee Campbell, Roland Charles, Robert Dalton, Michael Dawson, Mark Evans, Susan LaTempa, Gloria Lothrop, Everett McDonough, Sylvia Ruiz, Natalie Shivers, Darick Simpson, Jon Weedman, Bob Weinstein, Jon Wilkman, and David Yochum.

The substantial financial support required by the project came from Security Pacific Corporation, a community-minded bank, through executive vice president Ev McDonough, and from Bob Danziger, president of Sunlaw Co-Generation Partners I, an energy firm dedicated to a clean environment.

We owe special thanks to Amy Kitchener, the project coordinator, and to Coleman Grimmett and Bob Douglas, the project photographers; their hard work and good humor added immeasurably to the success of the project.

Our appreciation also goes to the administration and staff of the Los Angeles Public Library, particularly to: Susan Goldberg Kent, Elizabeth Martinez, Elizabeth Gay Teoman, Jane Nowak, Romaine Ahlstrom, Carol Baldwin, Patricia Clark, Cheryl Funada, Victor Gonzalez, Violet Kuroki, Roselynn Lee, Roella Louie, Sylva Manoogian, Tom Owen, Peter Persic, and Jae Min Roh.

Among the hundreds of volunteers and advisors to whom we are indebted, we would especially like to thank Thomas Breckner, Helen Brown, Roxanne Burgess, Michael Chan, Suellen Cheng, Ron Corbin, Devie and Hortensia Corral, Susan Ahn Cuddy, John Echeveste, Shanda Fernandez, Doug Flamming, Joe Flowers, Elmo Gambarana, Tomas Gaspar, Lynell George, Susan Gordon, Yolanda Guerra, Doris Hausmann, Herminia Herrera, Stephen Hollister, George and Iku Kiriyama, Michelle Lesse, Pyong-Yong Min, Eric Monkkonen, George Moreira, Renee Nahum, Peter Renich, George Sanchez, Andi Sica, Dennis Tafoya, Marilyn White, Verna Williams, and Sue Yee.

Thanks also to our project interns from area universities: Hsiang-Ling Chao, Maria Elena Fernandez, Sheila Gardette, Kay Goodloe, Darcie Iki, Laura Orozco, Hea-Won Paick, Heather Parker, Carlos Perez, Leticia Salcedo, Dean Scammahorn, Sepa Sete, Adrianne Shropshire, and Irma Valdivia.

And this project would not have been possible without the donors who came and shared their family albums. These people—including those whose images could not be reproduced in this short book—deserve gratitude not only from us, but from future generations as well: Emma Adams, Glenda Ahhaitty, Henry Ahn, Mary Alatorre, Councilman Richard and Angelina Alatorre, Mary Alvidrez, Berta Apodaca, Joe Arriola, Carol Baldwin, Marisol Bielma, Wajeha Bilal, Armida Tellez Bolton, Edward Brantley, Helen Brown, Josephine Burch, Velia Bustillos, Desiree Camarillo, Earline Campbell, Bartolome Cantor, Roscoe Castle, Beverly Cephus, Marguerite R. Chapman, Theresa Chavez, Robbie Chester, Emma Cho, William Chun-Hoon, William and Elma Chunn, Verlinda Clark, Renee Cochee, Elnora Cole, Joyce Corley, Hortensia Corral, Sandra Cox, Cordellia Crawford, Susan Ahn Cuddy, Ruth Davis, Linda De La Rosa, Rose Frances Andrade Dirks, Marilyn Dixon, Veronica Dizon, Julie Dominguez, Bob Douglas, Roger Egans, Jr., Miguel Elliot, Julio Elquezabal, Rodolfo Estrada, Cecil Fergerson, Olivia Fernandez, Shanda Fernandez, Bertha Figueroa, Liz Foisia, Kolokea Foisia, Jim Fong, Mitchell Foon, Robert Franklin, Ramona Frias, Masanori and Sakae Fujimoto, June Fujimoto, Cheryl Funada, West Gale, Petra Galindo, Irene Galvan, Josephine Garcia, Dorothy Giu, Luis Gomez, Yolanda Guerra, Andrew Guerrero, Cynthia Gutierrez, Paul Guzman, "Sweet Alice" Harris, Rosalind Harris, Arnett Hartsfield, Aldra Henry-Allison, Bill Herr, Kenjii Hirano, Darrell Hobson, Helen Hong, Arlene Inez, the International Institute of Los Angeles, Alice Ito, Manuel Jacquez, Jr., Carlo Jofily, Bettye Jones, Leilani Jones, Odus Jones, Edith Jung, Diane Kanner, Tessa Kelso, Emma Kim, Robert Kim, Yin Kim, George and Iku Kiriyama, Mildred Knox, Betty Krangle, Carrie Kwon, Ric La Paz, Audrey Lee, Holly Lee, Lisa Lee, Roselynn Lee, William Lempia, Stewart Lim, Katheryne Littleton-Bradley, Jess Lopez, Juanita Gamboa Lopez, Cheryl Love-Queen, Sam S. Low, Angelica Lozano, Tisha Lozano, Luis Lucero, June Lynch, Barbara McCoy, Charlene McKinney, Dorothy McLaughlin, Ben Manibog, Victor Martinez, Sita Maulupe, Ponciano Maya, Felix Medina, Pyong-Yong

Min, Rosemary Miranda, Maria J. Mojica, Jackie Momoli, Mary Lou Montagna, Marilyn Montenegro, Rosario Morales, Royal Morales, George Moreira, Dorothy Morgan, Eugene Moy, Ryo Munekata, Katherine Myers, Momo Nagano, Harrelson Notah, Father Paul Ojibway, Celia Ornelas, Jorge Orozco, Laura Orozco, Delia Ortega, Josephine Pancake, Jane Pang, Ildong C. Park, Sylvia Park, Woonha and Louise Park, Michael Parkinson, Richard Perea, Mary Ybarra Petterz, Los Pobladores, Rosalie Portillo, Geraldine Potter, Eric-John Priestley, Vincent Raggio, Mary Reinie, Lillie Reyes, Loma Reynolds, Esther Rivera, Jane Robbins, Diane Roberson, Alvaro Rodriguez, Gerald Rodriguez, James Rojas, Horace Rucker, Esther Salas, Gloria Salitrero, Dorothy Clark Sams, Martin Sanchez, Ofelia Deleon Sanchez, Carmen Sandoval, Socorro Santa Ana-Contreras, Jo-Ann Semon, Camilo Serrano, the Sherman Indian Museum, Yoshiro Shimoda, Mary Lee Shon, Amanda Smith, Ann Cunningham Smith, Martha Smith, Mary Smith, Renia Smith, Edward and Helen J. Soto, Viola Soto, Jennifer Sotomayor, Camille Steverson, Joseph and Trudy Tafoya, Randi Tahara, Edna Taylor, Jane Taylor, Robert Taylor, Jr., Raymond and Frank Telles, Edith Tom, Edward Toney, Sophie Toriumi, Armida Torres, George Toya, Mabel Troy, Irma Valdivia, Rosemarie Valencia, Laverne Vaughn, Lisa Gallegos Vazquez, Mars S. Ventura, Roberto F. Villagomez, the Wallace family, Burt Wallrich, Karina Walters, Angela Weil, Delroi Whitaker, Marilyn White, Barbara Williams, Grace Williams, Verna Williams, Earl Witscher, Magdalena Wodtke, Ada Chan Wong, Elsie Lee Wong, Lillian Wong, Cecilia Woo, Clothilde Woodard, Helen Lyons Wright, Roosevelt V. Wyatt, Sue Yee, and Jeannette Young.

Additional thanks to those who have helped to shape this book: to Marc Pouliot, Lane Barden, and Rob Marshall; to Dawn Davis, Jerome Chou, Grace Farrell, Sam Helfrich, Jim Levendos, and Hall Smyth at The New Press; and to Anthony McCall and Laura Howell at Anthony McCall Associates. Our appreciation also to Sojin Kim and Judith Hopkins, who are coordinating the continued efforts of the "Shades" project to reach more of L.A.'s communities.

Finally, we are grateful to our families. We thank our husbands, Raymond Cole and Hal Barron, for their editorial assistance, moral support, sense of humor, love, and understanding. And we thank all the people in our own family albums, whose photos have helped to give us a sense of who we are.

Introduction. About the Project

Part One by Carolyn Kozo Cole

In 1990, twenty-five years after the fiery uprising in Watts, researchers from the Southern California Library for Social Science and Research came to the Los Angeles Public Library looking for images of Watts to use in a commemorative exhibit. They weren't looking for images of run-down neighborhoods, burning buildings, or crowds charging police brigades: they wanted to see the neighborhood before 1965, when it was a racially diverse, but mostly African American, neighborhood of neat streets, small, attractive homes, and thriving commerce. That same year, I was put in charge of the Library's collection of 2.2 million photographs, and the researchers and I started to search for images.

Having previously curated six exhibits from the Library's collection, I knew how incredible it was; I also knew it was lacking in several areas. The only photograph in the Watts folder was of the Pacific Electric railway station. Not only were there no photographs of Watts in the files, but Boyle Heights, Jefferson Park, Central Avenue, Maravilla, and dozens of other smaller but established ethnic neighborhoods were also undocumented. Each of these Los Angeles neighborhoods has its own rich and vibrant history, yet images illustrating them were not available in any public archive. Los Angeles has the third largest central library in the nation and it was time to expand the photo collection to reflect the multicultural history of the city.

Over the next few months I spent a great amount of time thinking about where we would find photographs of these ethnic communities to complement the Library's collection. My thoughts led me to my own childhood in Virginia, where I would spend long summer hours in my grandfather's portrait studio, watching his assistant develop prints of family portraits and snapshots; it occurred to me that the city's missing history might be found in family albums.

During my first year of managing the photograph collection, I founded a nonprofit support group of friends to help expand and promote it. They enthusiastically responded to my call for help with a family album project. Together we roughed out an idea for the project and board member Ev McDonough presented it to Security Pacific National Bank, where he was executive vice president. Within six weeks we had funding for a pilot project in the African American community. It was called "Shades of L.A.: A Search for Visual Ethnic History."

In the following five months Project Coordinator Amy Kitchener and Kathy Kobayashi, a historian, helped us assemble a committee of community leaders, educators, and photographers to tackle the problem of locating black families from these early Los Angeles neighborhoods. At one time they had been confined to living within one district, but changes in laws and growing acceptance of integration allowed blacks in the 1960s and '70s to move to other areas of Los Angeles. In order to ask them to share their family albums with the Library, we first had to find them. Community leaders suggested we contact them through churches, community centers, social organizations, and ethnic newspapers.

We borrowed mailing lists, sent out thousands of flyers, met with neighborhood activists, followed up on their referrals, and also enticed college professors and students enrolled in ethnic studies programs to help out with their expertise and talent. Our next step was to host a series of "Photo Days." We would set up copystands at sites familiar to the African American community, and teams comprising volunteers, college interns, and library staff would sit with donors and leaf through their albums, looking, listening, and finally selecting the photos we would copy for the Library.

The biggest challenge was to persuade people to bring their personal and prized possessions to a public place and share them with strangers. Someone would have a great photograph taken of himself on a segregated beach, which would help document racial discrimination, but he might not want to be seen publicly as a teenager mugging for the camera. Whether it was the sight of an ill-fitting bathing suit or the recollection of embarrassing clashes with white bathers over crossed boundaries, our donors sometimes hesitated when we placed a "selected" post-it under their photographs. We would explain how their personal images would ignite memories for some, offer new information to others, and serve as a historical record for many.

On October 19, 1991, we kicked off our first Photo Day in the Vernon Branch Library at 42nd and Central Avenue, at the heart of what was a swinging night club district known as the "Stem." Today, the area is characterized by vacant lots, abandoned buildings, and a few modest store fronts.

When our first donor, Mr. Toney, walked in, he was nearly swarmed with pent-up enthusiasm. To our delight, the first images he pulled out of his grocery sack were of jazz clubs once located on Central Avenue. They were slipped into fancy deco-designed paper enclosures that identified the clubs with titles such as "The Last Word—East Side's Smartest Sepia Night Club." By the end of the day our two photogaphers and their 6x7 medium-format cameras had copied over 250 photographs—images that evoked sometimes funny, but always heartfelt, stories of black life in early Los Angeles.

A *Los Angeles Times* article reporting on that first Photo Day caught the attention of Robert Danziger, President and CEO of Sunlaw Co-generation Partners I, an energy firm located in nearby Vernon. Bob called the library and asked if his company could help with the project since he was already funding projects at Vernon's elementary school and video histories of local "old-timers." With his generous support we expanded the project to include the Mexican American, Korean American, Japanese American, Chinese American, Filipino American, Pacific Islander, and American Indian communities. With each Photo Day, hundreds of rare and wonderful images were added to the Library's archive.

Community response to the project was overwhelming. The phone in our office rang continually as self-appointed family historians answered the call to action. "You haven't seen anything yet!" they said, and brought in boxes and more boxes of photographs. Over 300 volunteers participated in the two-year project. We were also helped by the enormous amount of publicity resulting from the extensive local, national, and international media coverage. With each of the eight ethnic communities, it was always a thrill to open the family albums and listen to the stories begin.

About one year into our collection process, in the spring of 1992, some of the neighborhoods we had come to know and appreciate were the sites, once again, of devastating riots that tore Los Angeles apart. While the media flashed pictures of buildings going up in smoke and stores being looted, few spoke of another permanent loss—the thousands of irreplaceable photos which were incinerated in the fires. The loss reminded us of how fragile our histories are and added a sense of urgency to our project.

By mid-1993 we had copied over 5,000 photographs and had initiated an oral history program with a selected group of families. We curated traveling exhibits of the photos as a thank-you to the communities, and sent them back to the eighteen sites where we held the Photo Day sessions. Finally, on October 3, 1993, as part of the celebration for the grand reopening of the expanded and restored Los Angeles Public Library's Central Library, we exhibited 252 photographs, each one proudly representative of a participating family.

But there were still ways to expand and improve the project. We wanted to have the photos available to the public, not only by appointment in the History Department, but also at computer terminals throughout the Central Library and at the sixty-four branches throughout the city. Given our budget, our goals seemed unattainable, but IBM joined the Library in a partnership that propelled us to the forefront of technology in photo cataloging and imaging. It has been gratifying to see these wonderful images move from the limited scope of a family album to optical platters where they will be safe and available for generations to come. The project has inspired not only other libraries, but also historical societies, schools, museums, and even corporations to copy photographs from personal collections to construct a historical record. San Diego has a new archive that documents an early Italian community, and the Kern County (California) Library copied photographs of early Okie migrant workers and later Latino workers. These groups are also finding that it's not just copying the photographs that's valuable: it's the sharing of family stories that makes the project so compelling.

This book brings photos to yet another audience. It comprises only a fragment of the photographs we copied. Researchers have been eager to study them but then have expressed disappointment when more recent immigrant groups weren't available. We're remedying that with a second phase of "Shades," including families from the Middle East, Southeast Asia, and Central and South America. We also plan to include smaller and older communities, such as Jewish, Greek, and Italian Americans, who are proud of their heritage and history in Los Angeles, and are eager to be represented in the project. And we'll include Anglo families as well. The current Library photo collection tends to only represent Anglo families of prominence and wealth, but the "Shades of L.A." project can provide a broader view from a wider range of residents. Perhaps, given the history of Los Angeles, indeed the history of this country, the project will never be completed, but will continue to expand and to embrace new waves of immigrants.

Introduction. About the Book

Part Two by Kathy Kobayashi

No matter how many times I look at these photographs, I find new ways of enjoying them. When I watch other people look at them, I am struck by their enthusiasm and the wide range of their responses. Sometimes they are fascinated by the images that are most different from their own experiences, seeing things they have never seen before. The photos of the segregated beaches, for example, with the "prohibited" sign marking them off, are new to many people (pages 92 and 99). Other times there is a spark of recognition — "That could have been me." I like the one of the little boy playing with the garden hose in his driveway, the family car looming behind him (page 39), which reminds me of the simple pleasures of childhood. Each photo is layered with meaning, and people see different layers, depending on their assumptions, interests, memories, and even their moods. At times the photographs are familiar and even universal, yet they are also surprising, and sometimes even mysterious.

It is hard to predict how you will respond to the photos or what uses you will find for them. Historians may find images that perfectly illustrate issues they have been working on for years. In his prize-winning history, *Becoming Mexican American: Ethnicity, Culture and Identity in Chicano Los Angeles, 1900-1945*, George Sanchez used photos from the "Shades of L.A." archives, some of which appear in this book. Filmmakers and set designers may use the photos to inform their re-creations of everyday life and fashions from the past: The makers of *Devil in a Blue Dress*, the film of Walter Moseley's novel, used "Shades of L.A." photos for ideas about what black Los Angeles looked like in the 1940s. Some people may be drawn to a particular face; others may start out looking for photos representative of their own ethnic group, only to find themselves identifying more strongly with an image from a different group. And many of us feel like we're peeking in on someone else's family album — which we are — interested in other people's lives and inevitably comparing them to our own.

The photos are arranged in the book following themes that are common to family albums, rather than chronologically or by ethnic group. This highlights both the commonalities that connect the various families in the photographs and the differences that distinguish them. It begins with formal family portraits and more casual shots of families at home. As with many albums, children and teenagers receive special attention. We also see people at work, in their community organizations, and in their churches. Then we watch as people celebrate holidays and enjoy their leisure, and finally we share in their rites of passage: births and birthdays, marriage, and death. The rich photographs are accompanied by short captions that are based on the recollections of the people who own the originals and who often appear in them.

Besides these common themes, the photos also reflect the specific histories of particular ethnic groups, and the historical timeline chart on pages 116 to 119 allows you to situate the photos within those histories. The timeline, for example, shows how early Chinese immigration was cut off by exclusion and followed by a wave of Japanese immigration, which was then cut off by exclusion and followed by a wave of Filipino immigration. This history is reflected in the photos, which include the Congregational Chinese Branch Church in 1908 (page 71), one of the earliest Asian American photos in this book; a well-established Japanese American family in the 1920s (page 77); and the Filipino Recreational Hall in the early 1940s (page 93).

As you look at these photos, a few points may help guide you in your exploration. First, the photos show people who have often been visually overlooked in the past; African Americans, urban American Indians, immigrants from Mexico, China, Japan, Korea, the Philippines, and the Pacific Islands, and their children and grandchildren have been largely missing from photographs in the public record. The photos also reflect the history of Los Angeles and Southern California, a region many people don't think has much of a history, from the turn of the century until the 1960s. Some images show where people came from before settling in Southern California and where they travelled to after they lived here, but the focus is on the ethnic history of the Los Angeles area, a place where diversity has characterized the past and the present, and will continue to shape the future.

The photographs are all the more interesting because the ethnic history presented in this book isn't an "official" history, as constructed by a city historian or an ethnographer. Rather, it is an intimate look at peoples' lives, viewed from the *inside*. The photographs offer personal views of families and communities from the albums and cardboard boxes of people who have saved and treasured them over generations. They show family celebrations, community events, and everyday life. The casual photo on page 88 shows a group of African American men making ice cream for a birthday party in Los Angeles in the 1940s. Another picture shows three happy sisters, all dressed up in matching outfits, sitting in front of their family's first television set (page 25). This may seem all too ordinary, until we remember that most of the images we see today, especially images of ethnic people, are taken by outsiders for their own purposes. These outsiders—photojournalists, artists, TV and film crews, professional photographers—may portray people as downtrodden, criminal, or exotic, or they may create wonderful and sympathetic images, but those images are still externally created.

Furthermore, the photos in this book are not simply a random collection of personal views. One of the most important aspects of "Shades of L.A." is that it shows how people have defined their own history. As they decided to take and preserve these photos, they were interpreting their history, and not simply being the subjects of it. They express, for example, the pride and dignity of their work—whether they are women cannery workers (page 57) or small business owners (pages 49 and 55). They honor the memories of their parents and grandparents, and keep them connected to future generations, by saving photographs of their funerals (page 106 and others) and by visiting their cemeteries (page 107).

That history, of course, cannot be a complete one. An important caveat: these photos do not represent the whole economic spectrum. They come not from the poorest, but from people who had access to cameras or photographers, and they tend to show people in their better moments. There are, for example, many more photos from comfortable, middle-class African Americans than from the poor, an unavoidable bias which nonetheless is a useful corrective to the fact that the large and vibrant African American middle class in Los Angeles has often been overlooked. Still, these images do represent particular truths. They capture moments from people's lives that they want to remember and to pass down to their children—not what others have decided was important.

This book validates that sense of history. The people who have shared these photos—the keepers of history in their own families—were often tentative at first, wondering whether the images they had long treasured would be of interest to people other than themselves and their own families. Others came with a deeper, long-standing conviction that what they had was a tremendously important resource, and were excited that someone had finally asked them to share it with the larger public. As we experience the photos from all these people, we support them in their history making. We learn from them, and we cannot help but think about our own family photos and what they can tell us about our communities and ourselves.

In addition, the photos have special visual qualities. Some of the photographs in this book are beautiful by any standard, with excellent composition and lighting. Estela Gomez standing on the beach in 1963, for example, or the two Japanese American children in Halloween masks in 1925 are striking images in any context (pages 47 and 75). In general, however, this book requires a different approach than most art photography, documentary photography, or photojournalism books. Many of the photos are snapshots, with little consciousness of technique or artistry, and even photos taken by professional photographers seem to primarily reflect the family's vision of itself, rather than the vision of the photographer. Most of the time we do not even know who took the picture.

Still, the photos are striking. Some have an engaging freshness—teenage boys in their convertible, or Korean Americans enjoying a backyard party (pages 42 and 81). Others are wonderful for the way people have made standard—even iconic—poses all their own. The portrait of Henrietta Arciniega and her six sisters, on her wedding day in 1931, is so compelling that even people who do not know the family have ordered copies to hang in their own homes; in the way it evokes the beauty of weddings and of family ties, it touches people as personally as their own family photos, perhaps even more. Sometimes we sense an exceptional photographer behind the lens; other times the beauty seems almost accidental. And undoubtedly, the photos will take on different meanings—will look different—as they are seen by new eyes and placed in new contexts. As the same image moves from a family album to a historical text or a gallery wall, it will be transformed.

Finally, the photos are a small sample of a much larger collection, and they serve as a model for future collections in other communities. This book includes only 119 of the more than 5000 photos in the "Shades of L.A." collection at the Los Angeles Public Library. The collection, in turn, only scratches the surface of what is out there in other family albums and cardboard boxes. Our hope is that the people who see this book will look at their own family albums, and perhaps those of their neighbors, with fresh eyes and deeper appreciation.

This book, then, is only a beginning.

Shades of L.A.

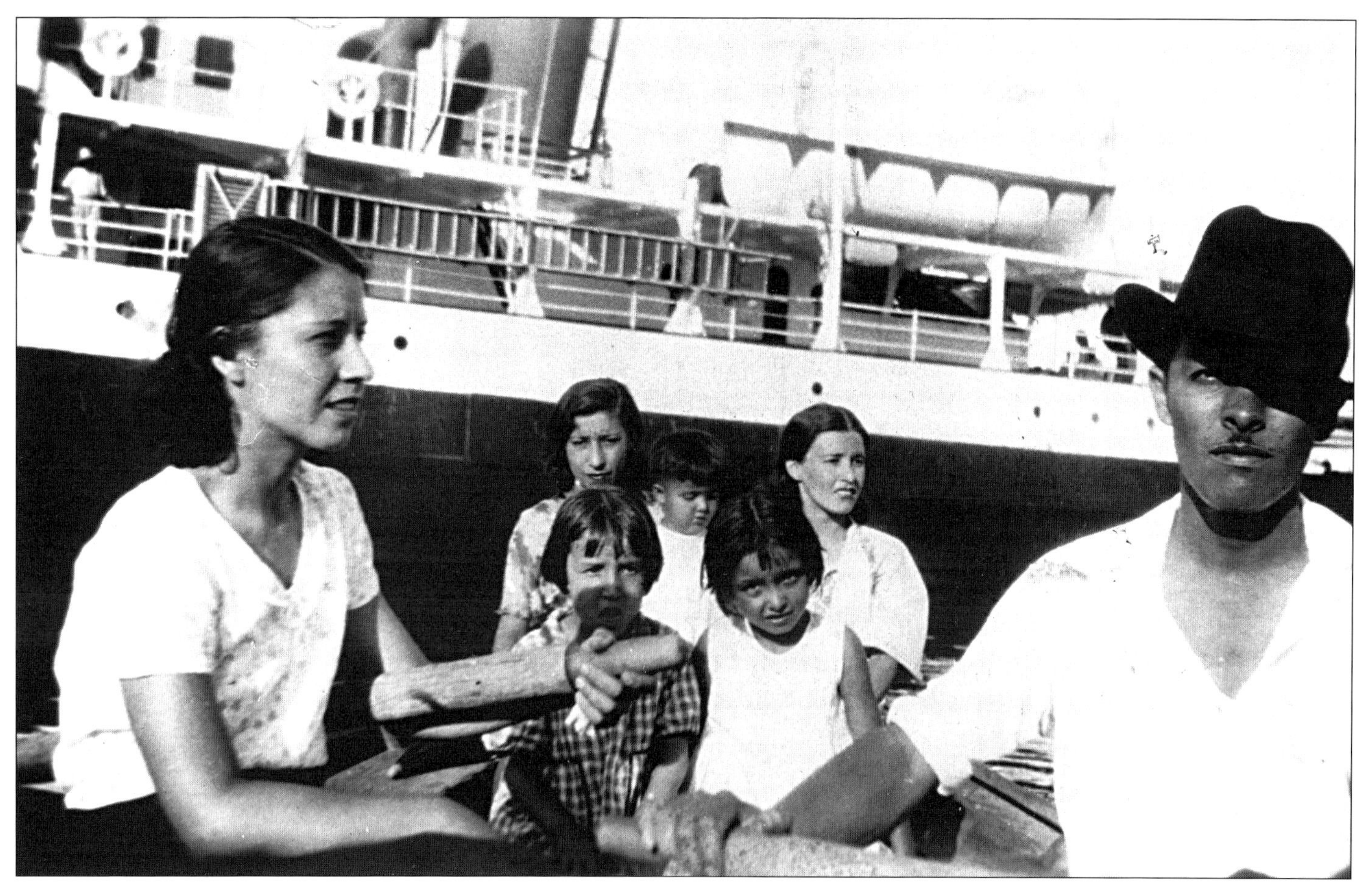

Maria Emery Garcia *(left)*, her daughter Gloria *(front right)*, and her brother Jorge Emery *(far right)*

returning from Baja California to San Pedro in 1935.
(Mexican American)

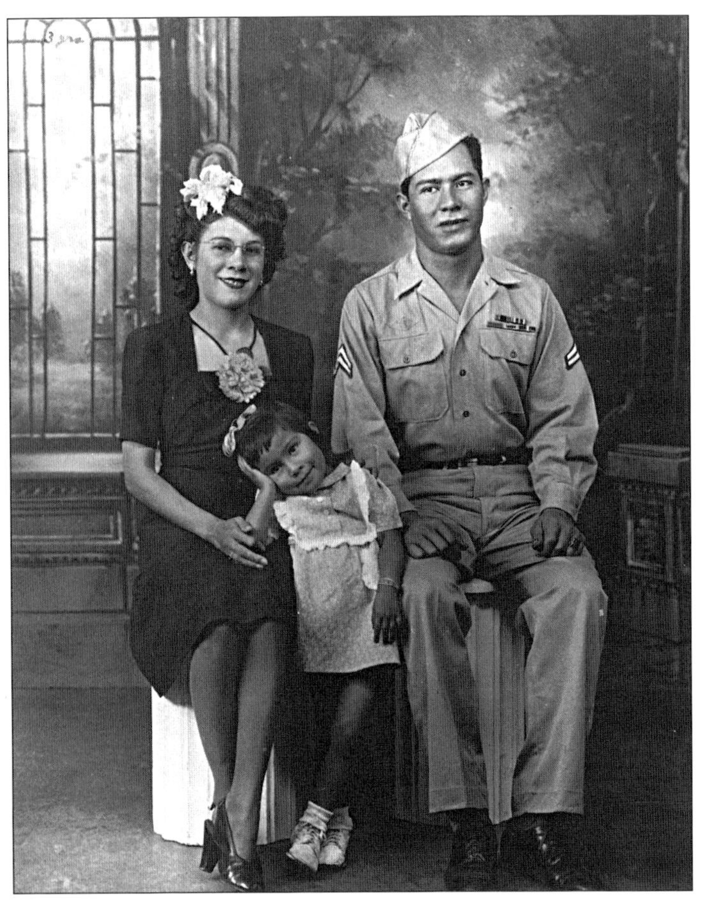

Joe Nabor and Sarah Holquin Nabor with their daughter Jo-Ann in 1945.

Joe, a Yaqui Indian, and his wife, a Hopi-Navajo, met and married in New Mexico. Sarah moved to Los Angeles during World War II, and Joe joined her after his honorable discharge from the 15th Cavalry of the U.S. Army.

(American Indian)

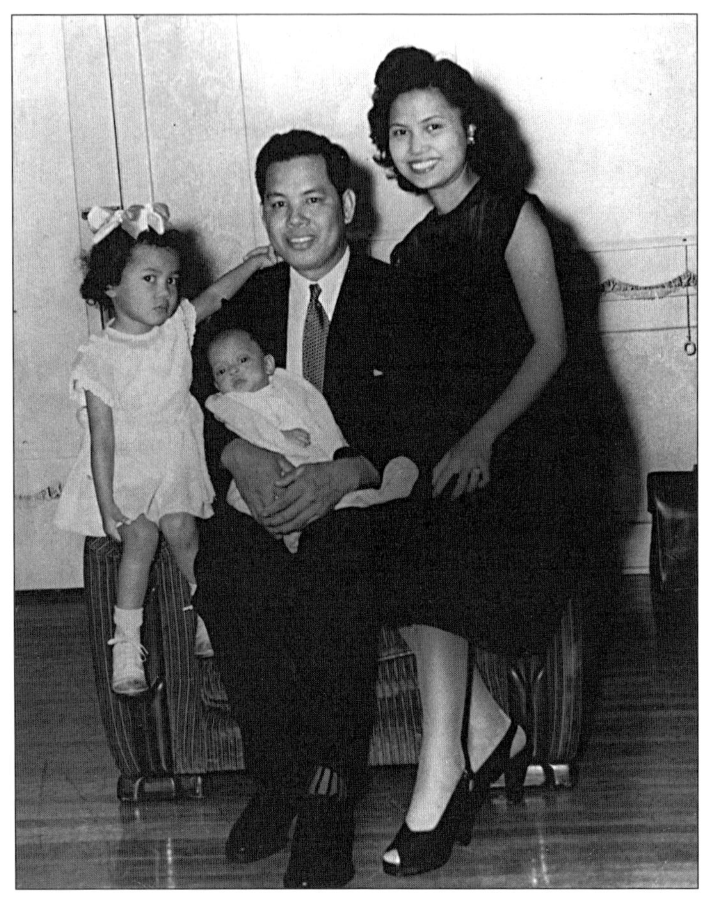

Casiano Coloma,

second minister of the Filipino Christian Church in Los Angeles and his family.

(Filipino American)

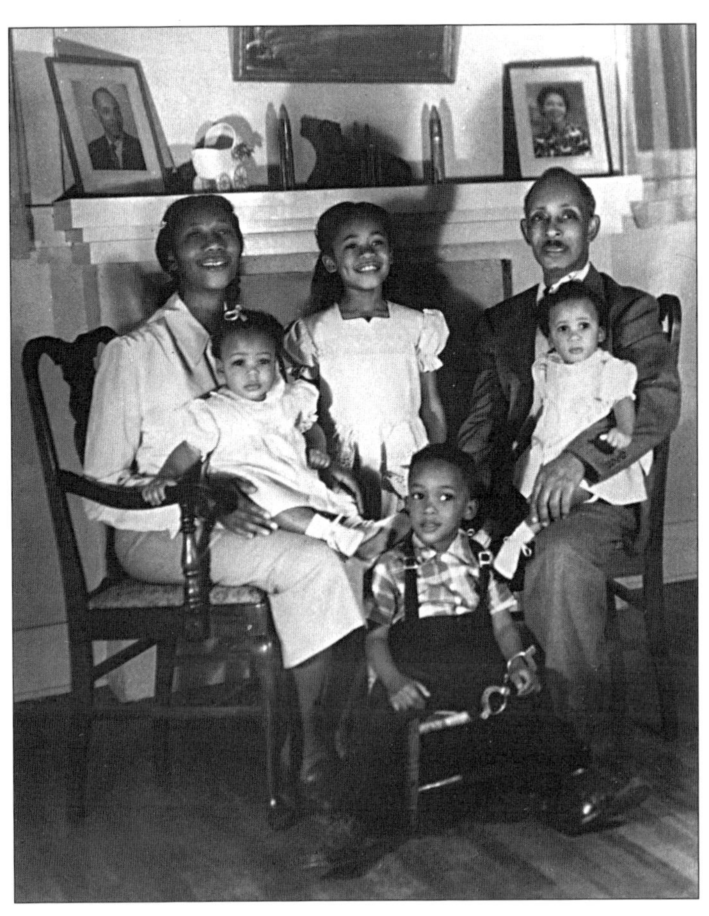

Marilyn White *(center, standing)* and her family

in their home at 231 West 43rd Street
in Los Angeles, 1954. Her brother locked himself into the handcuffs hours before the photographer arrived, and the key remained missing until too late.
(African American)

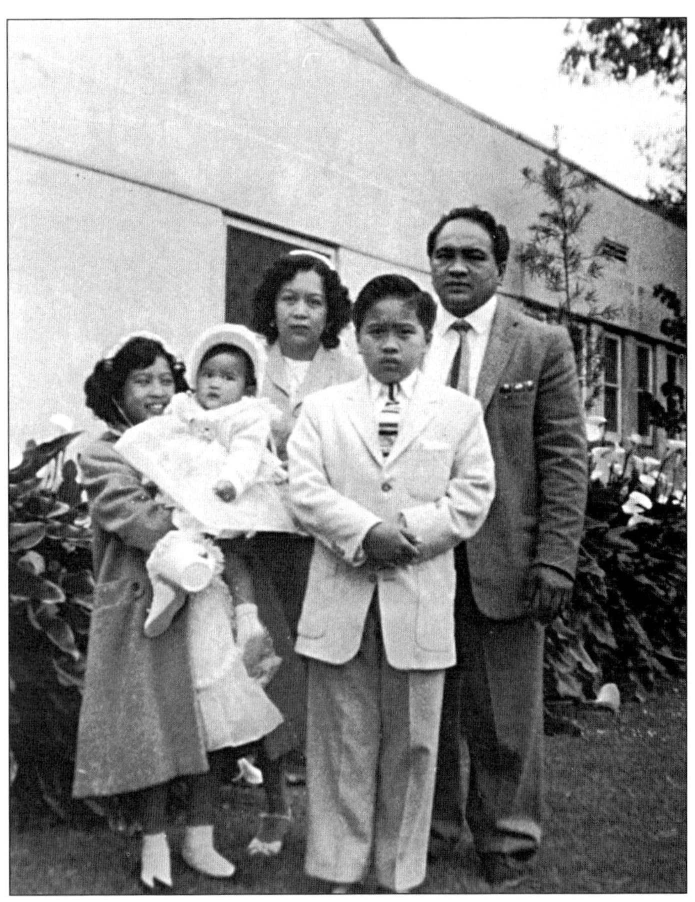

Edward Kwan, Jr., his wife Helen and children Roselynn, Sharon *(the baby)*, and Edward III

at an Easter celebration in Exposition Park near USC, 1958.
(Pacific Islander American/ Hawaiian)

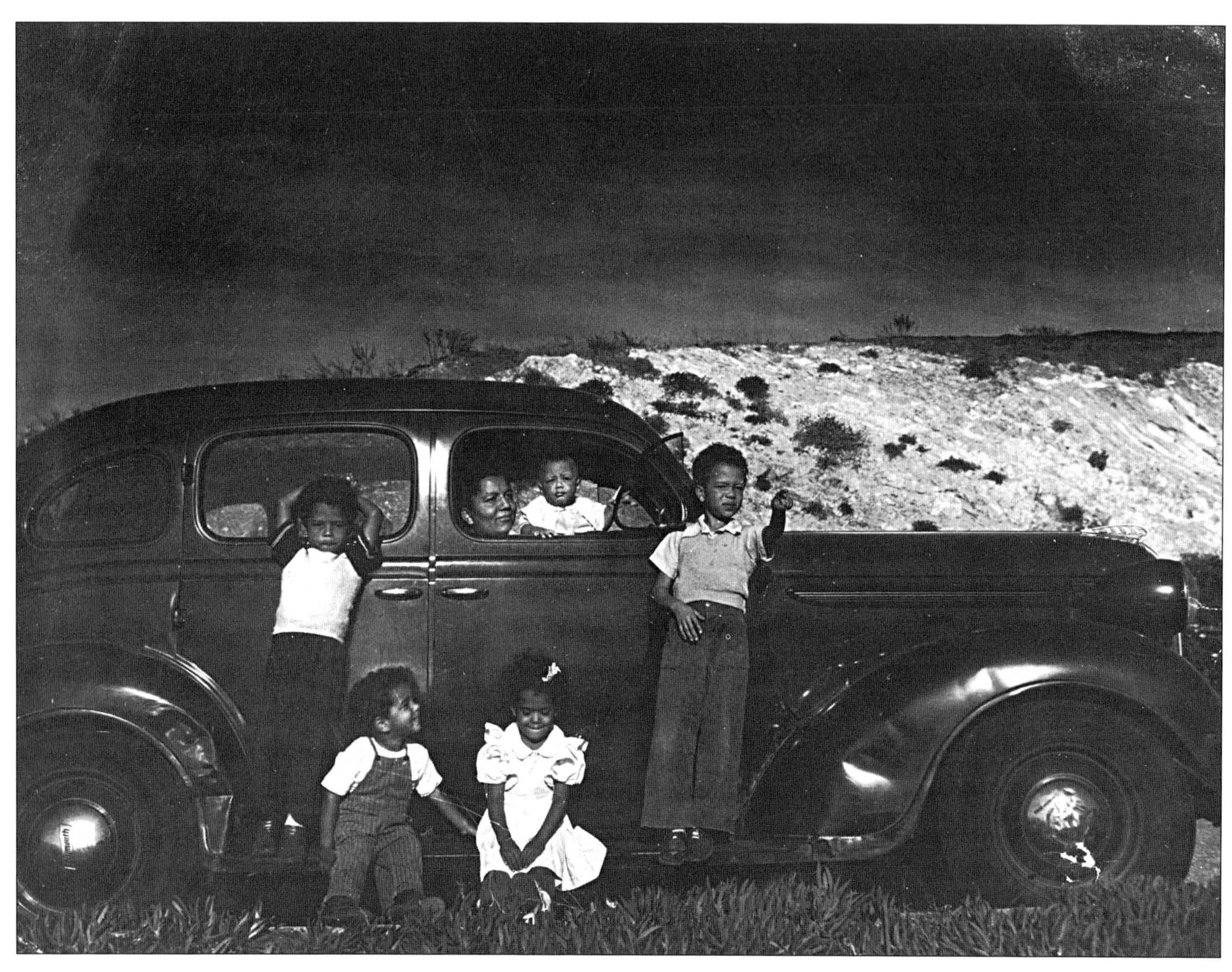

The Carr family

at Point Fermin in San Pedro, 1945.
(African American)

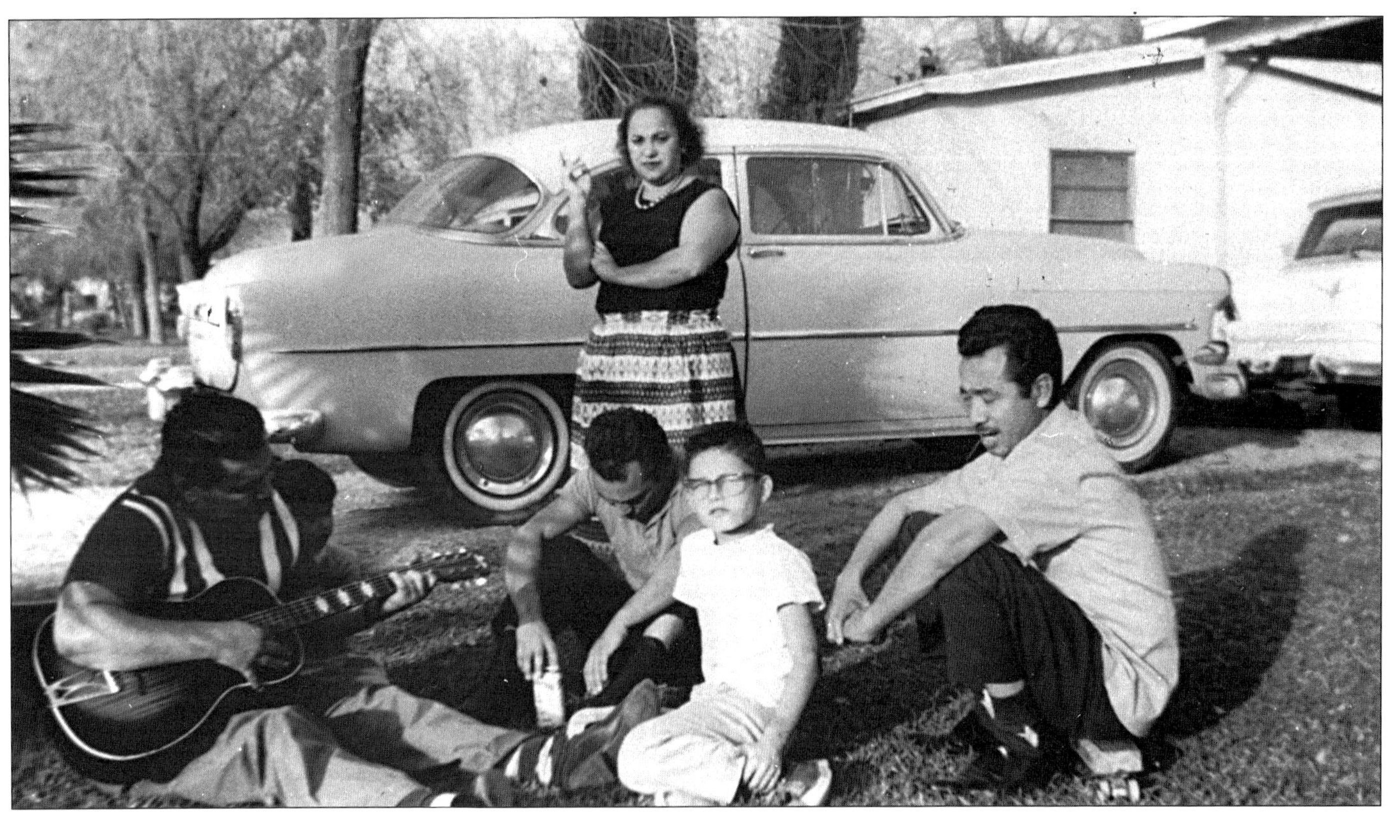

A family gathering in Fresno,

ca. 1950s.
(Mexican American)

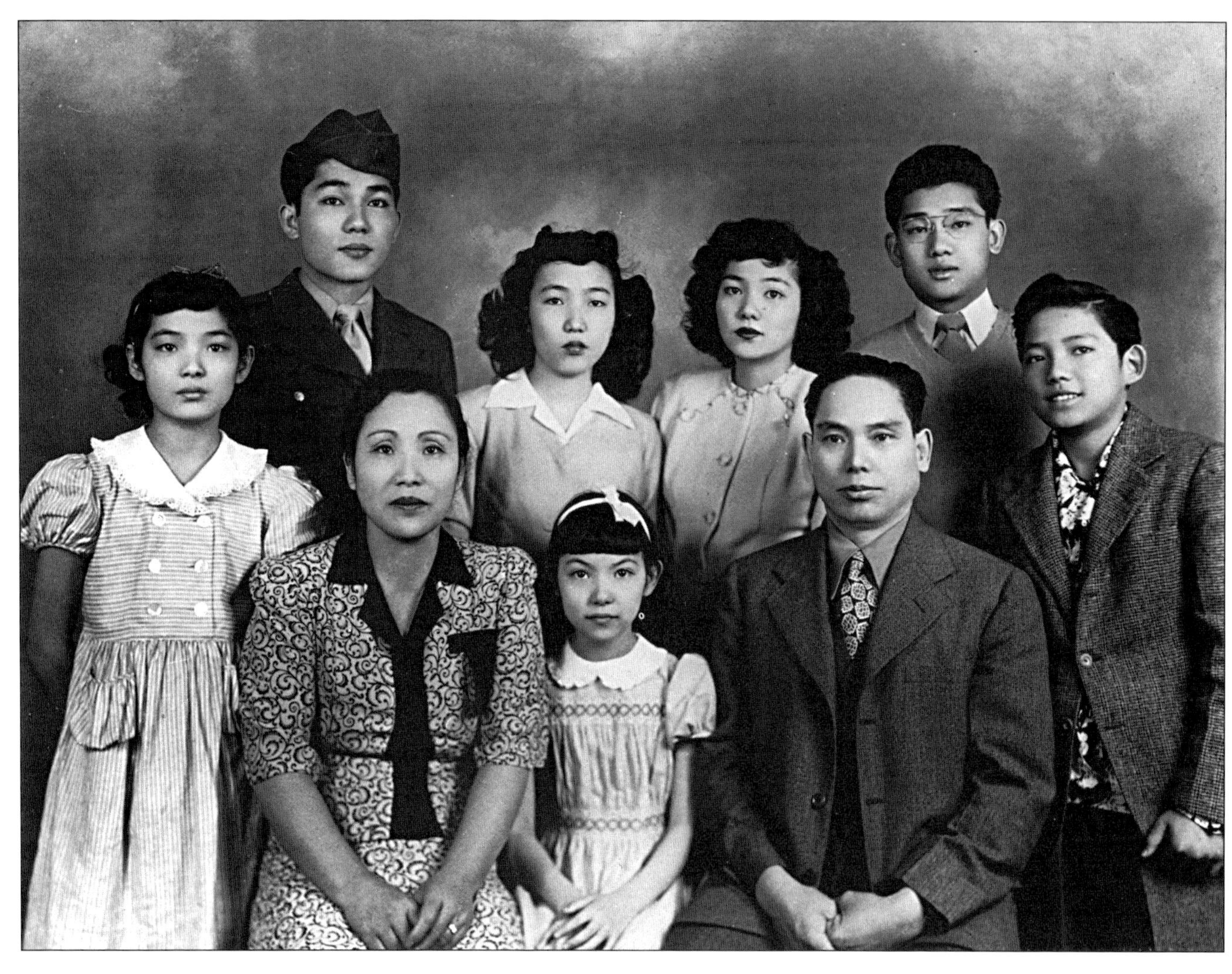

The Mitsunaga family

in Salt Lake City, Utah, five years before moving to Los Angeles, 1946.
(Japanese American)

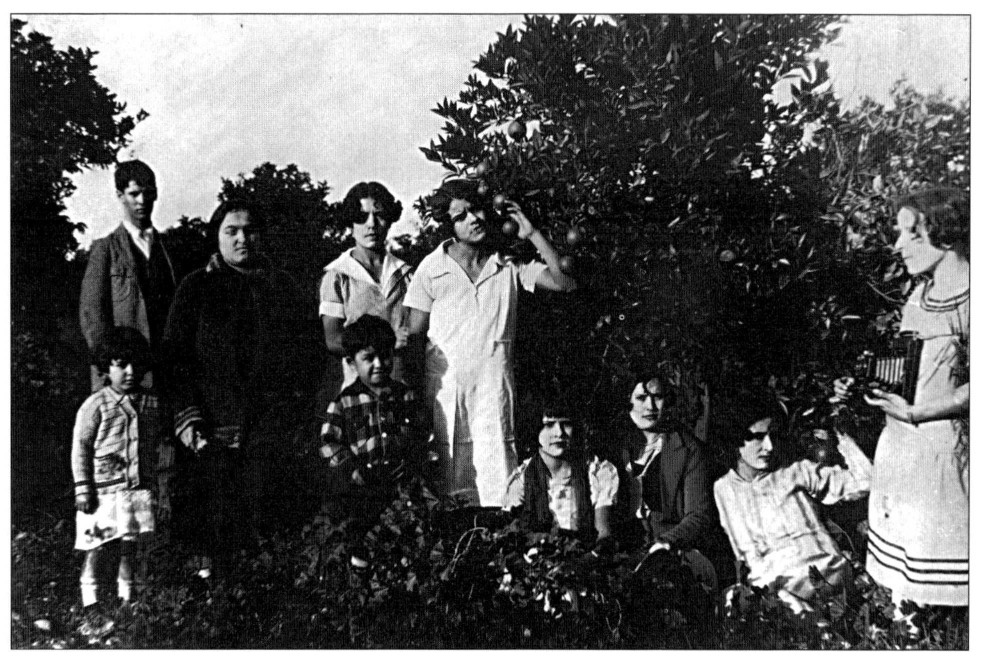

Maria *(with camera)*, Elpidia *(to her right)*, Maria de Jesus *(holding oranges)*, and Luz Soto *(to her right)*

at an orange grove in Fullerton, 1928. *(Mexican American)*

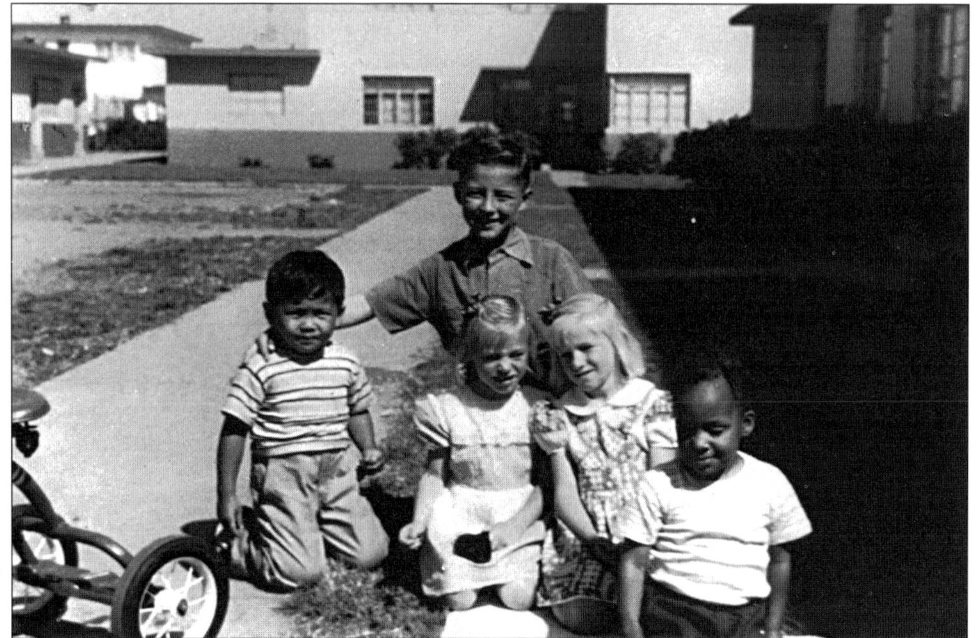

Debra Debise *(second from right)* with her friends in the Jordan Downs Housing Project, Watts, 1957.

In its early days in the 1940s and 1950s, Los Angeles' public housing reflected the progressive ideals of housing reformers and included racially integrated projects.

Hisataro and Sugi Kiriyama, and their first son in Japan, ca. 1908.

(Japanese American)

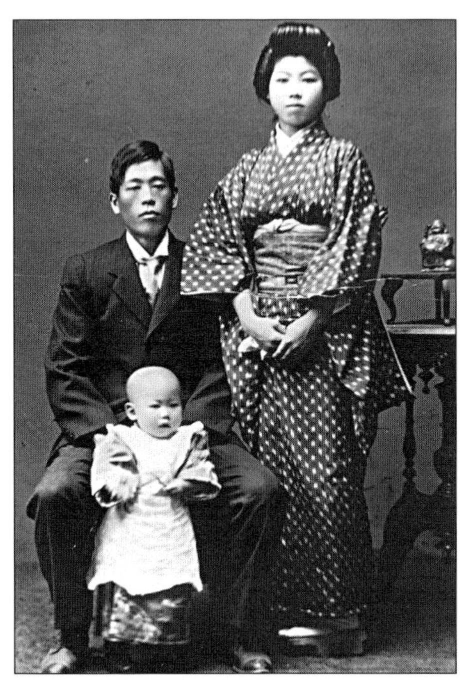

Hisataro and Sugi Kiriyama, and their children in America, 1929.

(Japanese American)

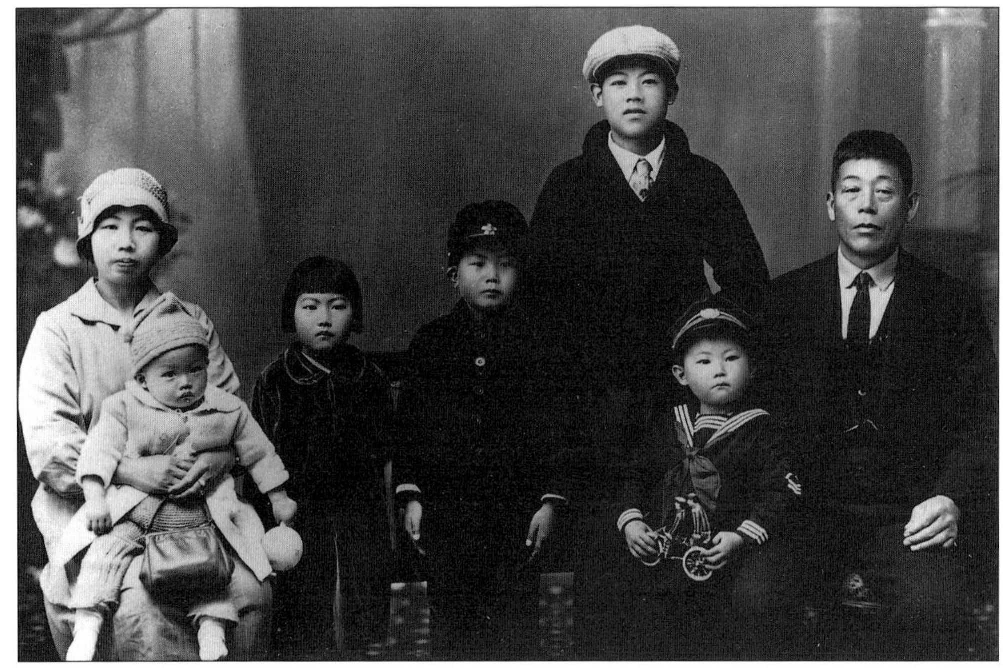

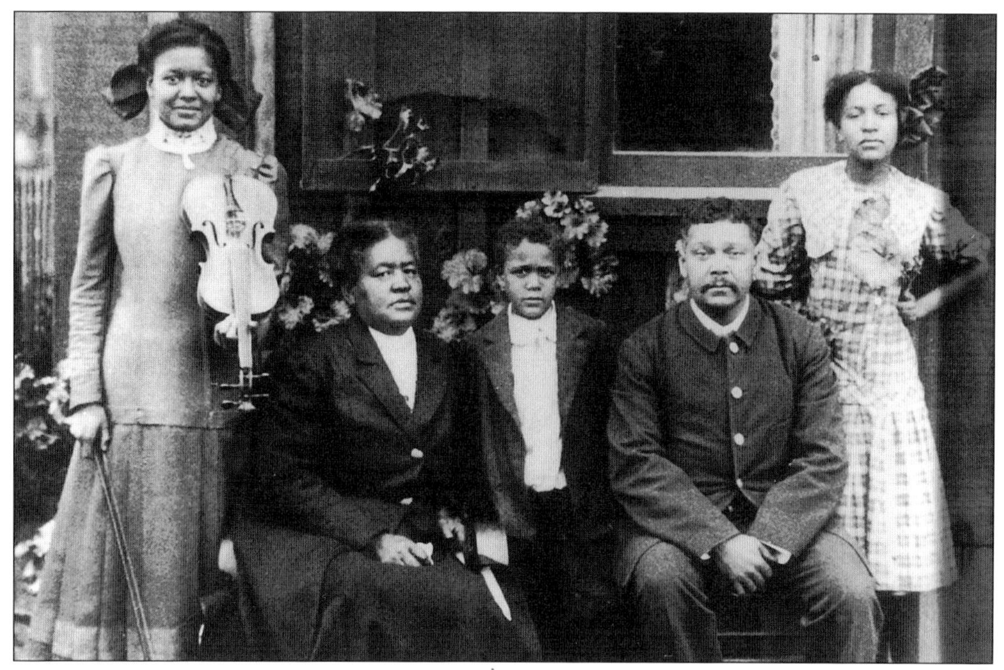

Ruth, Lettie, Oliver, Robert, and Gladys Lishey

in Watts, 1910.

(African American)

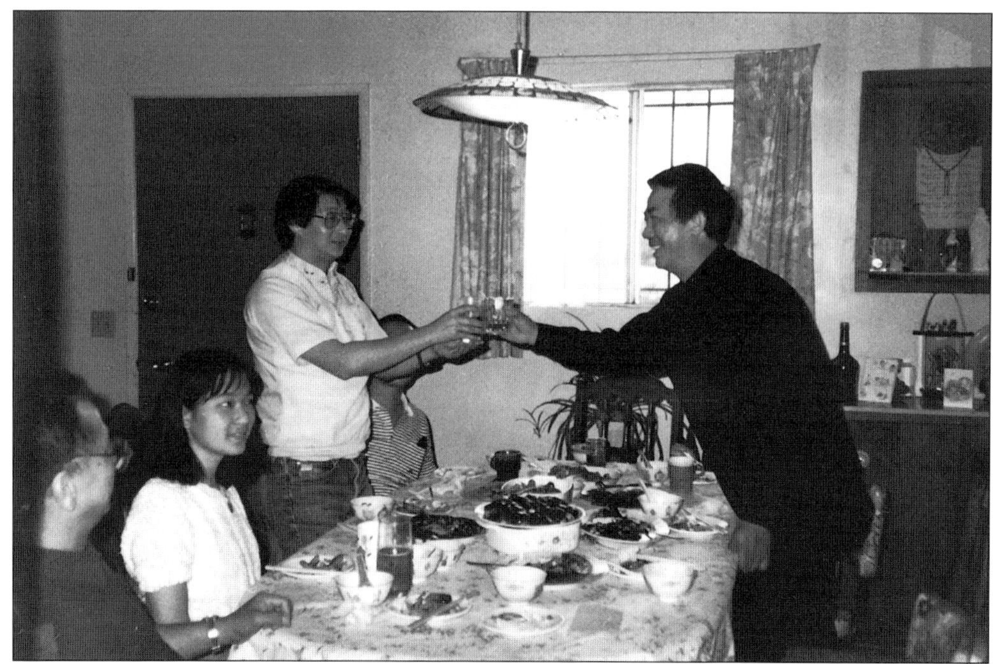

Members of St. Bridget's Catholic Chinese Center

in Los Angeles celebrate a meal at home.

(Chinese American)

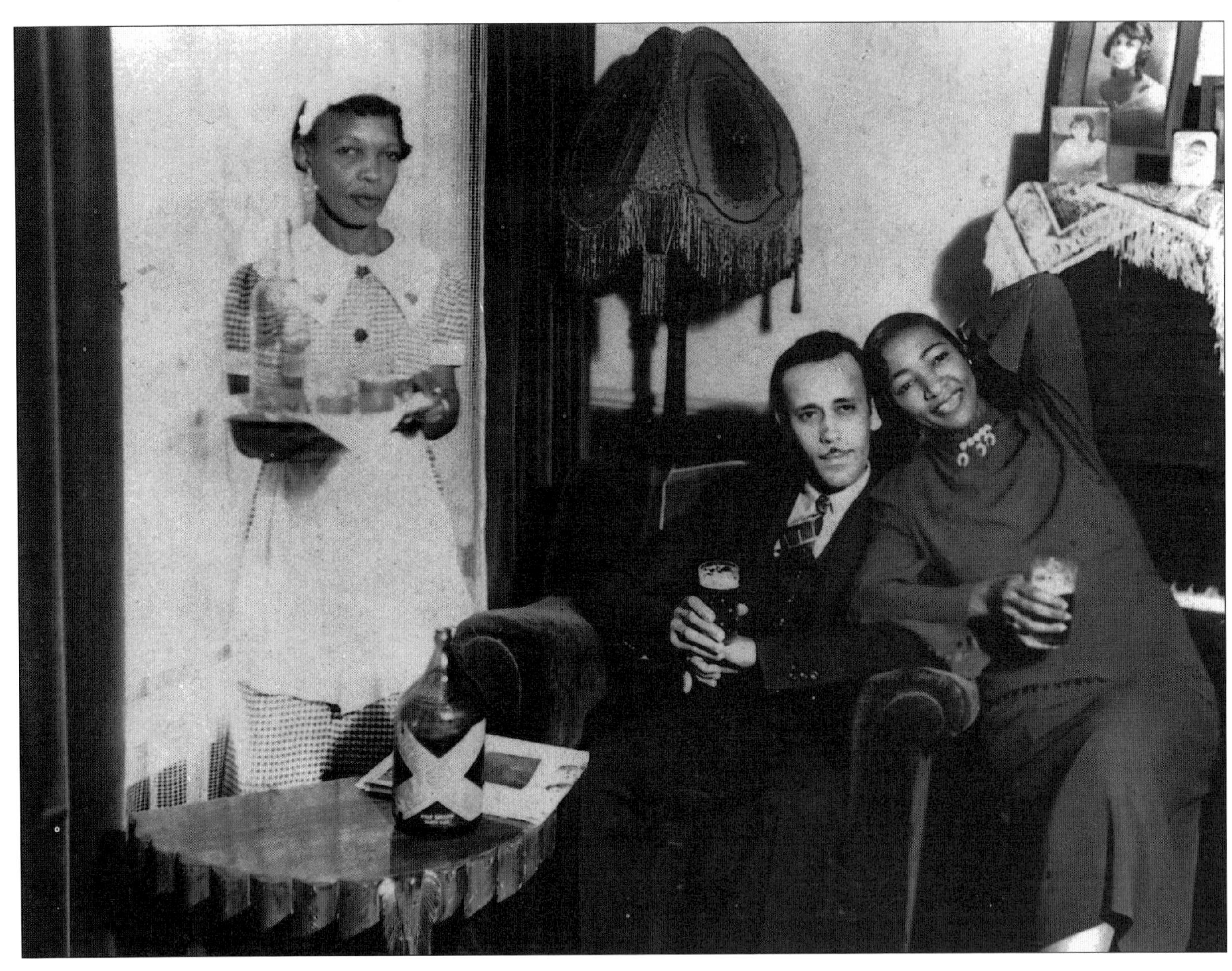

Henry Pickens and Watie Belle Rozier Pickens

with the family maid, 1929.
(African American)

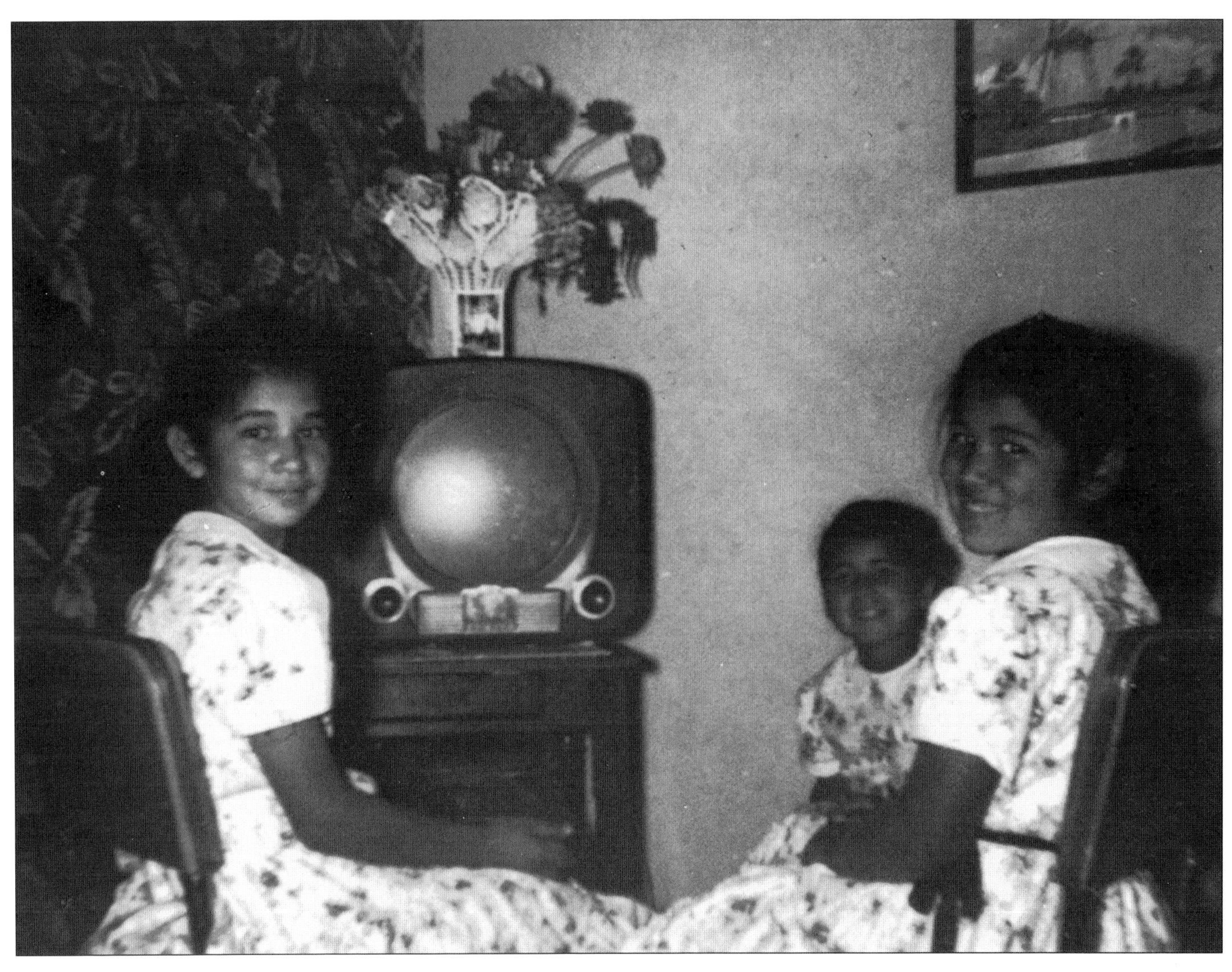

Leonor, Virginia and Angelica Lozano *(left to right)*
seated around the family's first television in their home, ca. 1953.
(Mexican American)

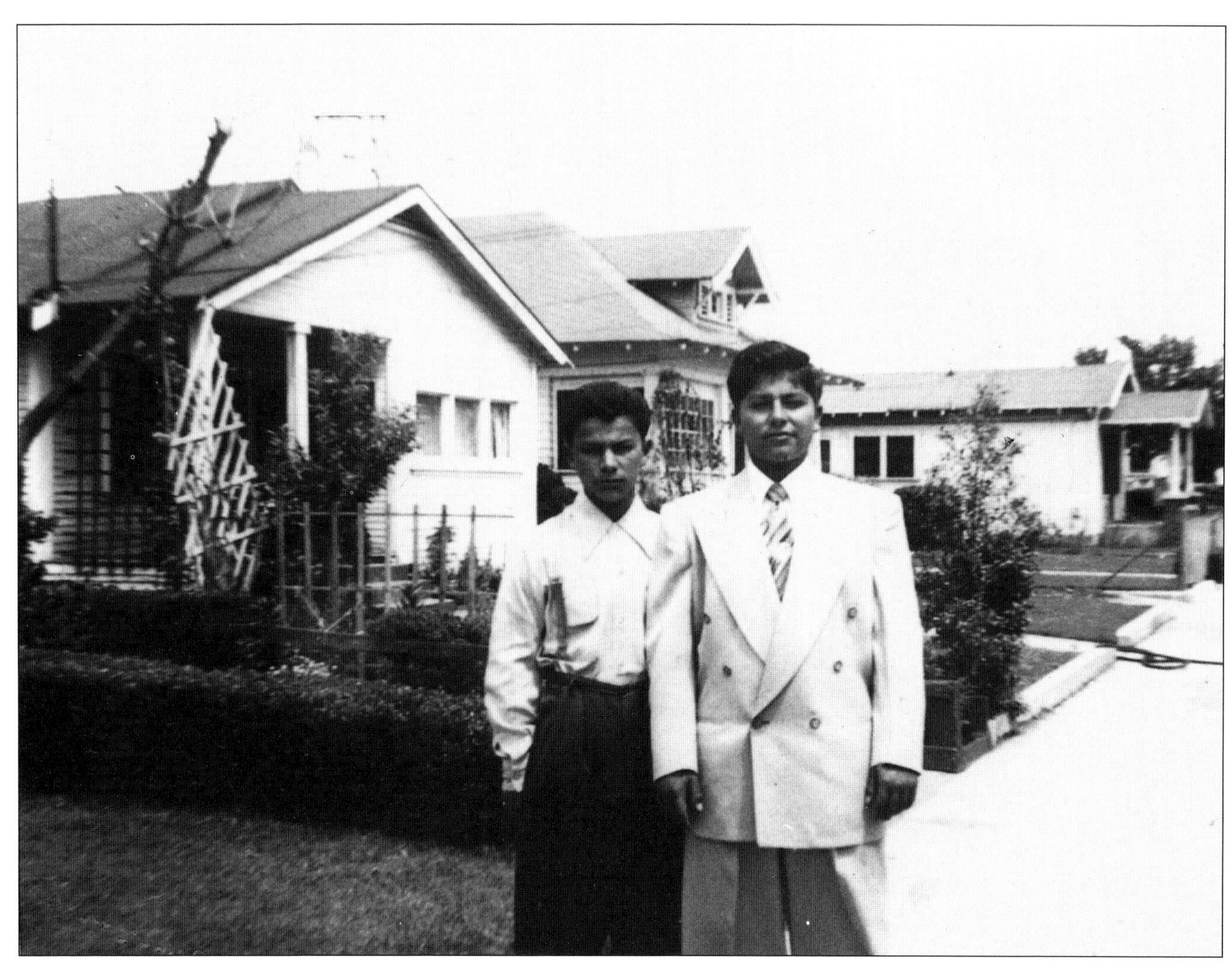

Richard Garcia *(left)* and John Urrea

in front of John's house on Young Street in Wilmington, California.
(Mexican American)

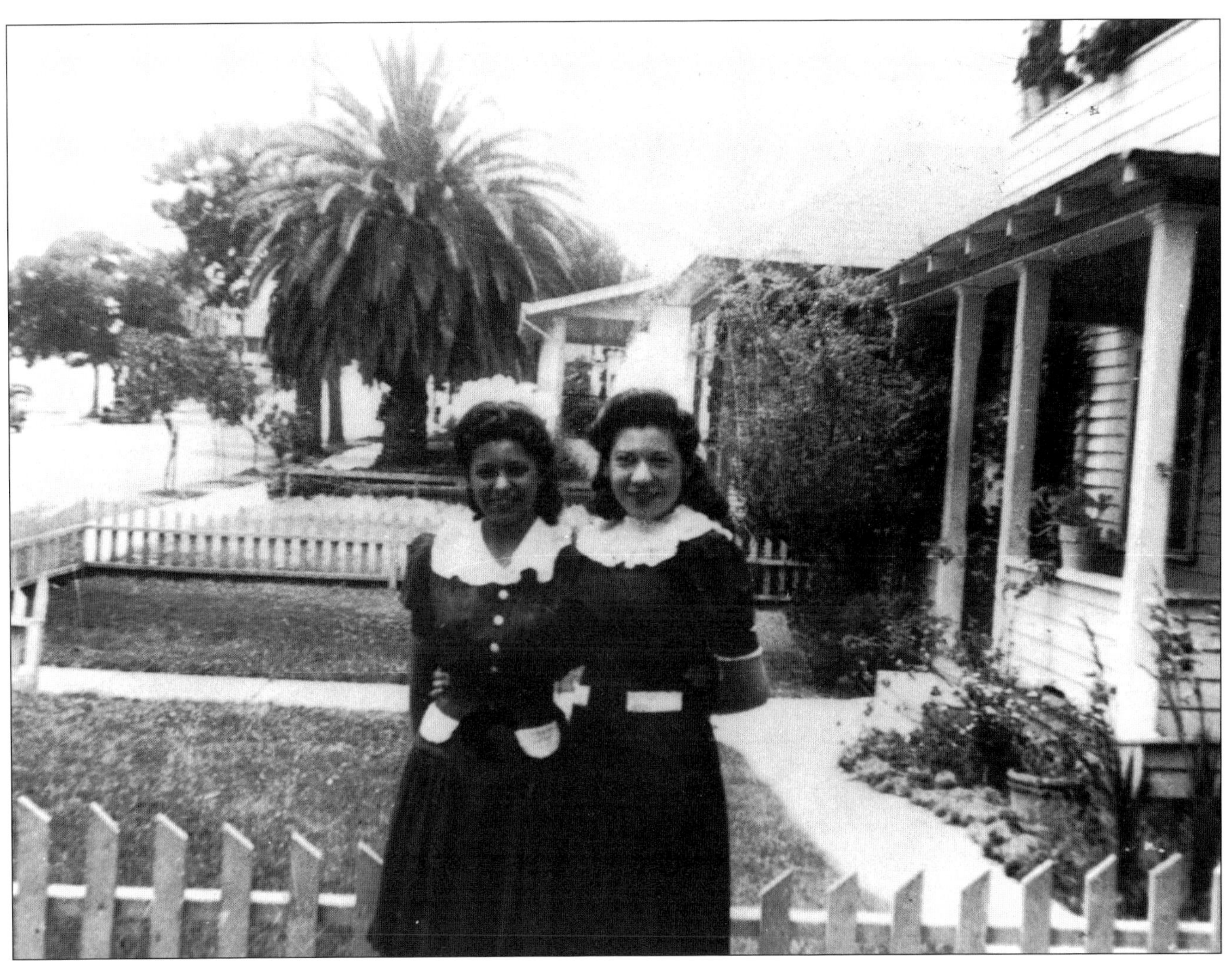

SISTERS LILIA AND VIOLA RODRIGUEZ,

in mourning for their father, pose in front of their home on Sepulveda Street in San Pedro.
(Mexican American)

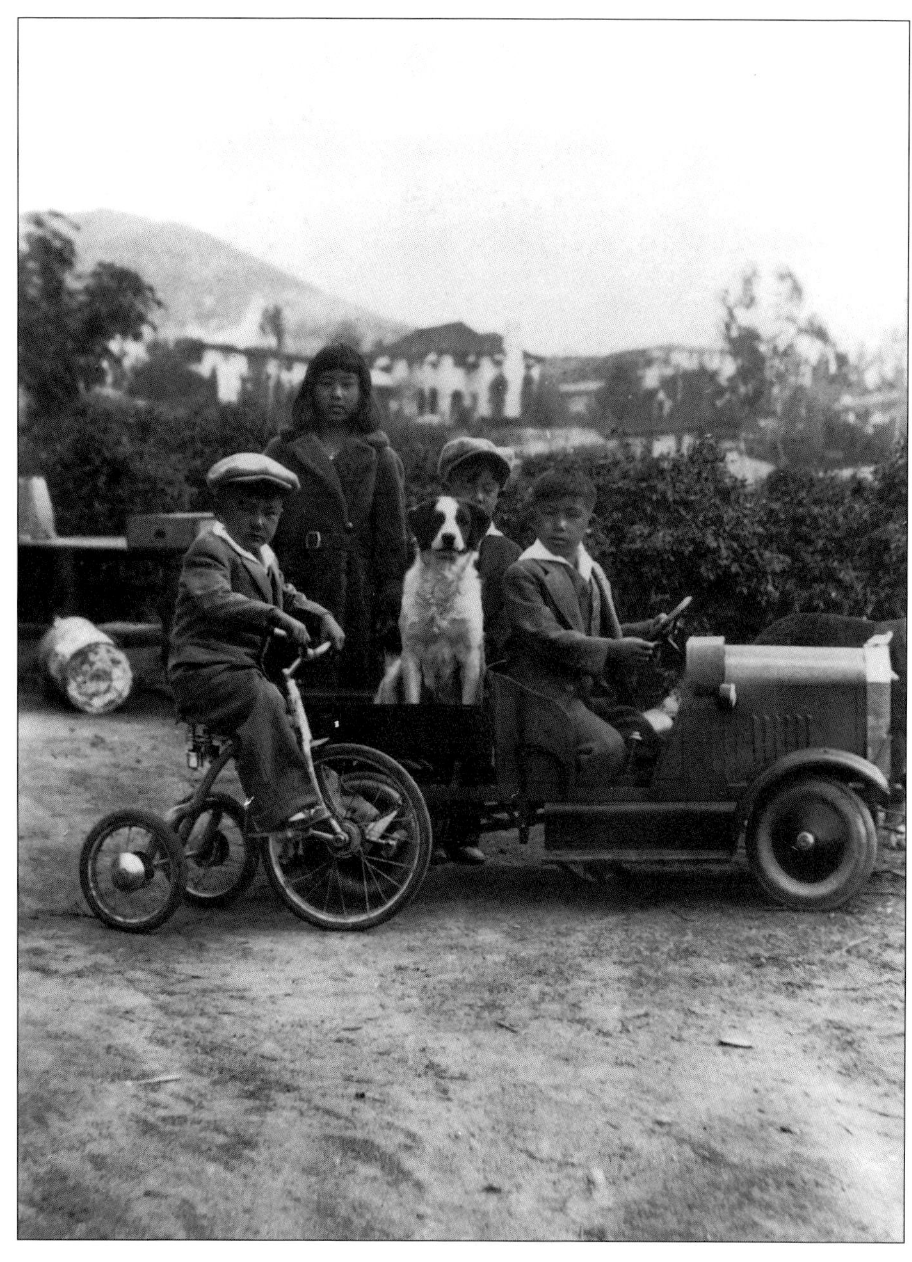

Hitoshi and Aiko Kuromi, their cousin, Mikio Kawakami, and their brother, Isamu Kuromi

on Los Feliz Boulevard in Los Angeles, ca. 1920s. The Kuromi and Kawakami families leased land in the Los Feliz area to grow flowers for the wholesale market.
(Japanese American)

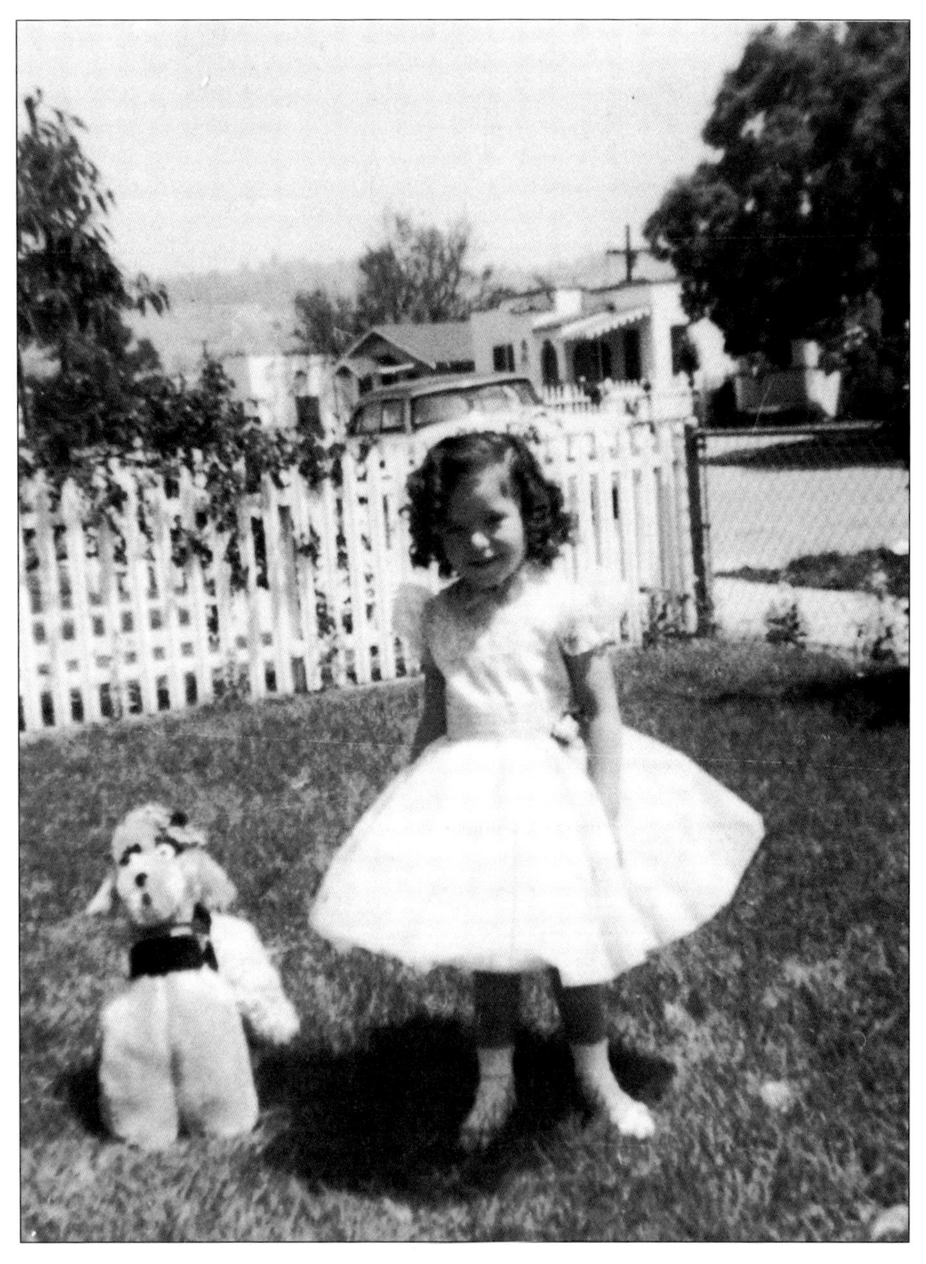

Angela Weil and her poodle

on Cabot Street near Elysian Park in Los Angeles, 1962.

(Mexican American)

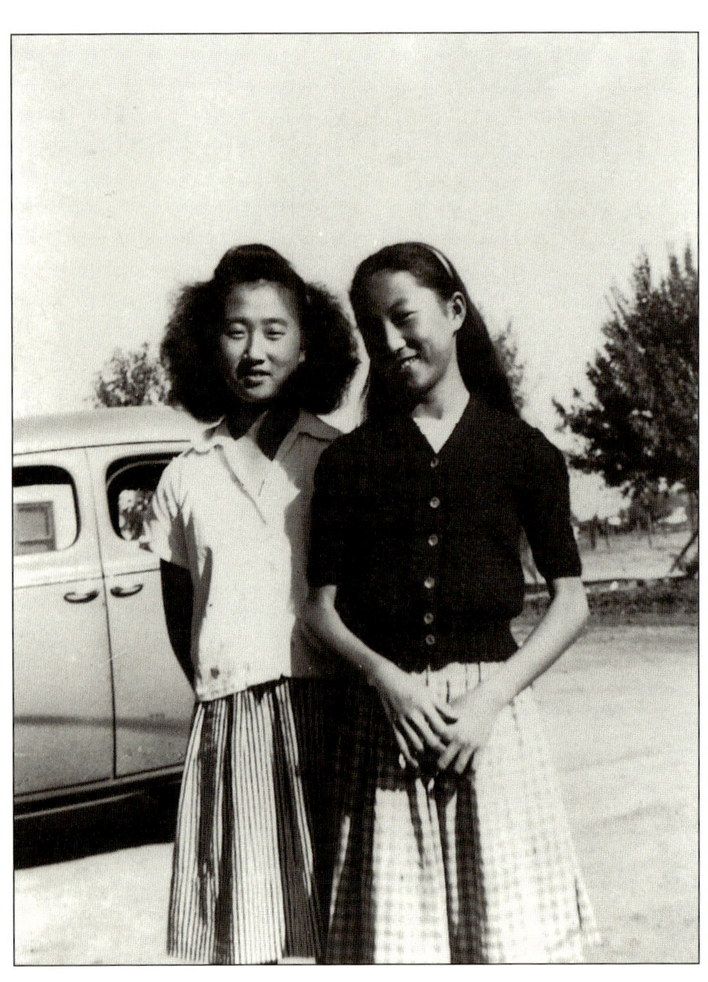

Emma Kim *(left)* and her sister Ada

in Delano, California, 1944.

(Korean American)

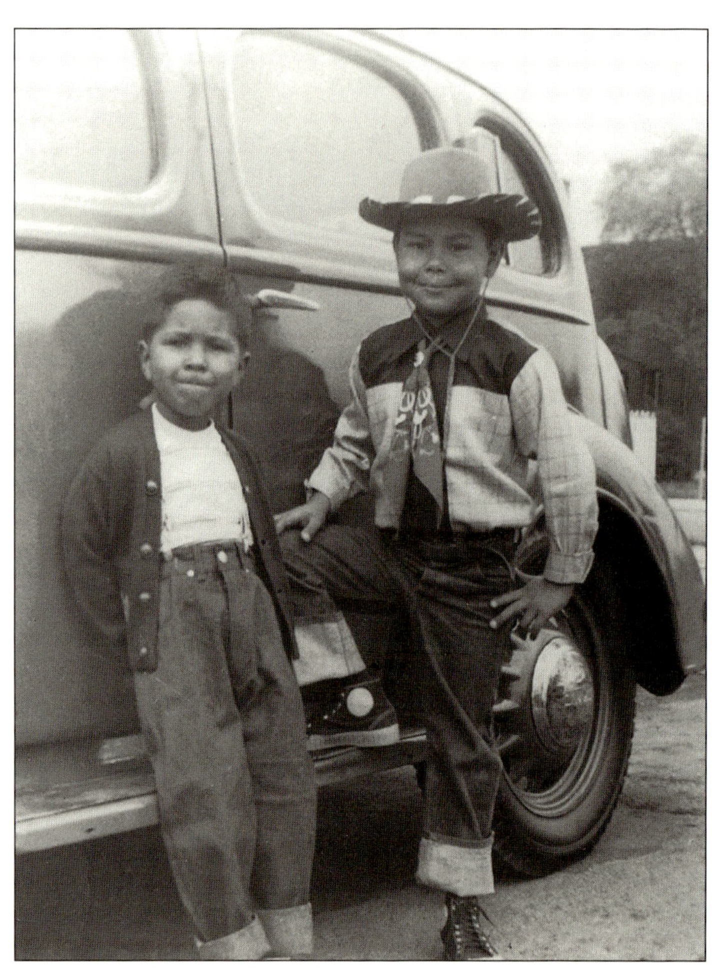

Fred Martel *(right)* and a friend

on Bridge Street in Boyle Heights, 1947.

(Mexican American)

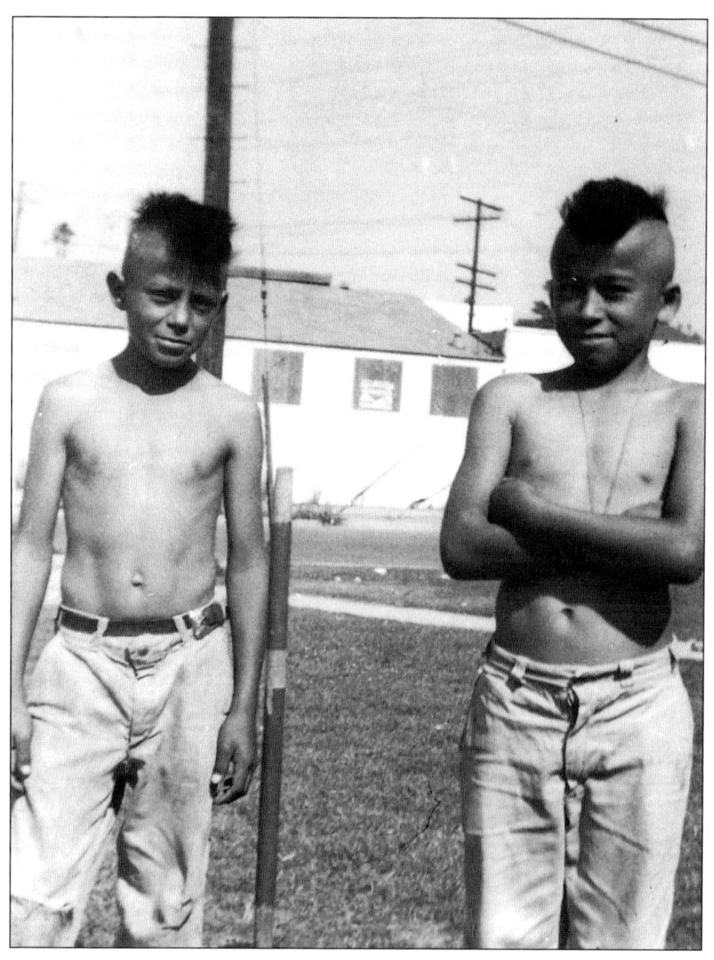

John and Danny Mojica

in Lincoln Heights with their new Mohawk haircuts, in support of the Lincoln High School "Mohawks" team, July 1958.

(Mexican American)

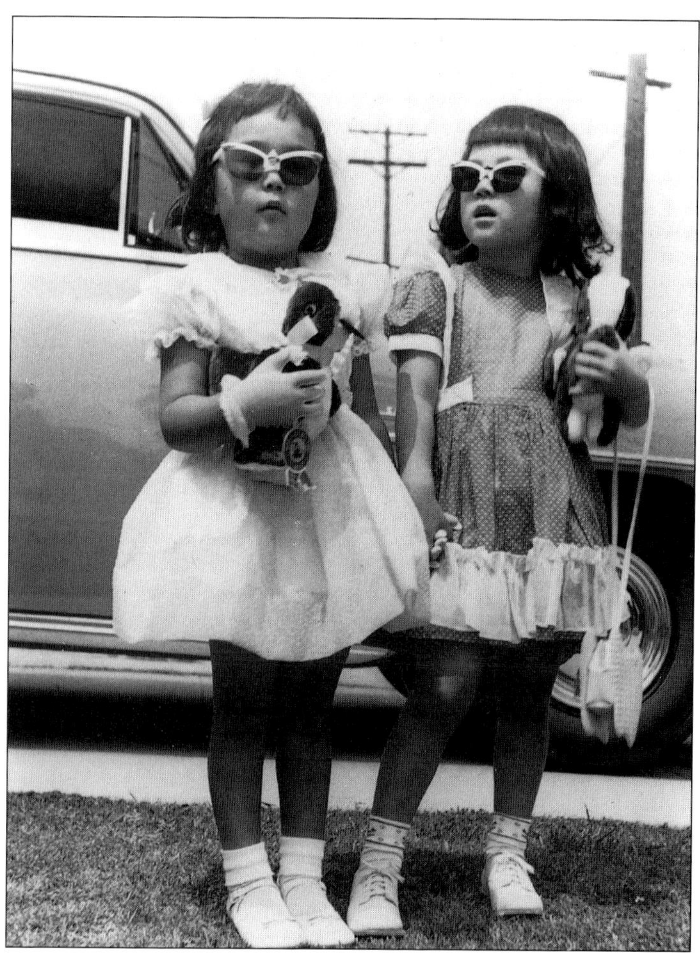

Six-year-olds Diane Funada *(left)* and her best friend, Naomi Okamoto,

dressed for Easter in Los Angeles, April 1956.

(Japanese American)

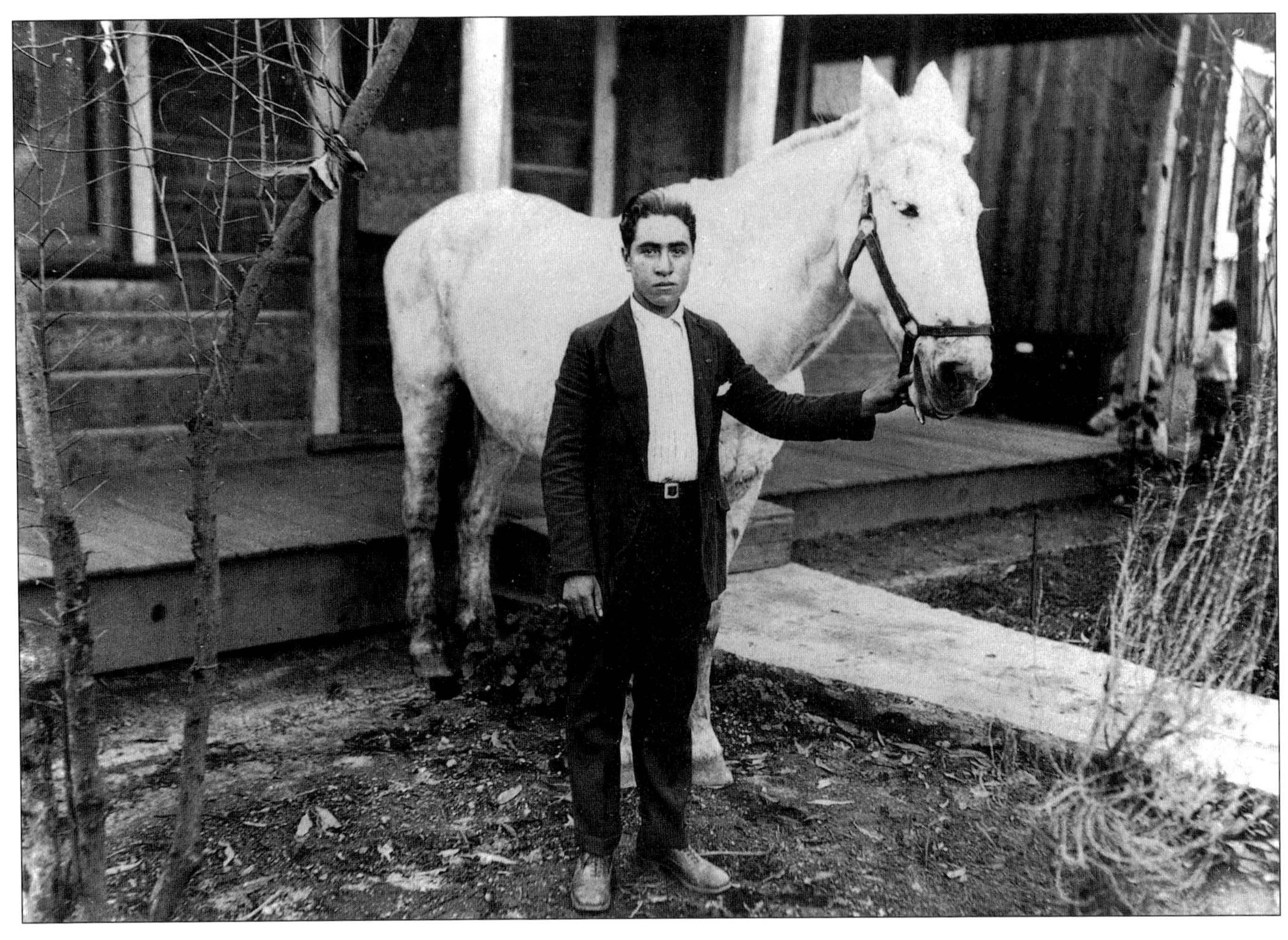

Alfredo Bedoya and his horse

in the San Gabriel Valley.

(Mexican American)

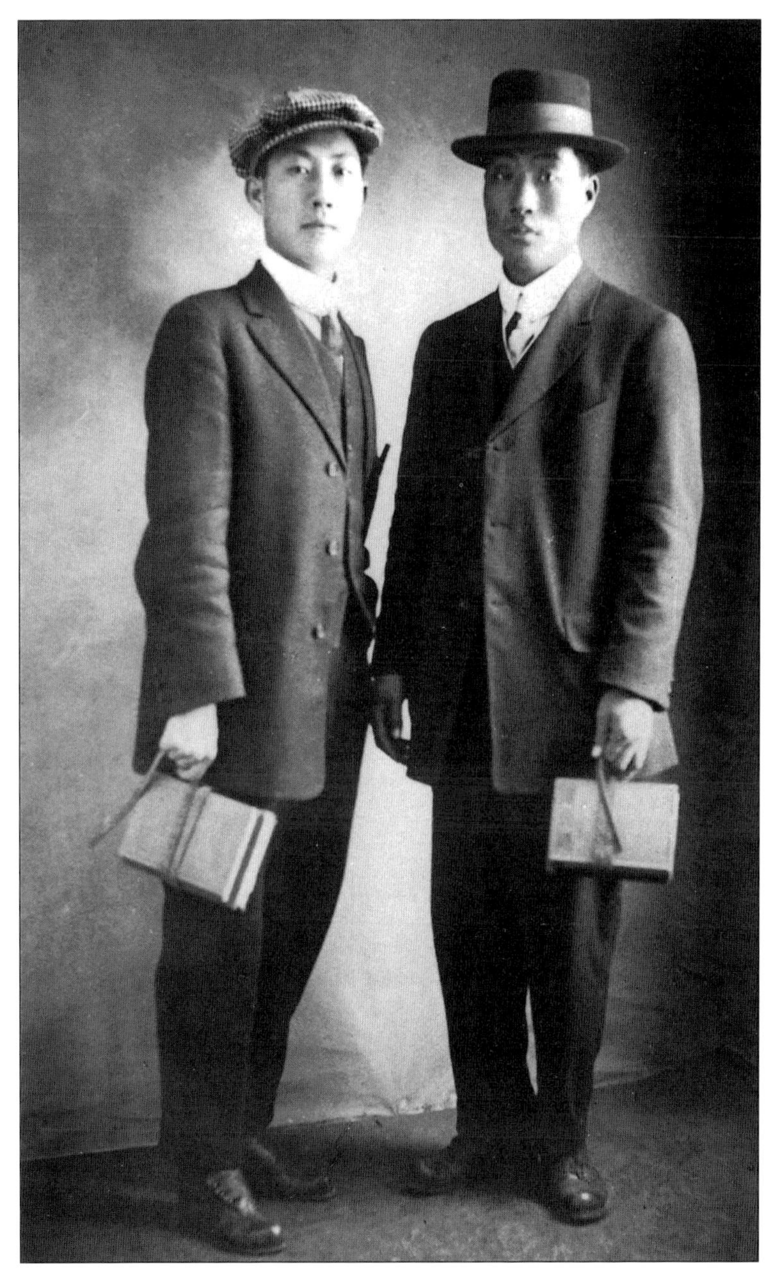

Students in Claremont, 1907.

(Korean American)

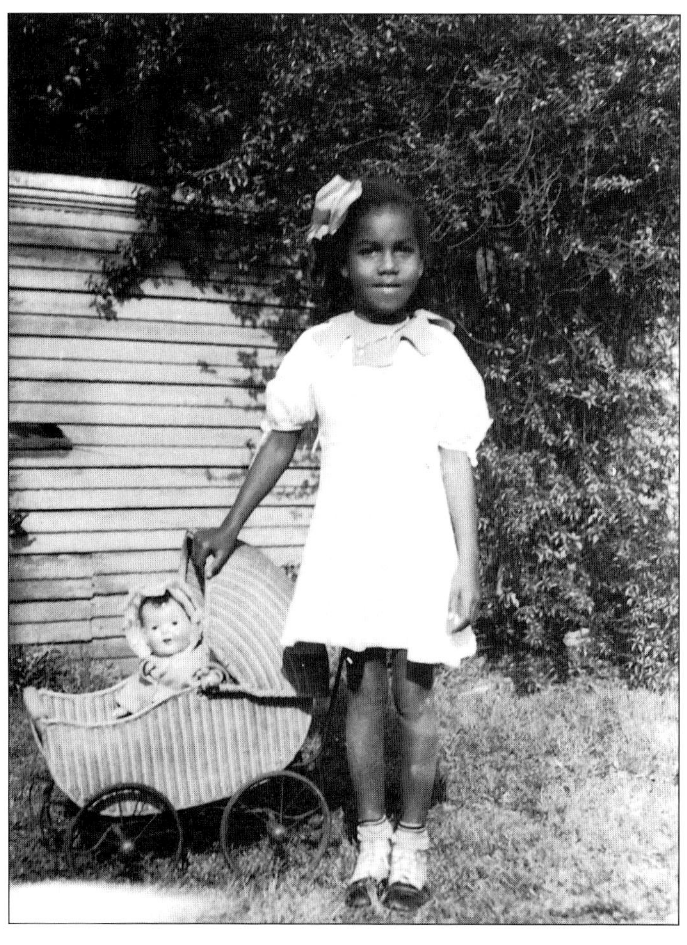

Pat Thompson

at 42nd Street and Central Avenue in Los Angeles, 1939.
(African American)

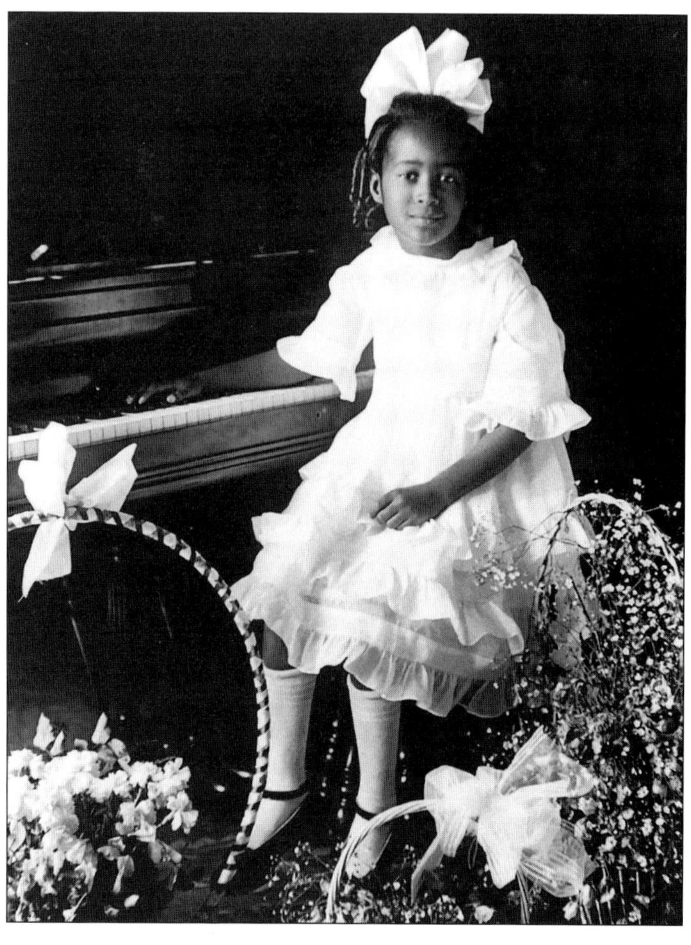

Seven-year-old Juanita Terry,

at her piano recital, June 1919.
(African American)

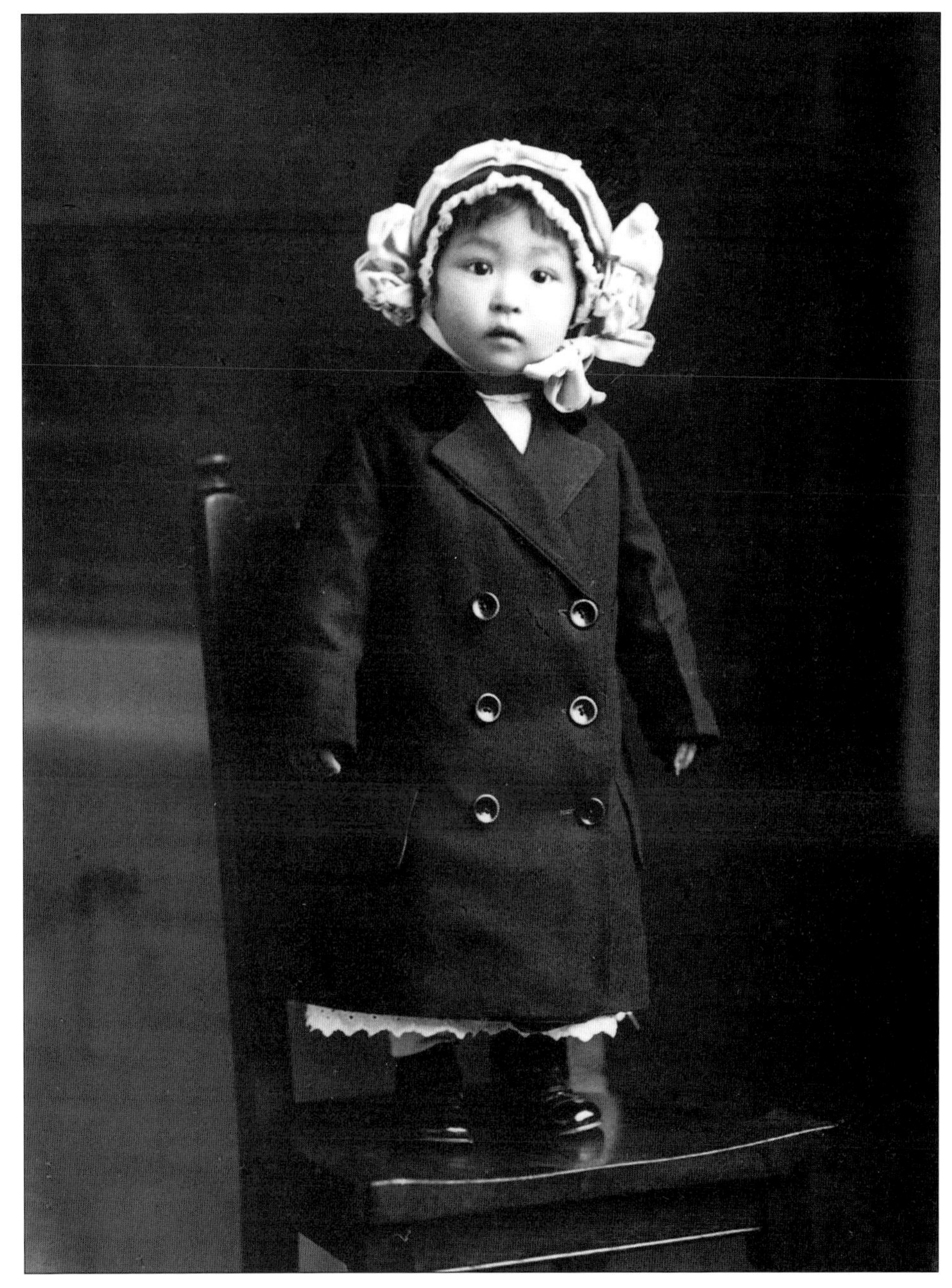

Unidentifed girl.

(Japanese American)

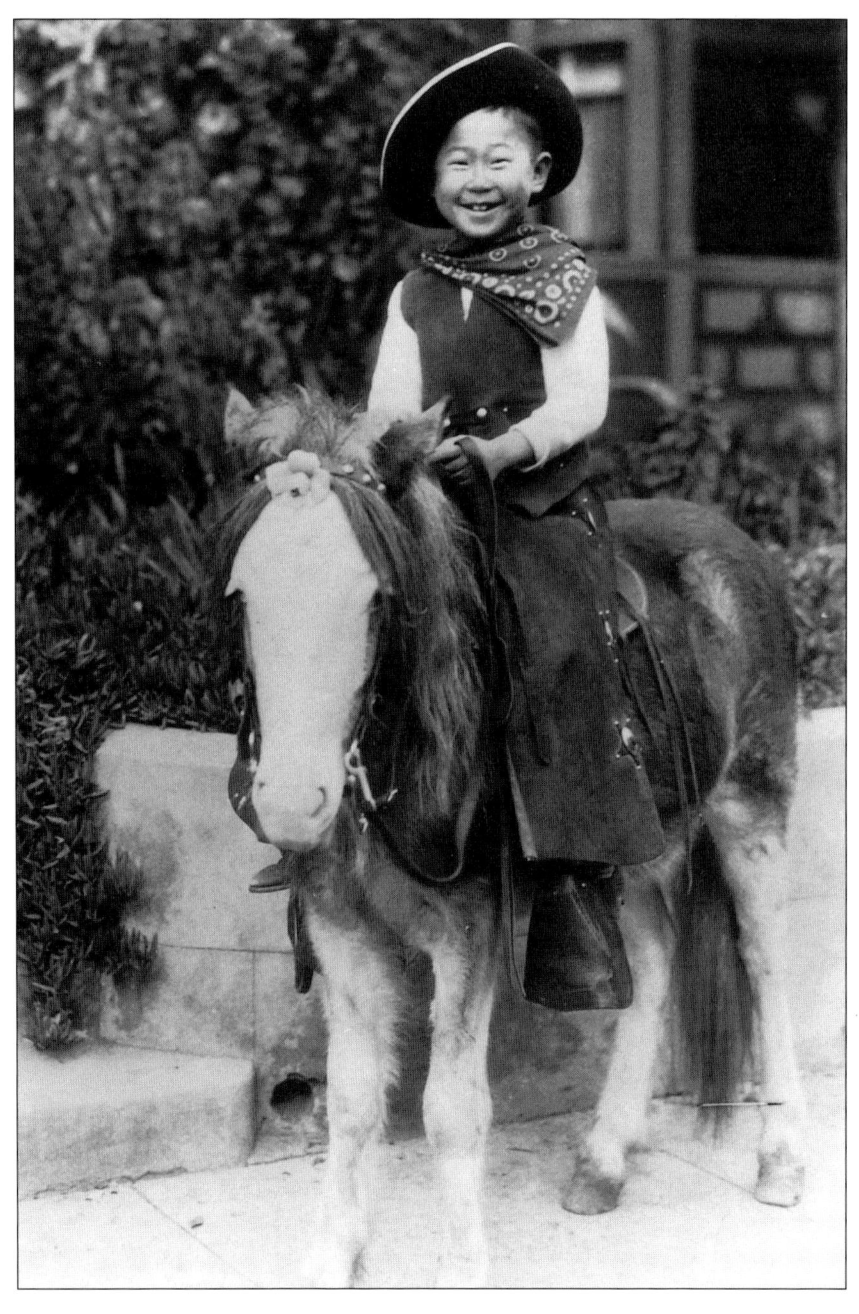

Four-year-old Ralph Ahn

poses on the photographer's pony at
First and Flower Streets in downtown Los Angeles, 1930.
(Korean American)

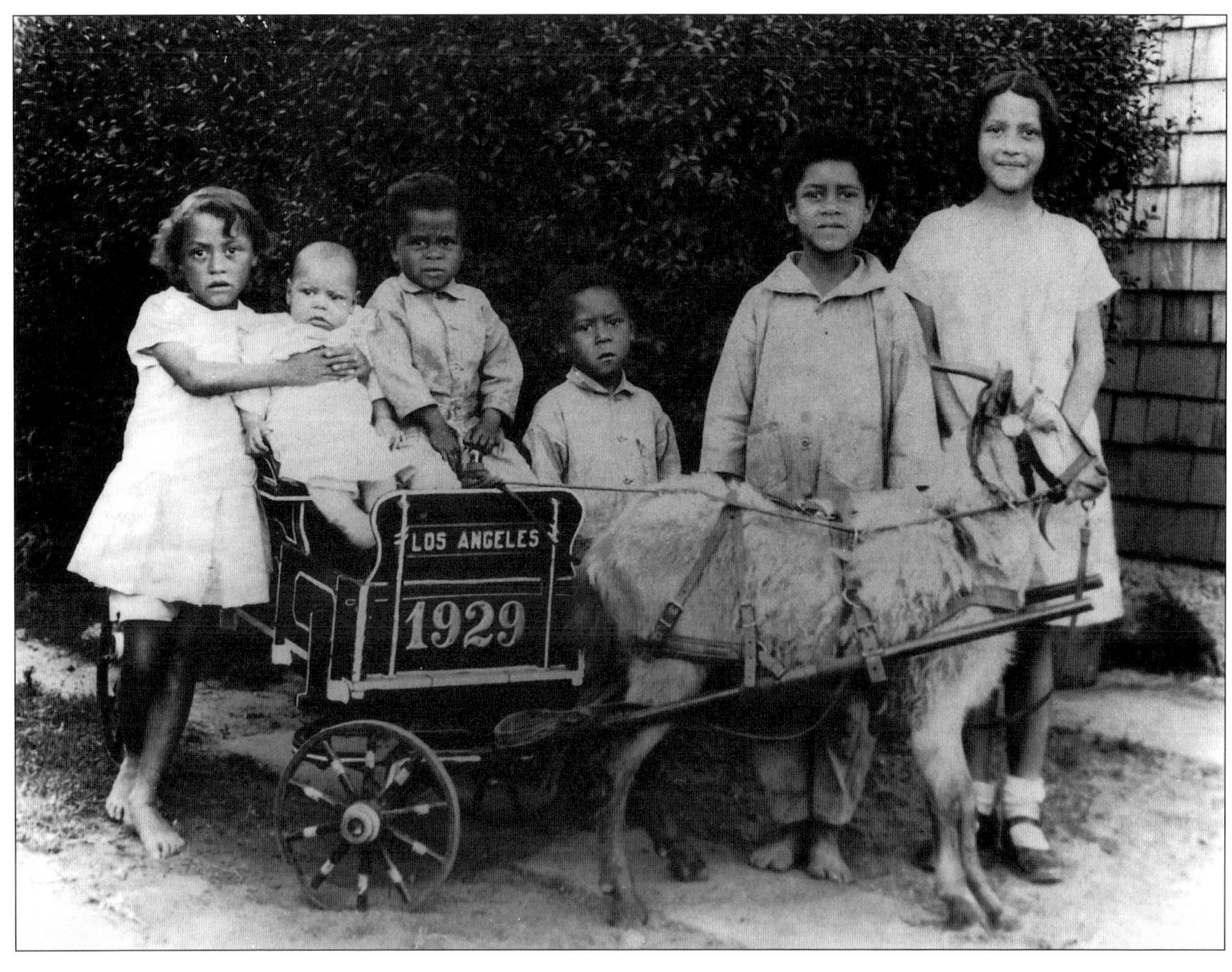

Doris, Leon, Edwin, Frank, Earl, and Mildred Day

at their home on East 47th Place in Los Angeles, 1939.

(African American)

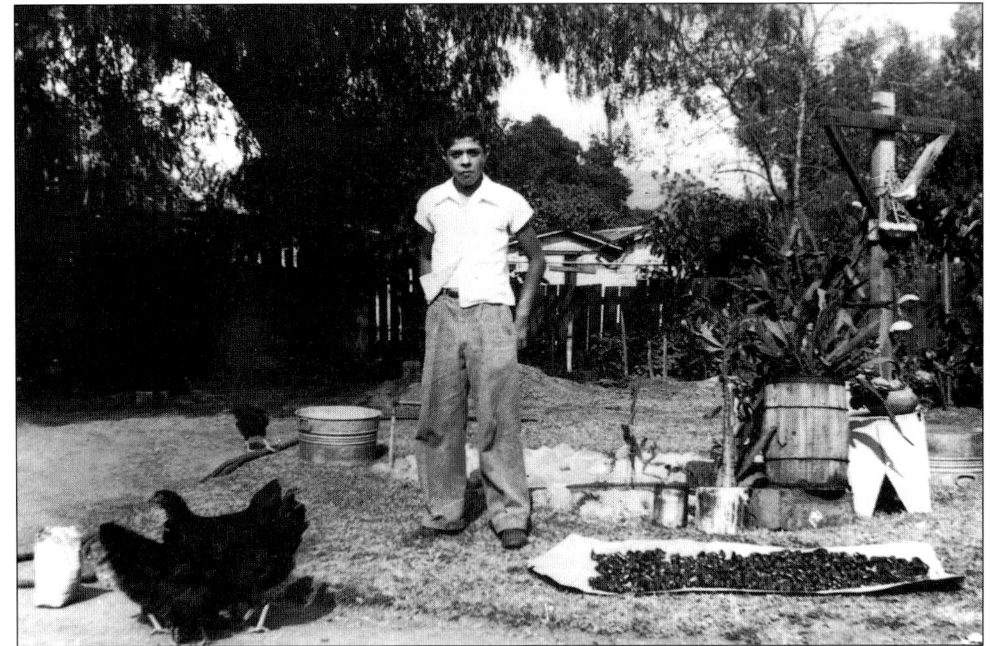

Arthur Bustillos

in his backyard on Fisher Street in East Los Angeles, ca. 1940. *(Mexican American)*

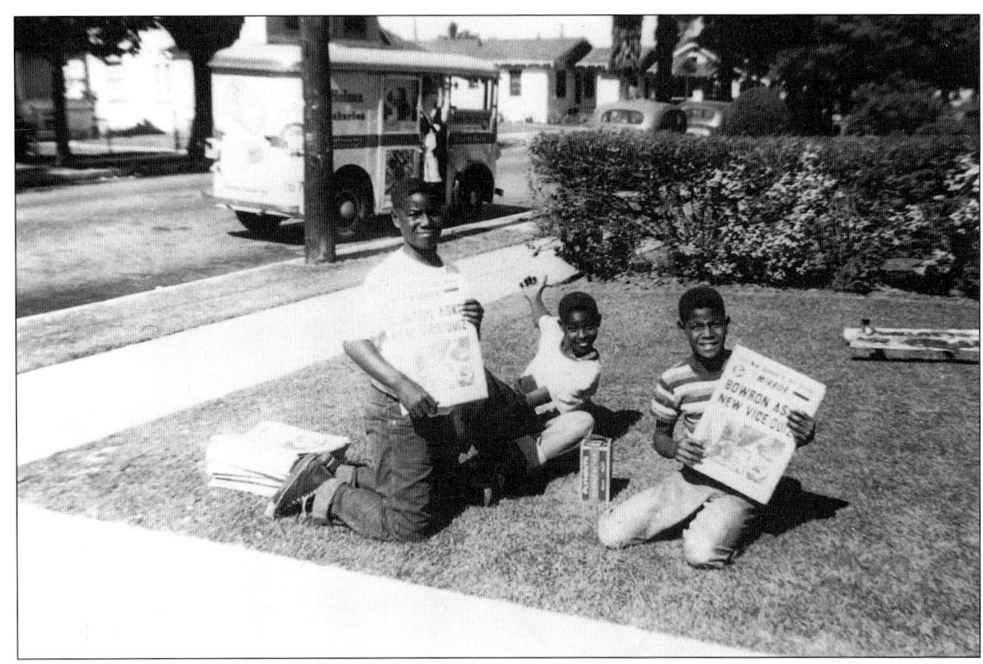

Newspaper carriers for the L.A. Mirror

on East 48th Street in Los Angeles, ca. 1945. *(African American)*

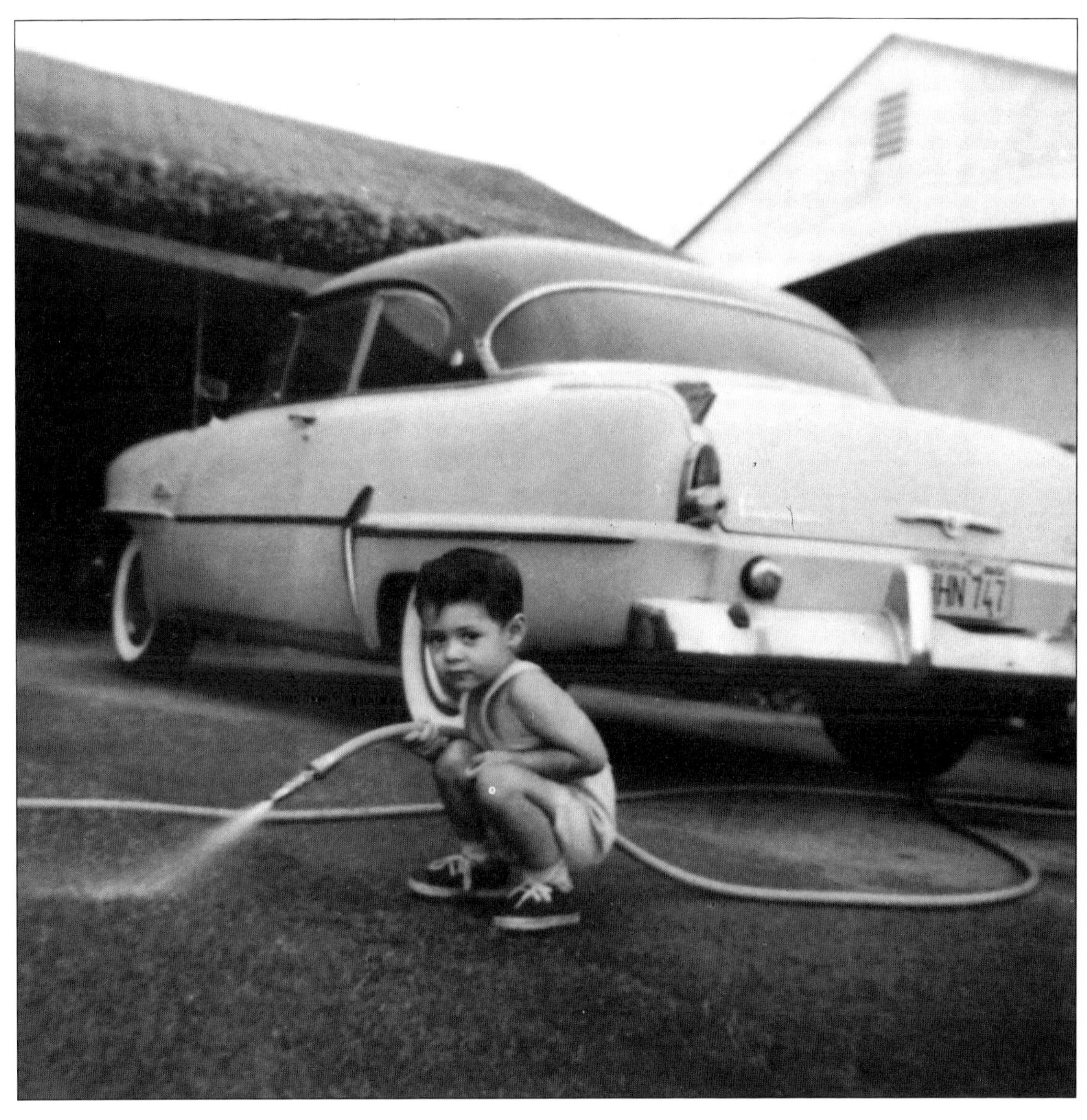

ARNOLD BUSTILLOS

playing at his home on Dubonnet Avenue in Rosemead, March 1959.

(Mexican American)

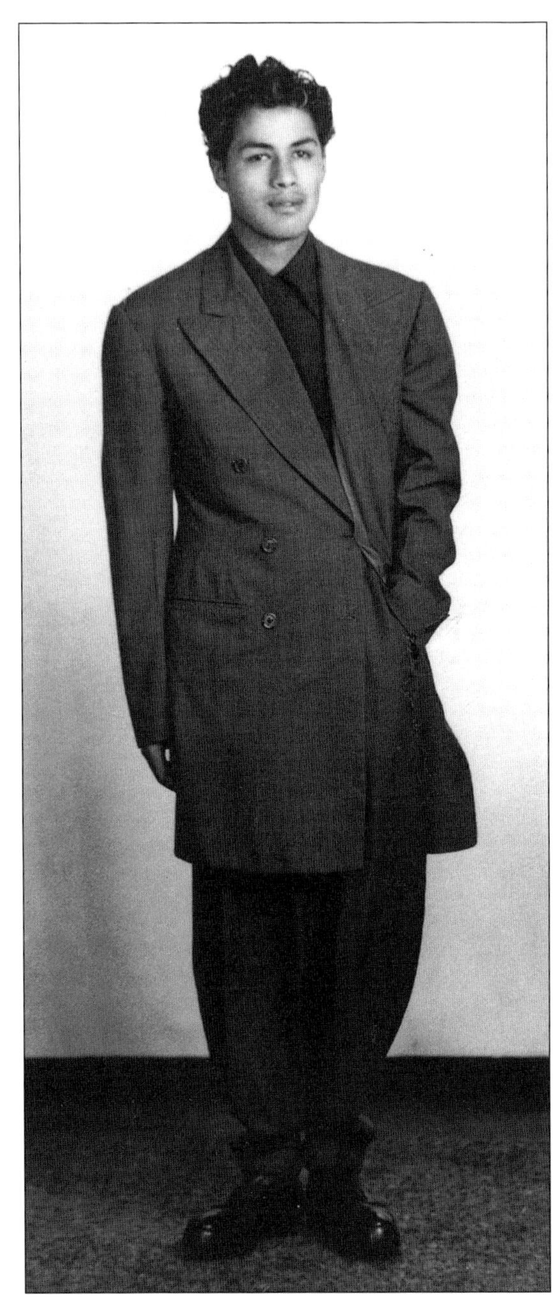

Frank Lopez in San Fernando, 1944.

Frank is in his drapes, a variation on the zoot suit style widely popular in the 1940s.
(Mexican American)

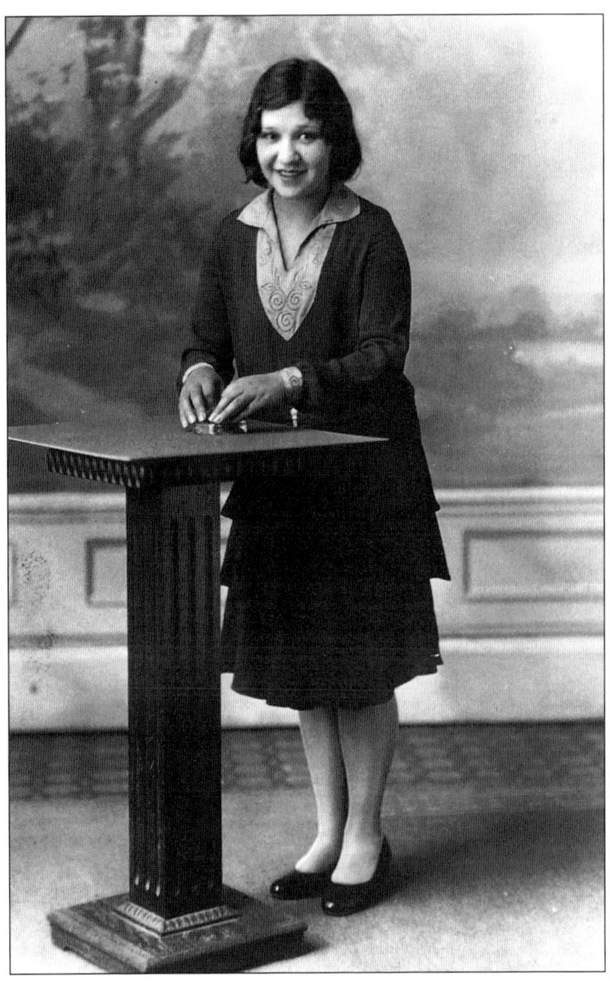

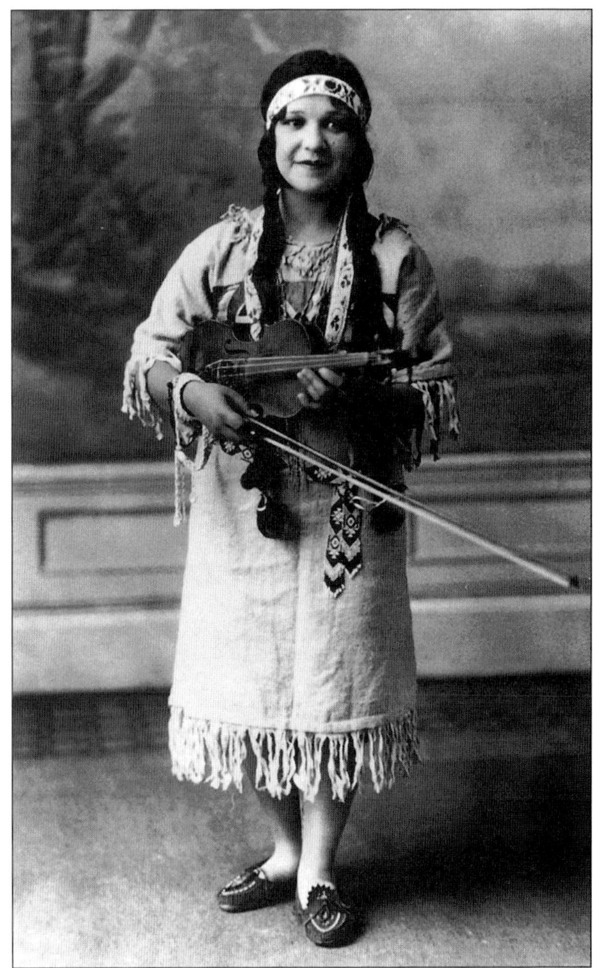

Student at the Sherman Institute in Riverside, ca. 1940. This boarding school was one of many founded in the late 19th and early 20th centuries to educate American Indian children off reservations and to encourage their assimilation into more mainstream American life. These photos are from the files of the Sherman Indian Museum, and are thus different from most of the photos in this book, which come from family albums.
(American Indian)

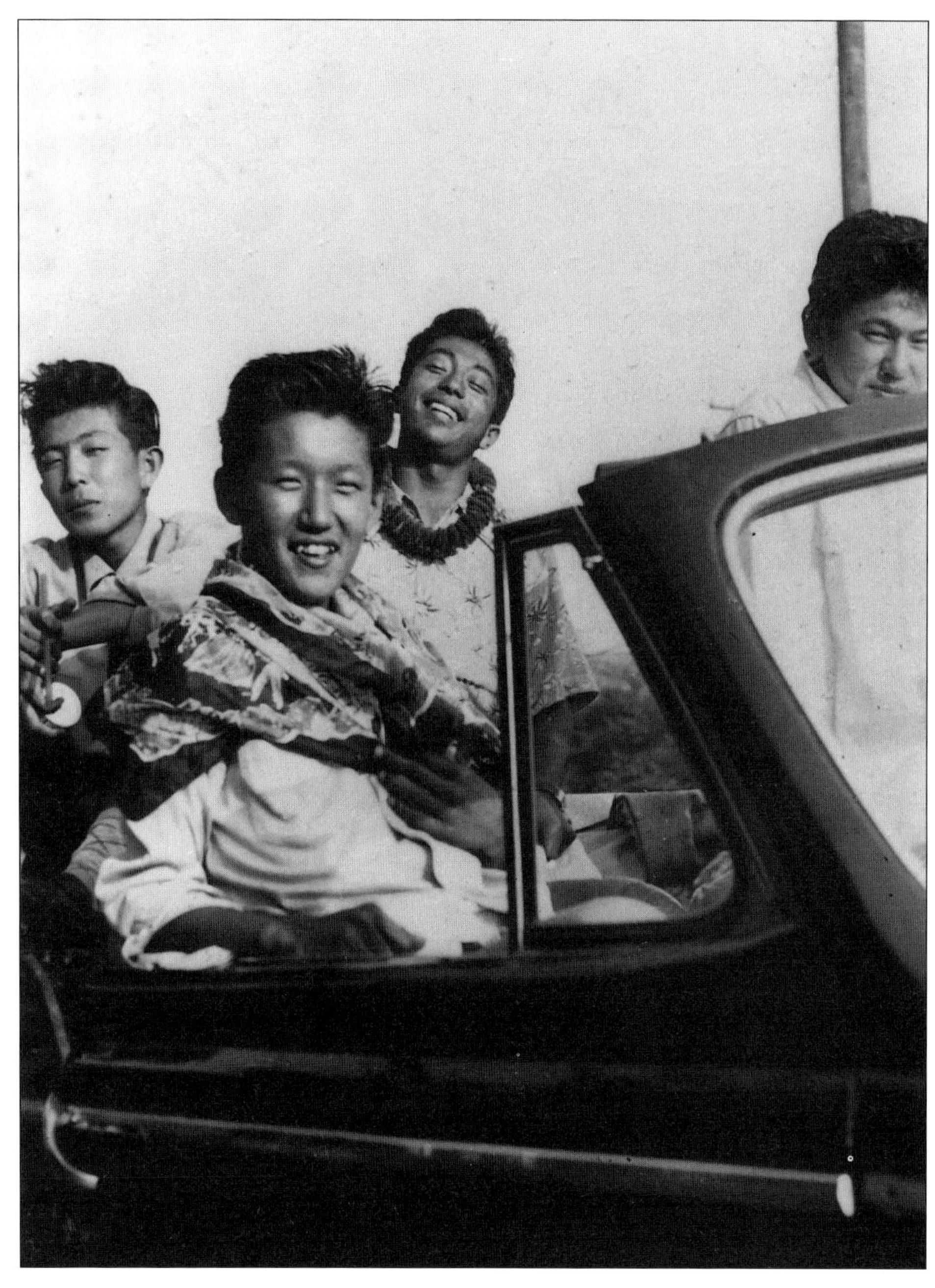

George Toya and his friends in Los Angeles,

ca. 1949.

(Japanese American)

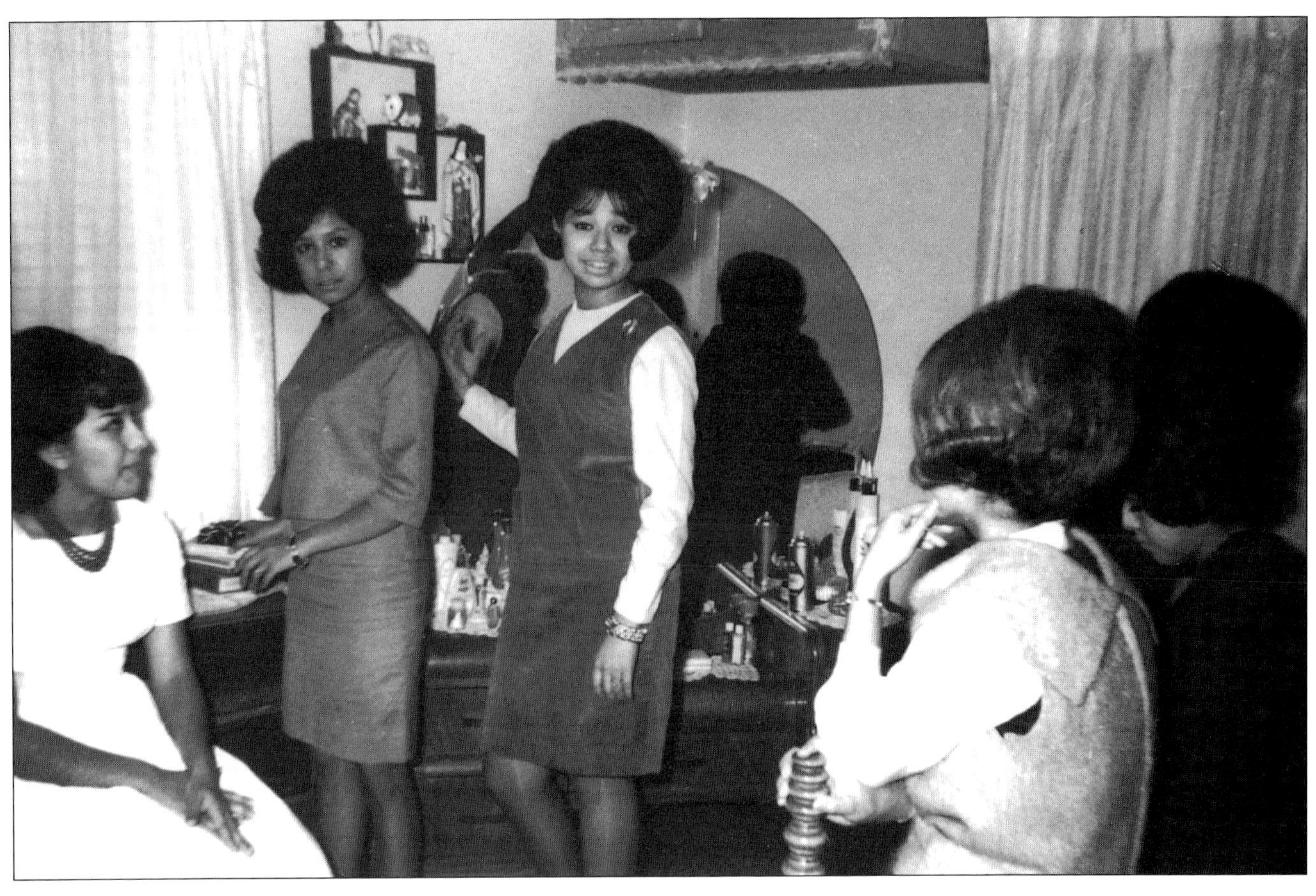

MARYLOU MARTINEZ *(far left)*, MARY PUGA *(center)*, AND FRIENDS

getting ready to go to a party, 1964.
(Mexican American, African American)

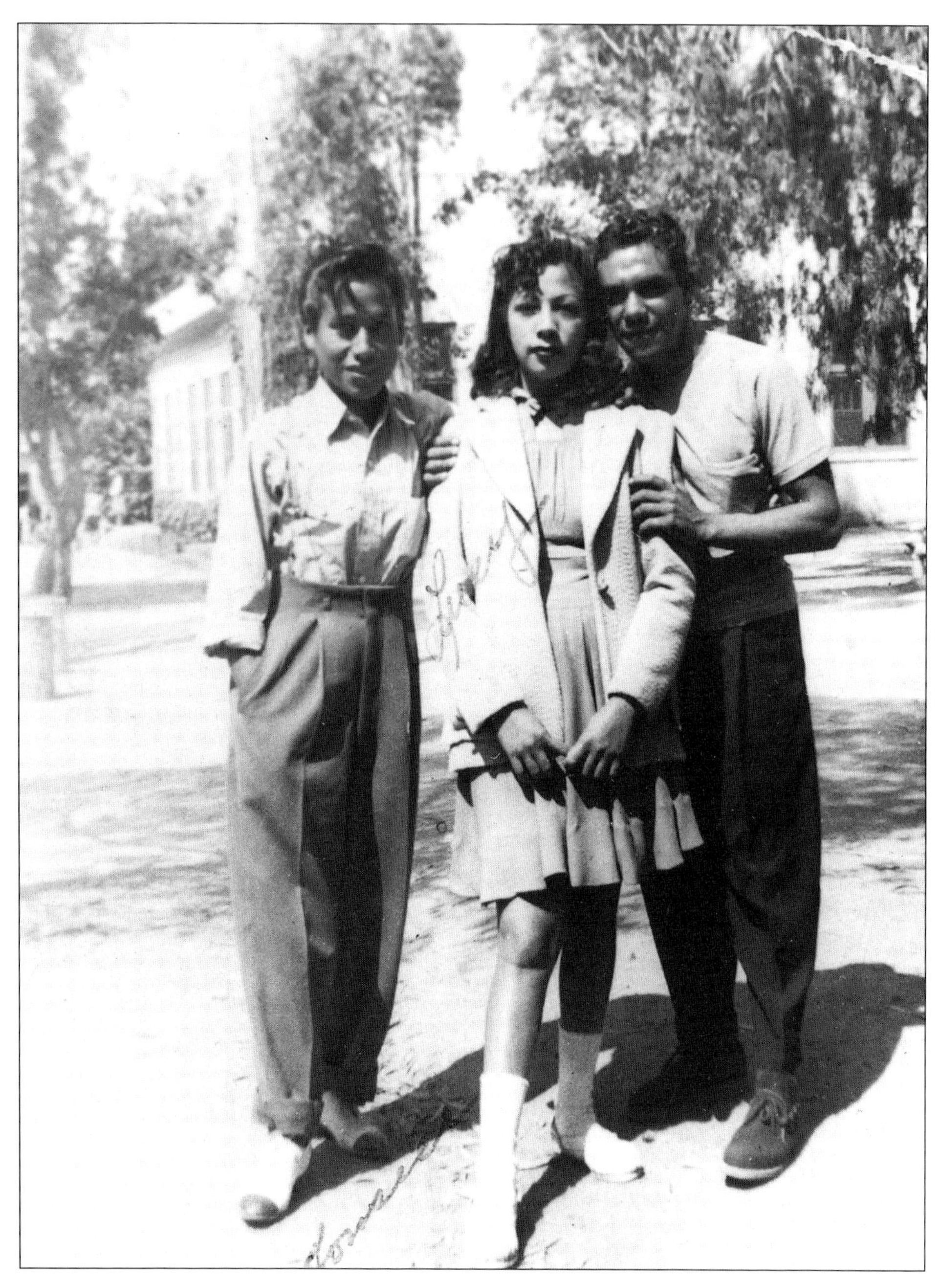

Lucy Fonseca *(center)* and friends

at San Fernando Junior High School, 1939.

(Mexican American)

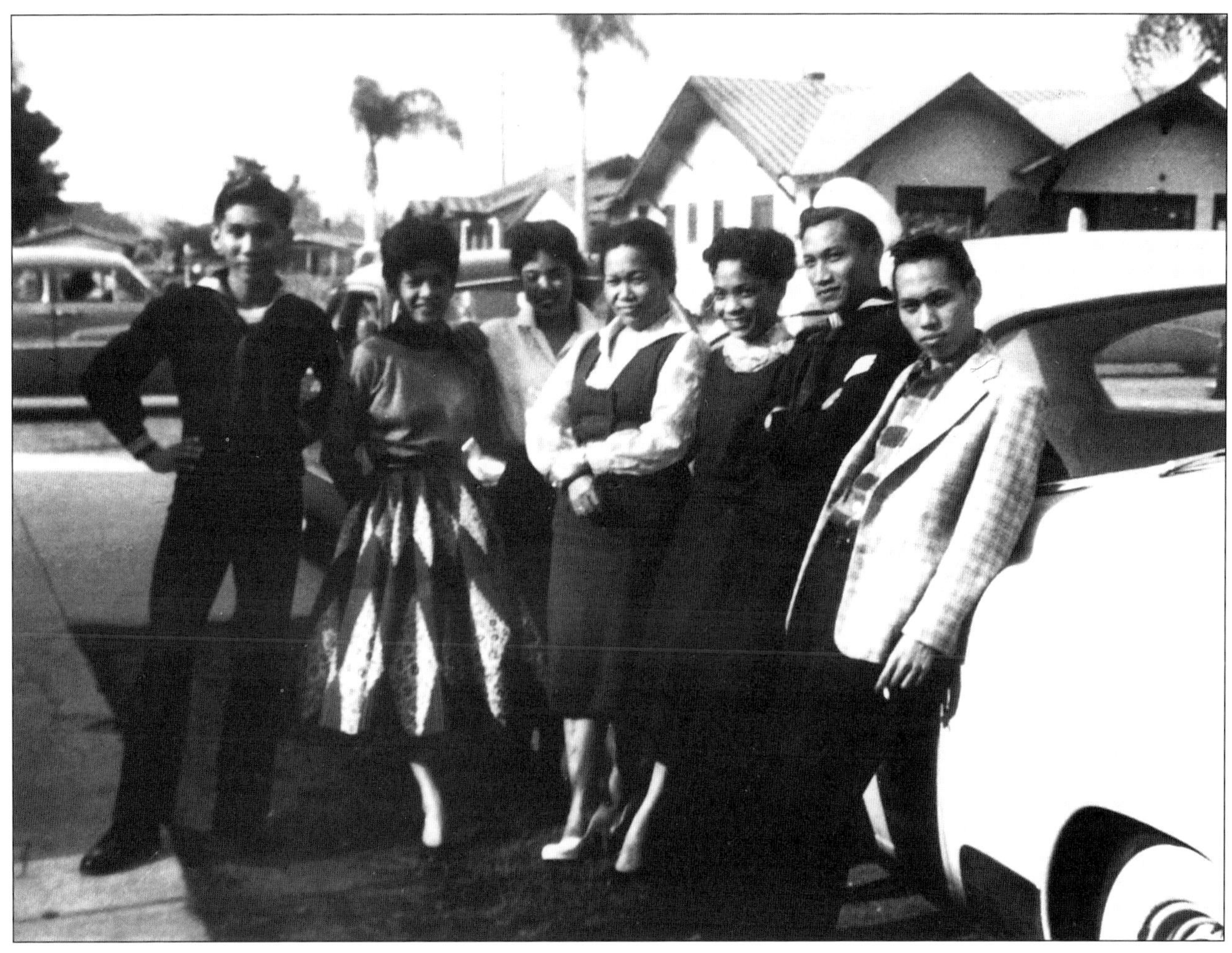

Friends and relatives of Royal Morales near Jefferson Boulevard and Normandie Avenue in Los Angeles, ca. 1953. They are *(left to right)* Sam Reyes, Carmen Quinones, Kathy De La Rosa, Mrs. Quinones, Bonnie Quinones, Tim Reyes, and Ronnie Behasa. *(Filipino American)*

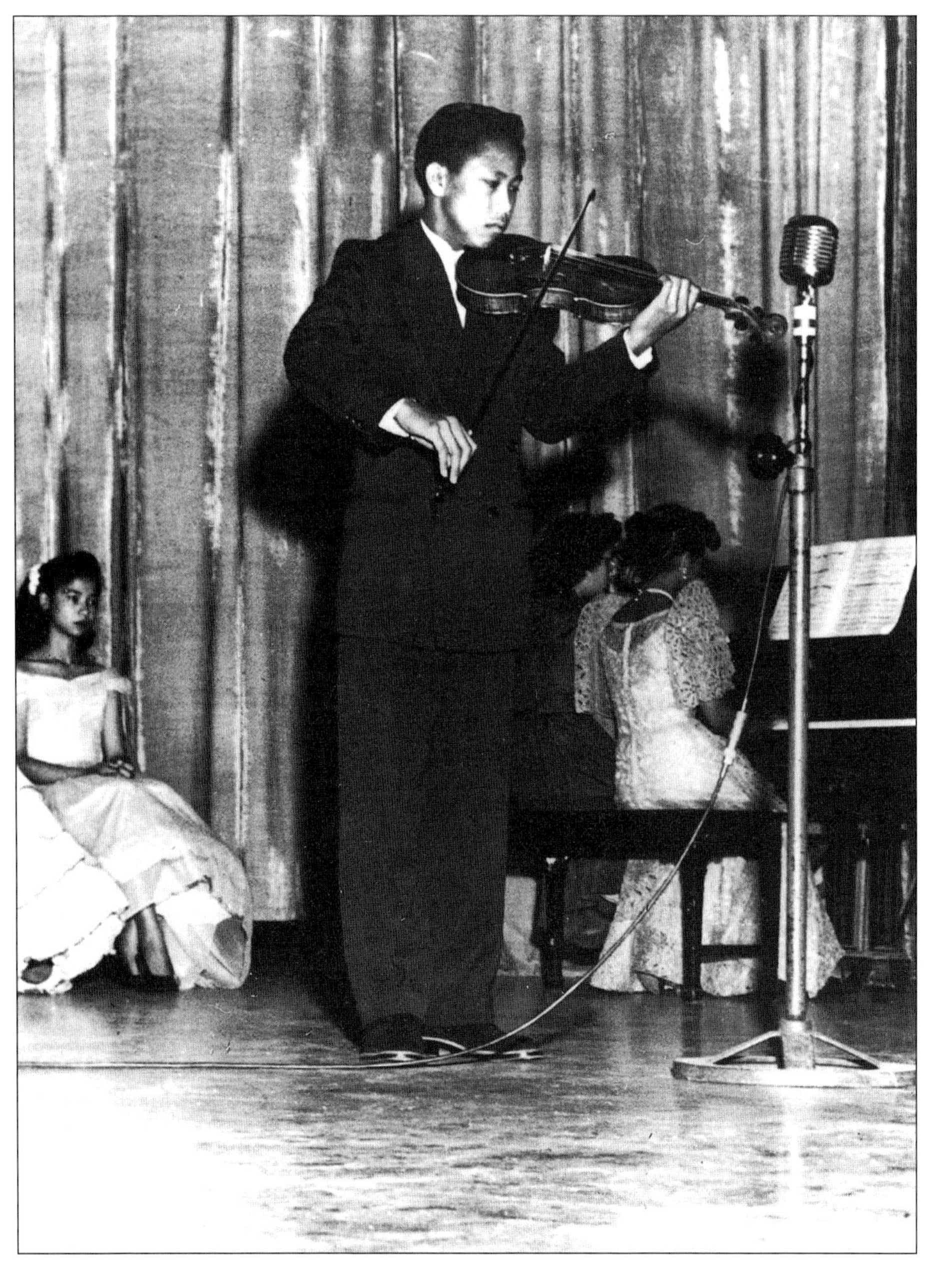

Vicente Noble, Jr., accompanied by Anita Noble on the piano, at a Jose Rizal Day celebration, June 1953. Jose Rizal was an important writer and leader in the Philippine movement for independence in the 1900s. *(Filipino American)*

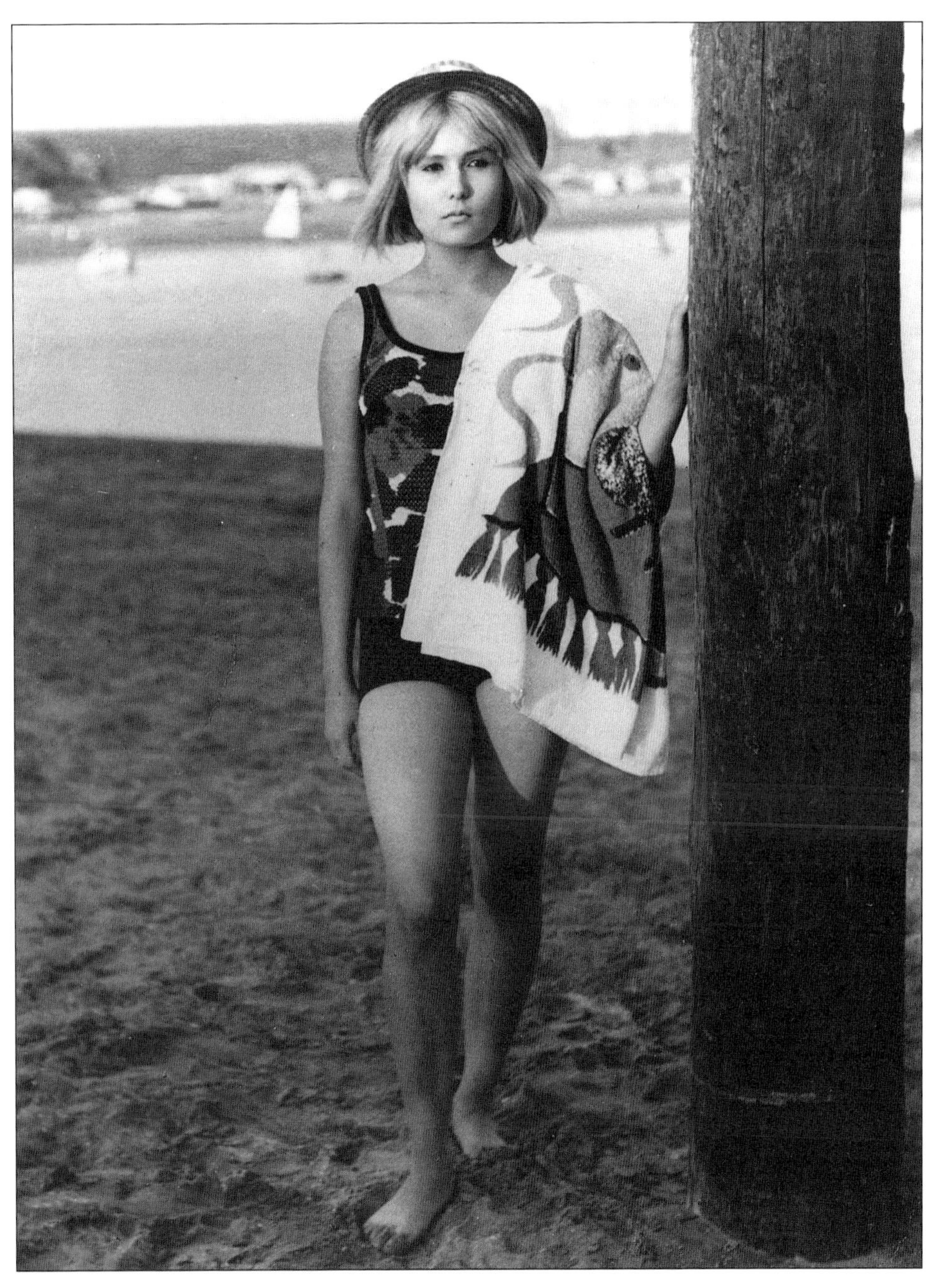

Estela Gomez, 1963.

(Mexican American)

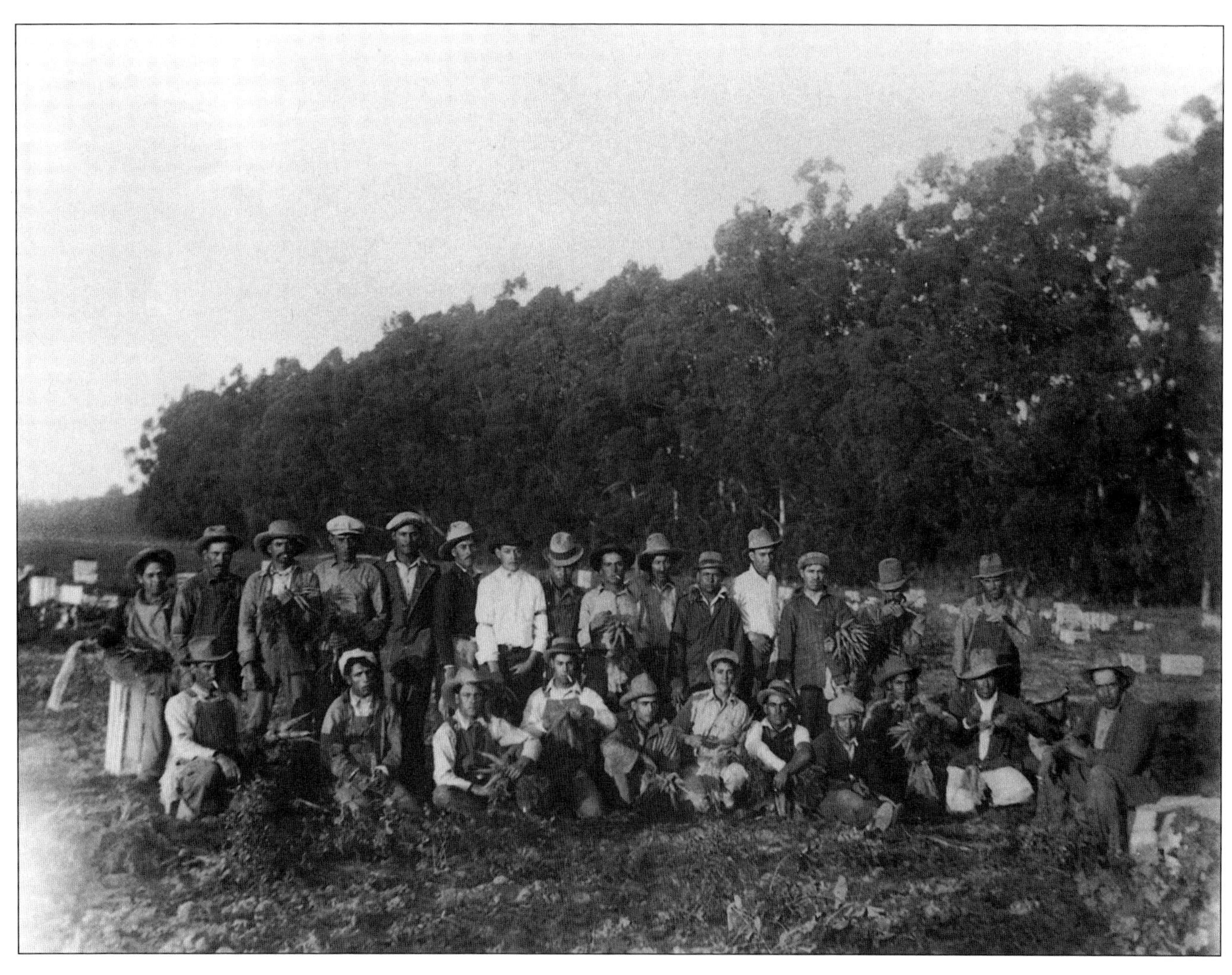

Isidro Ordonez *(top row, far right)* and
his nephew Polo Ordonez *(bottom row, sixth from left)*,

harvesting carrot crops in Ventura County, 1929.
(Mexican American)

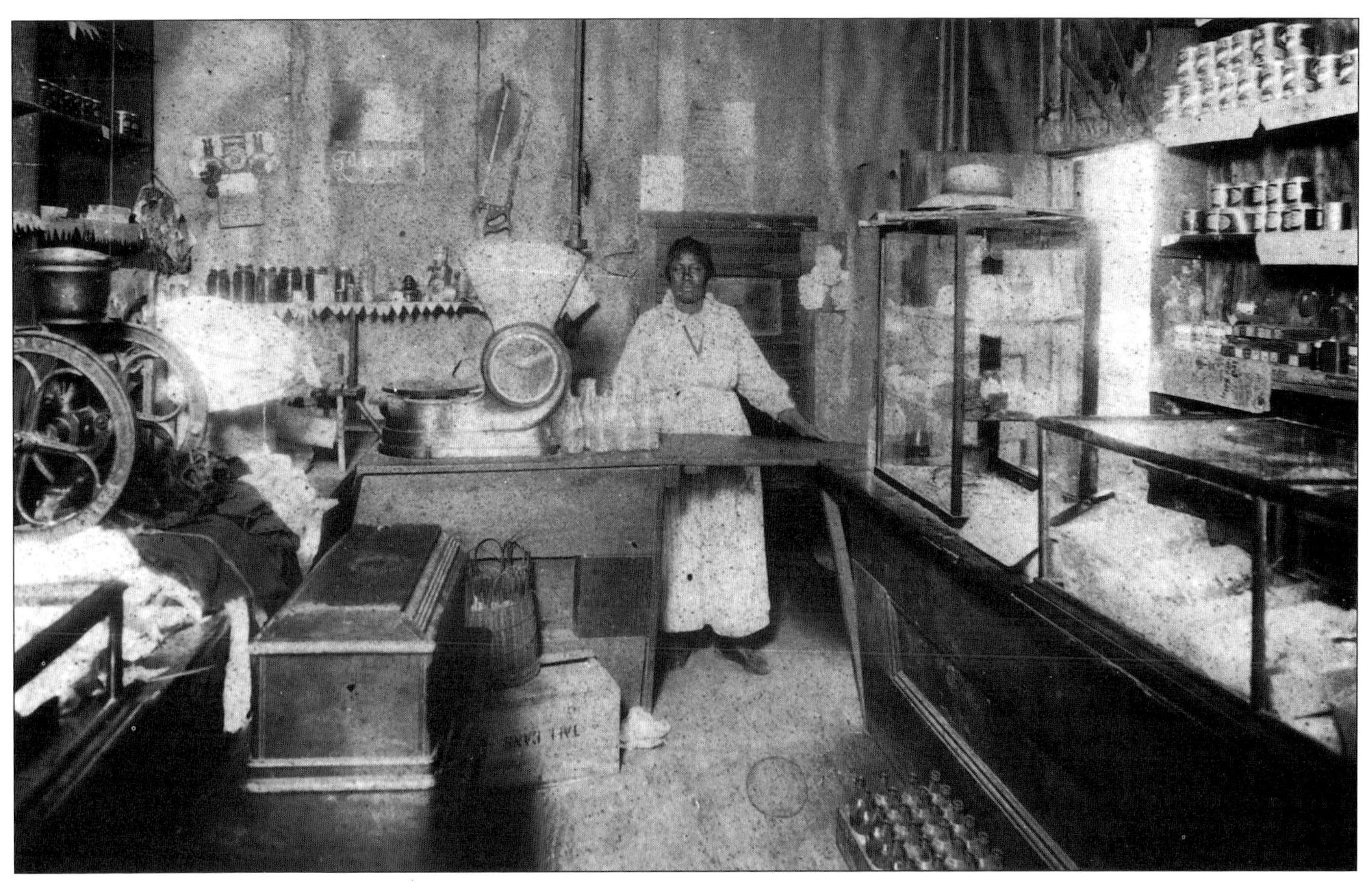

Liney Jones Rozier

at the family store on 51st Street and Holmes Avenue in Los Angeles, 1906.

(African American)

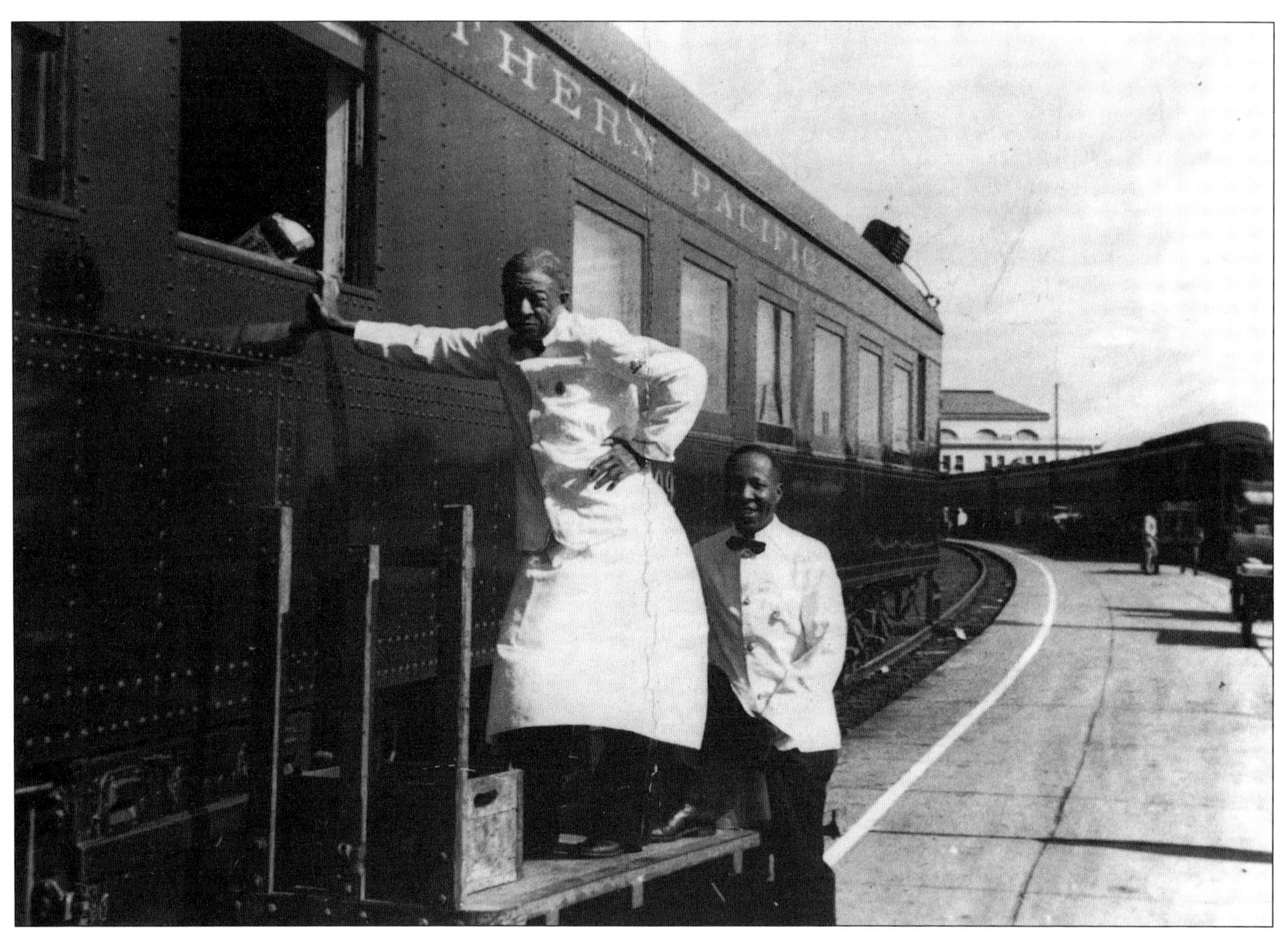

Charles McKinney and Frank Carter,

waiters on the Southern Pacific, at Union Station, 1940.

(African American)

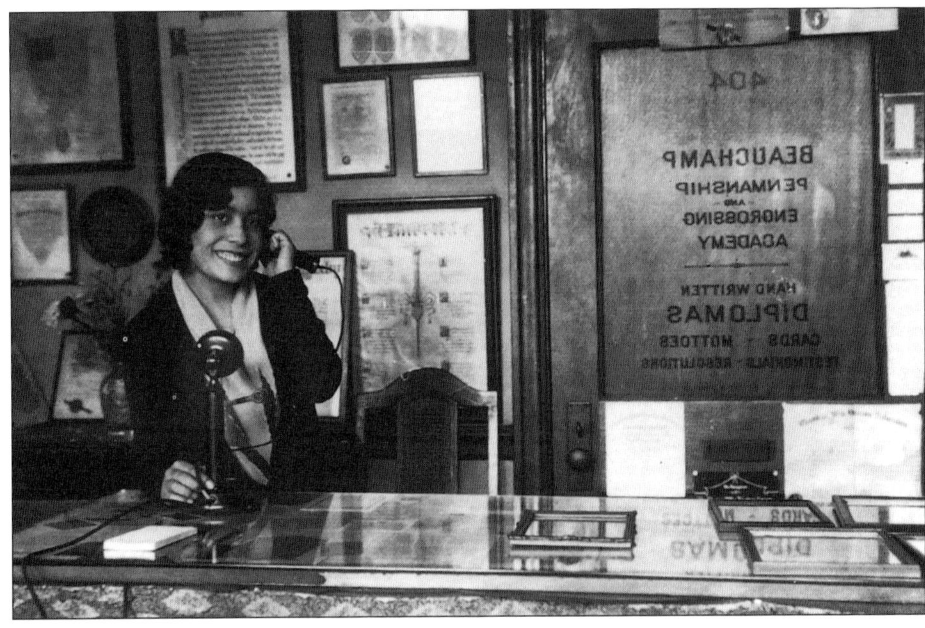

ARMIDA TORRES,

the office manager of Beauchamp Penmanship and Engrossing Academy at 145 South Broadway in downtown Los Angeles, early 1920s.
(Mexican American)

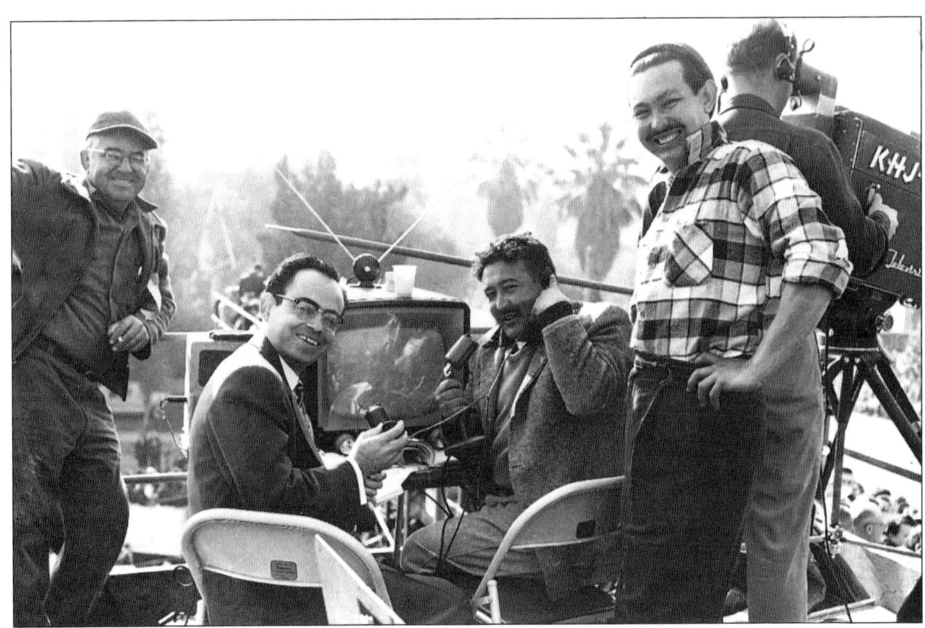

TED FREGUZO, EDDIE RODRIGUEZ, AND PETE RODRIGUEZ

in charge of the first television and radio simulcast, in Spanish of the Rose Parade, 1952.
(Mexican American)

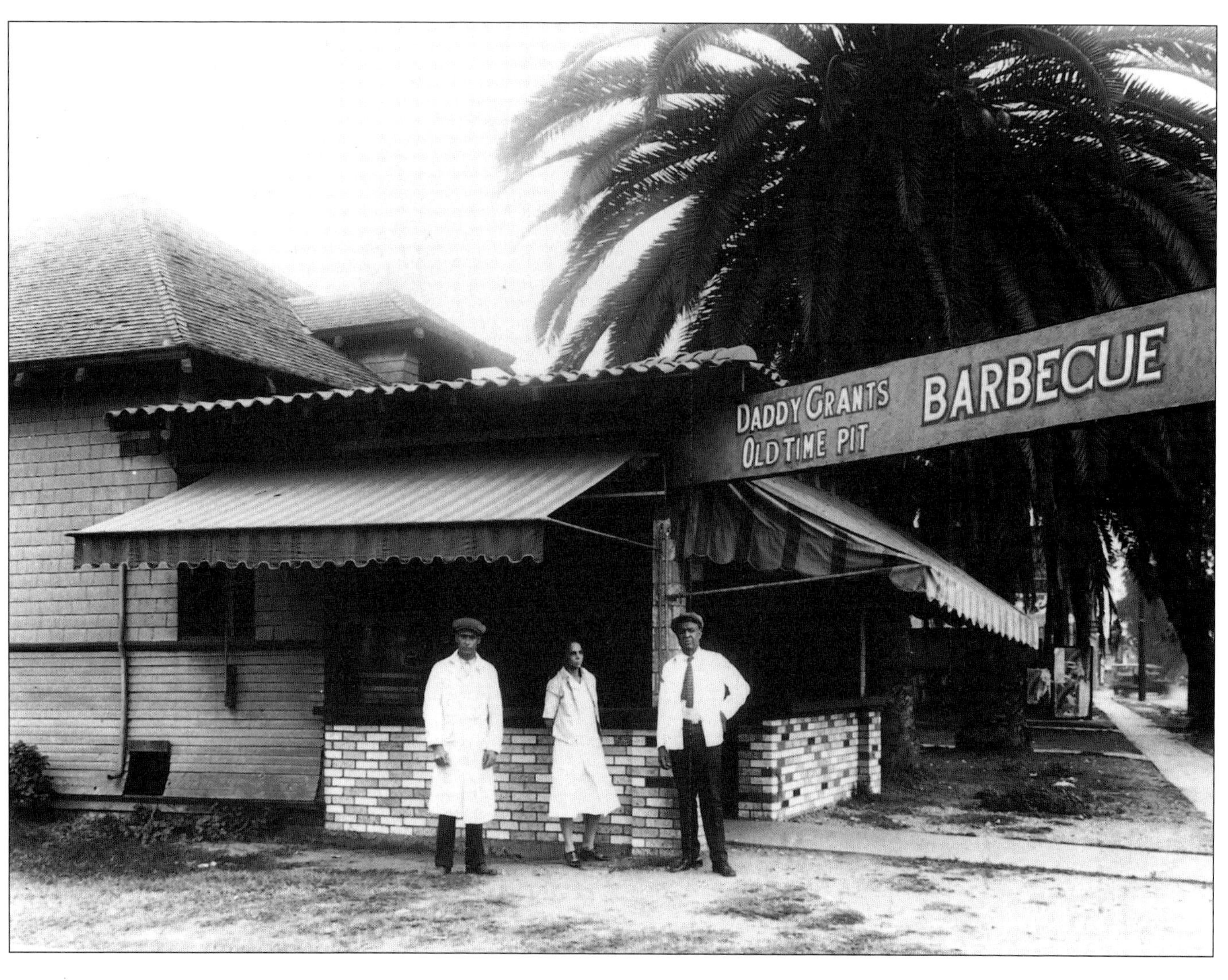

Lemuel "Daddy" Grant *(far right)*

in front of his Old Time Pit Barbecue on Washington Boulevard in Los Angeles, ca. 1930.

(African American)

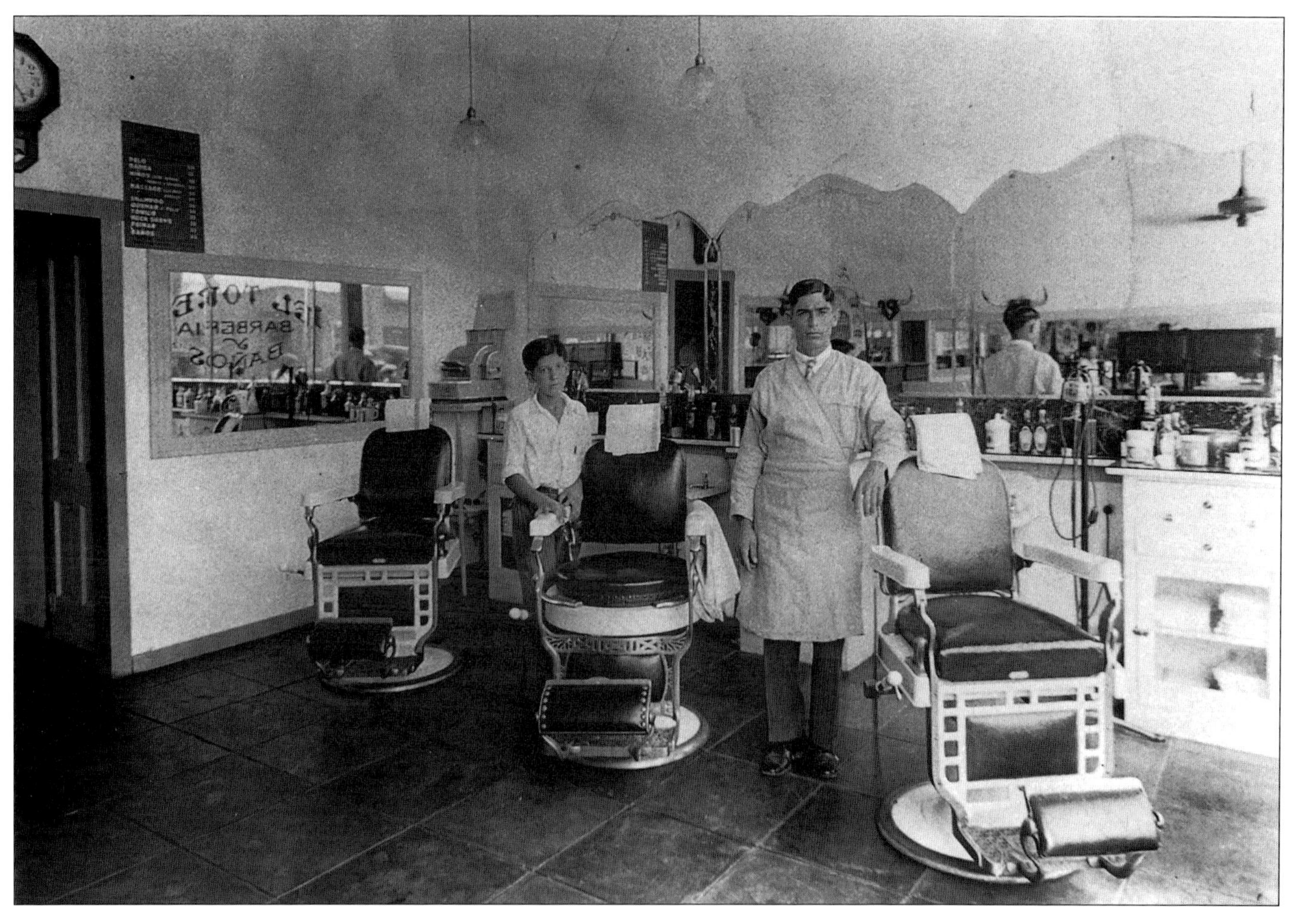

Young Antonio Sandoval *(left)*

in Lan's Barber Shop on Ford Boulevard in Maravilla Park, East Los Angeles, 1929.

(Mexican American)

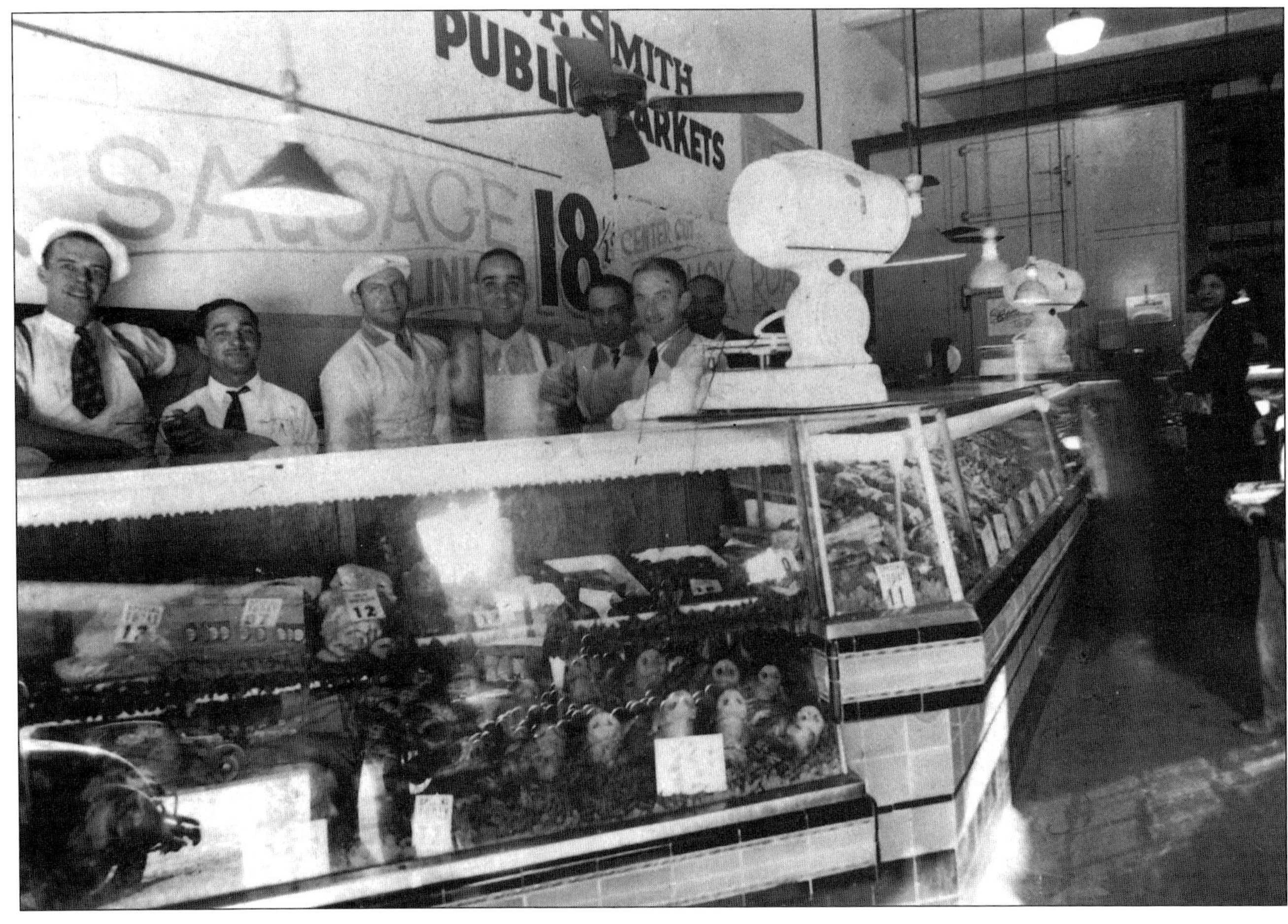

THEODORE TROY *(second from left)*

at work in the E.F. Smith Public Market.
It was the first 24-hour market on Central Avenue, ca. 1939.
(African American and others)

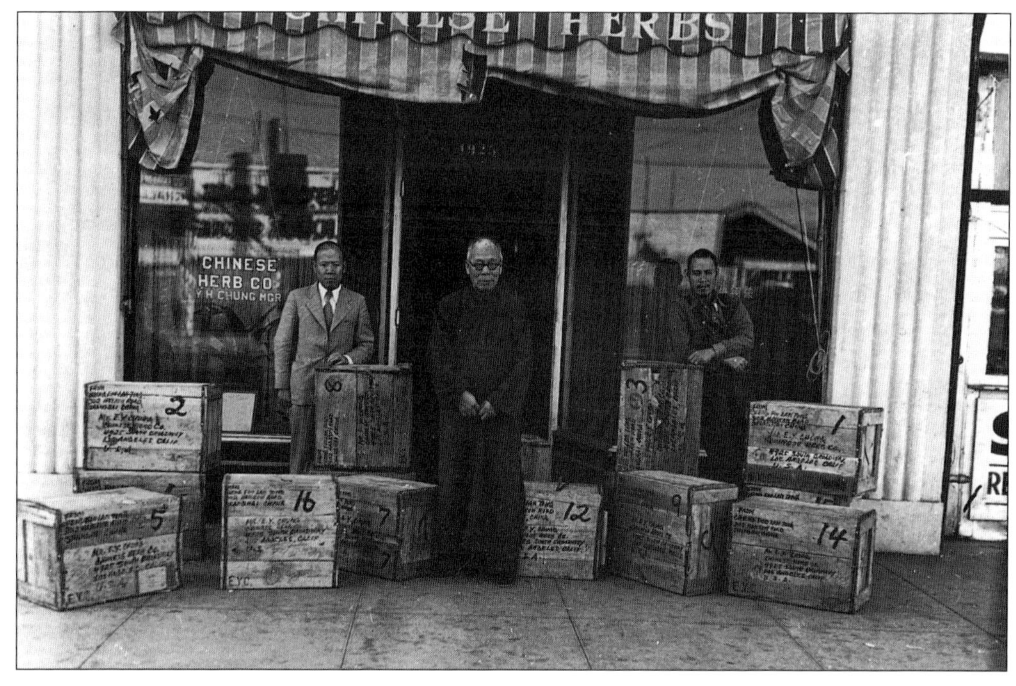

Yick Hong Chung *(center)*
and sons Elbert *(left)*
and Sam *(right)*,
in front of their
Chinese Herb Company on South
Broadway, 1938.
(Chinese American)

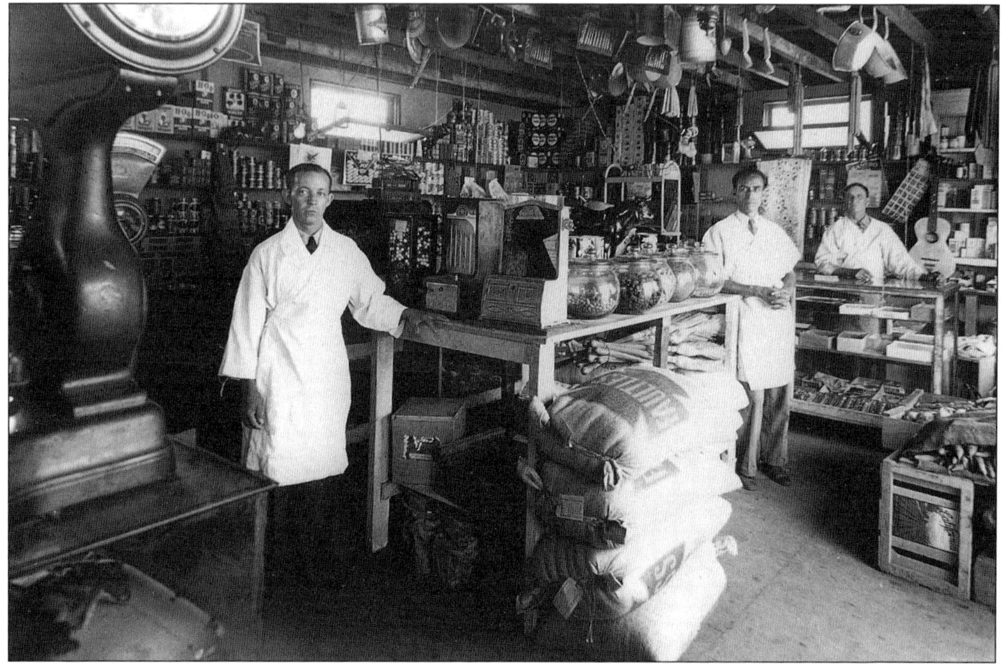

Uncle Aurelio Dominguez *(left)*
in his grocery store on
Solano Avenue near Elysian Park
in Los Angeles, 1925.
(Mexican American)

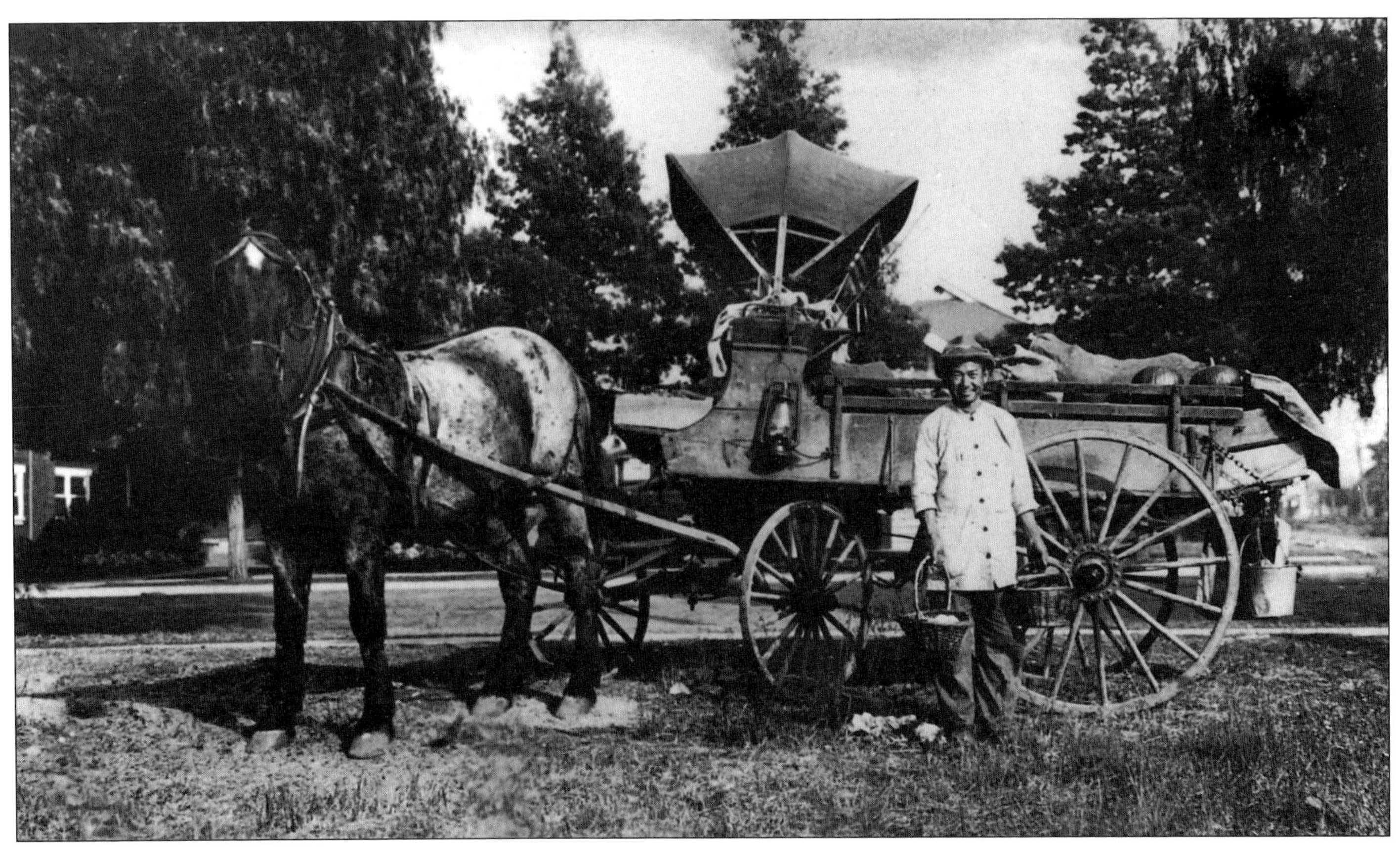

Chan Yip Leong,

born 1867, selling fruit and vegetables east of the plaza, 1914.

(Chinese American)

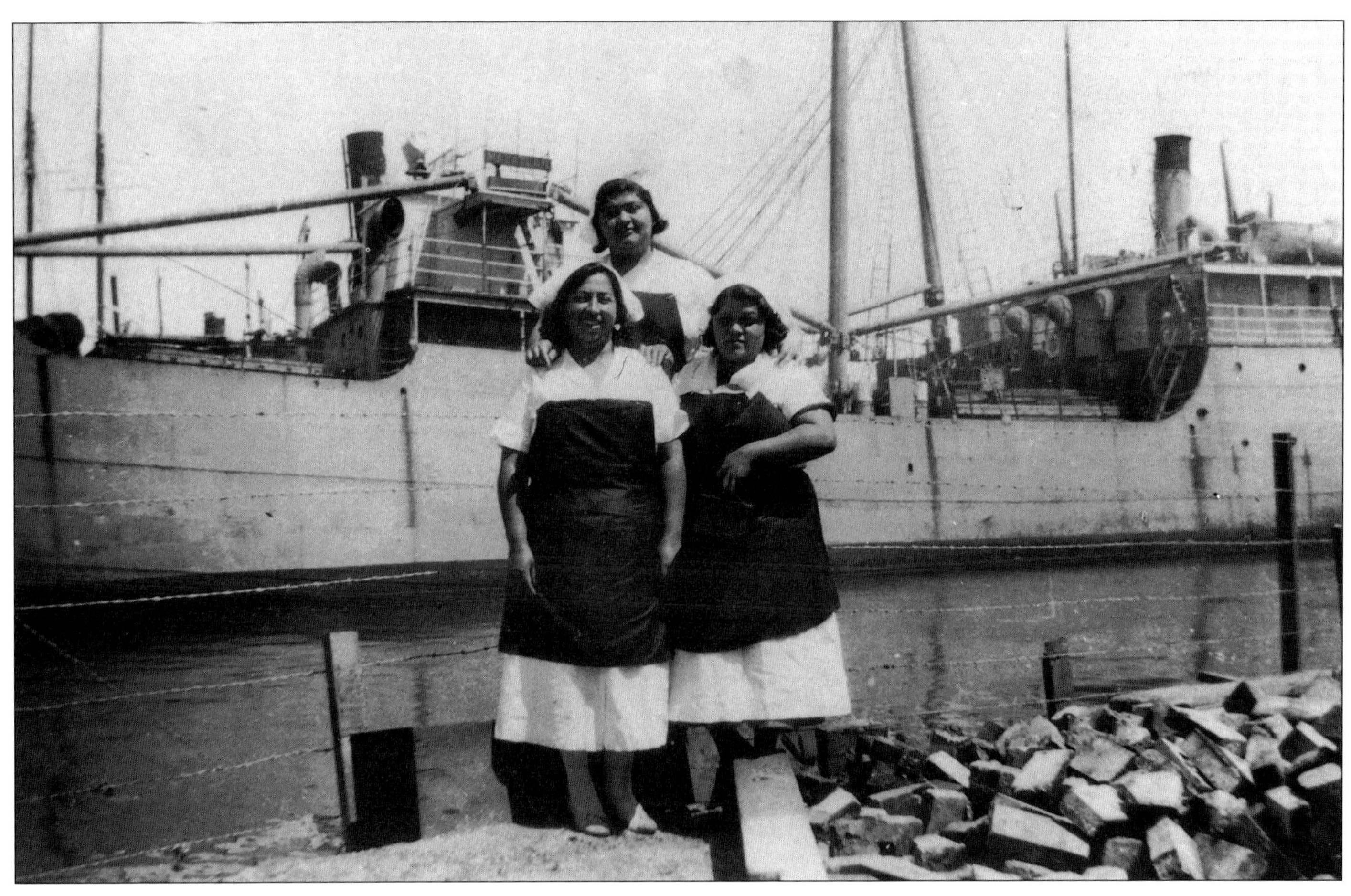

Jenny Gonzalez *(top)*
AND TWO OTHER CANNERY WORKERS
in the Los Angeles Harbor area, ca. 1930s.
(Mexican American)

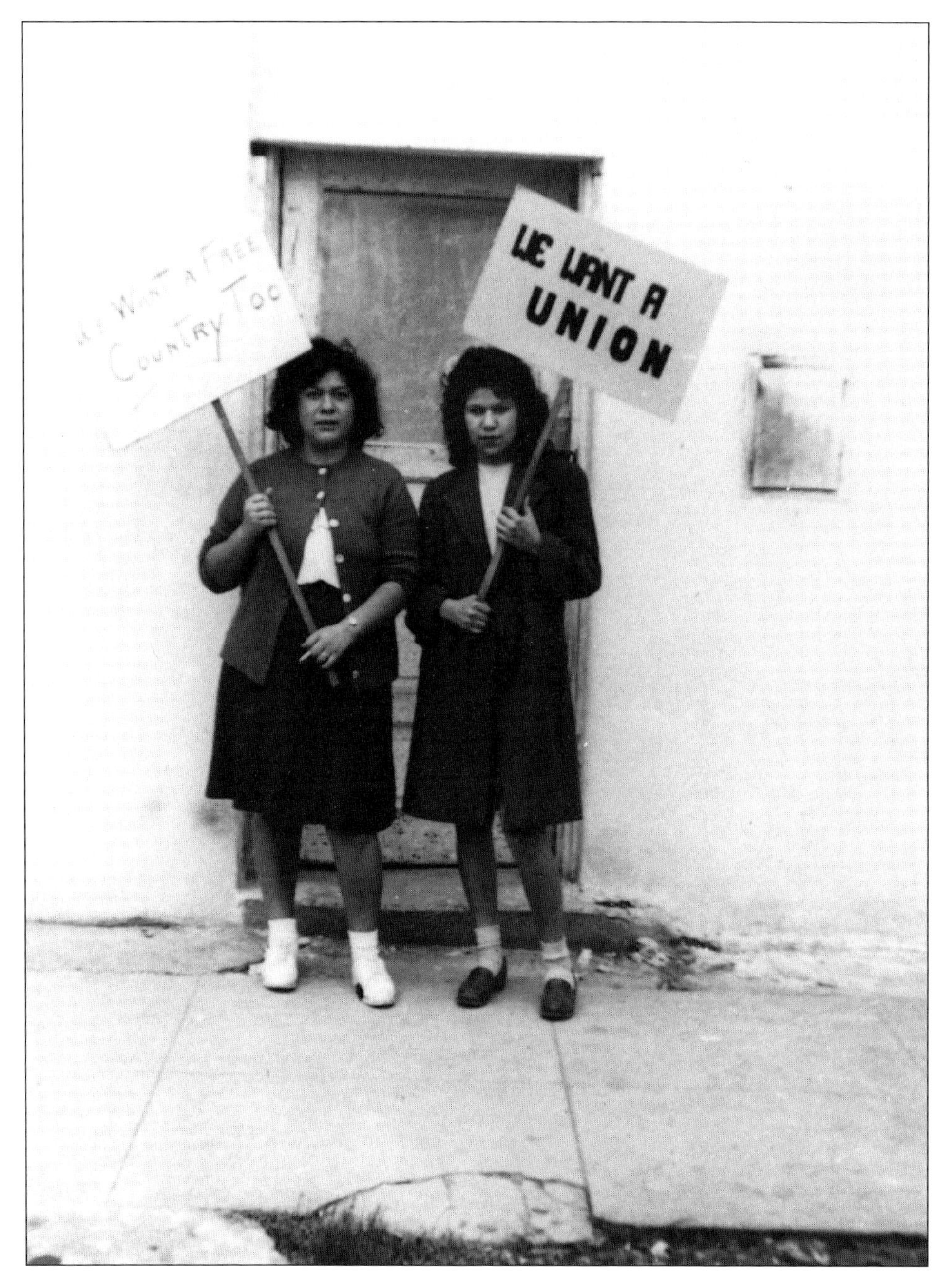

Rosie Albrann *(left, age 19)* and Ramona Fonseca *(right, age 17)*

on strike outside of the Barenveld Shirt Factory, protesting the lack of a union, 1943.

(Mexican American)

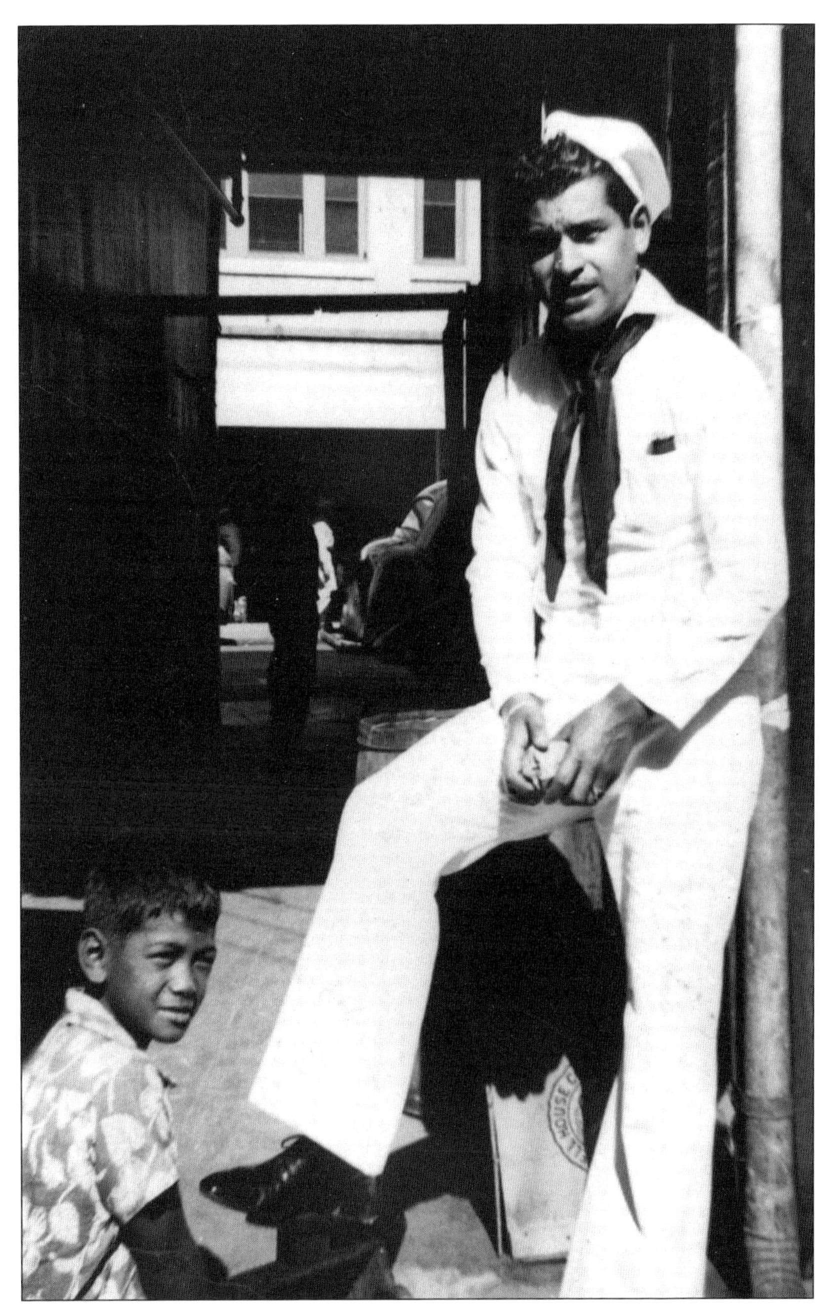

Daniel Lopez *(right)*

probably in San Diego, November 13, 1944.

(Mexican American)

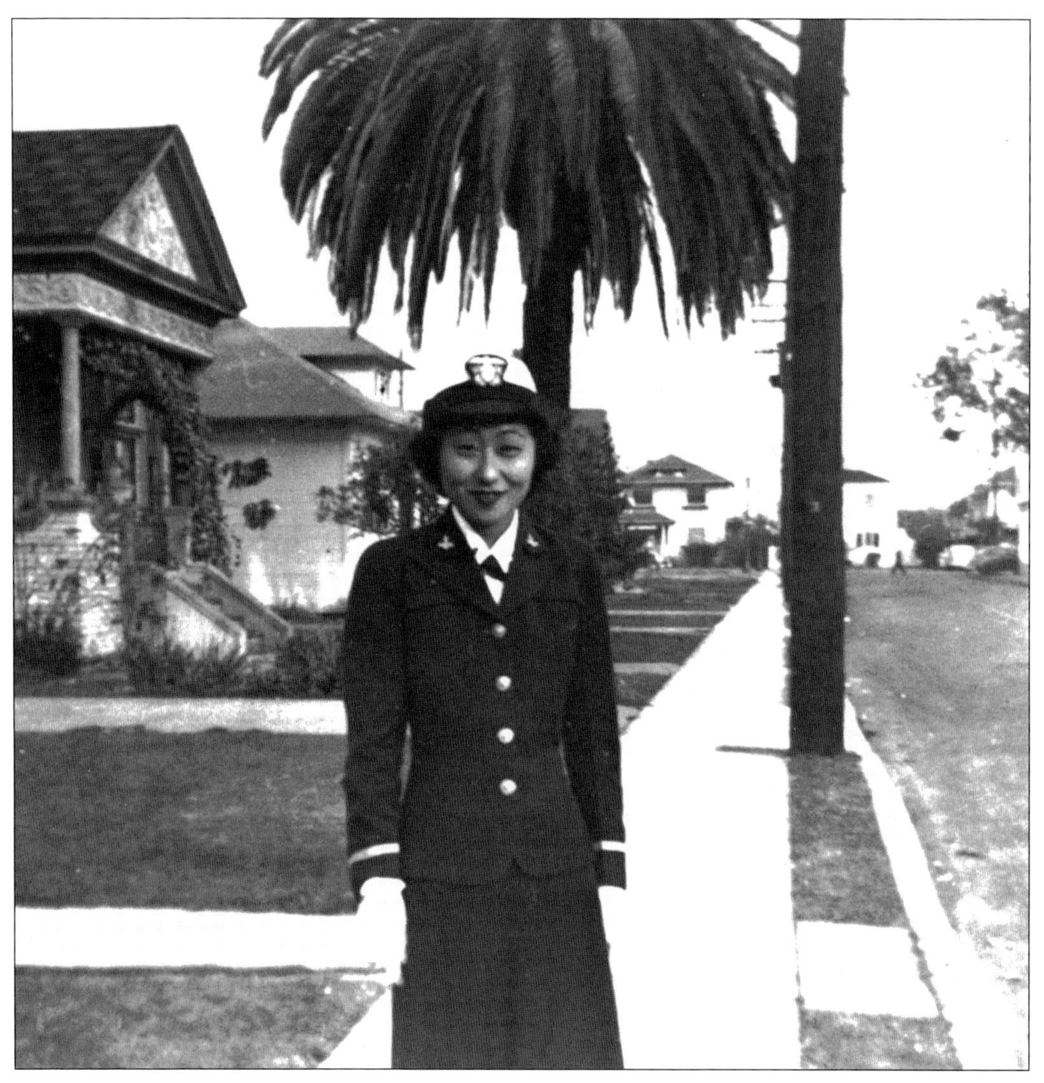

Susan Ahn

on 37th Place in Los Angeles, 1943. She was the first Korean American in the WAVES, the women's division of the U.S. Naval Reserve in the 1940s. She also went to Pensacola Gunnery School to become the first woman gunnery officer.

(Korean American)

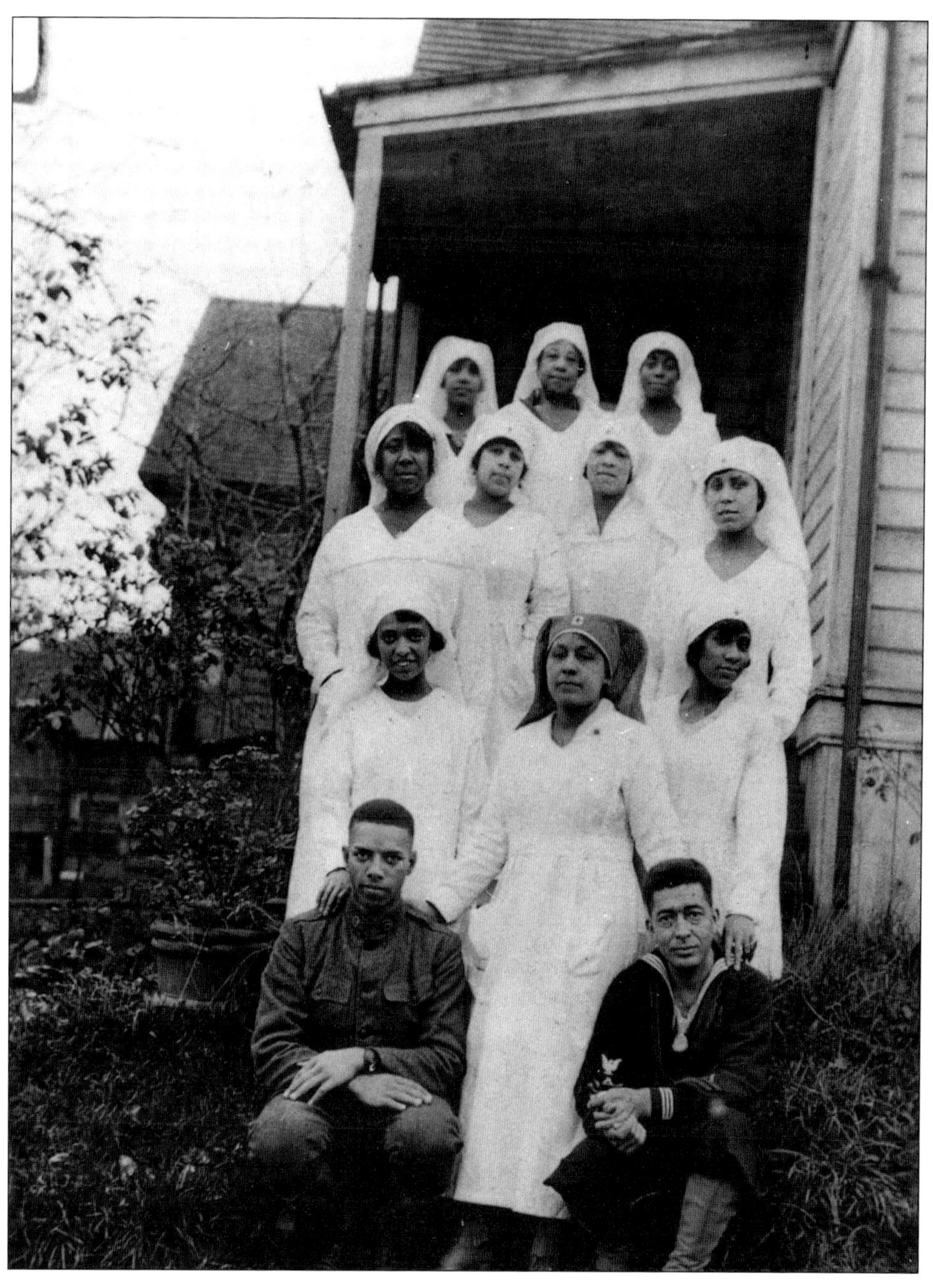

Red Cross volunteers

on 22nd Street near Hooper Avenue
in Los Angeles during World War I, ca. 1918.
(African American)

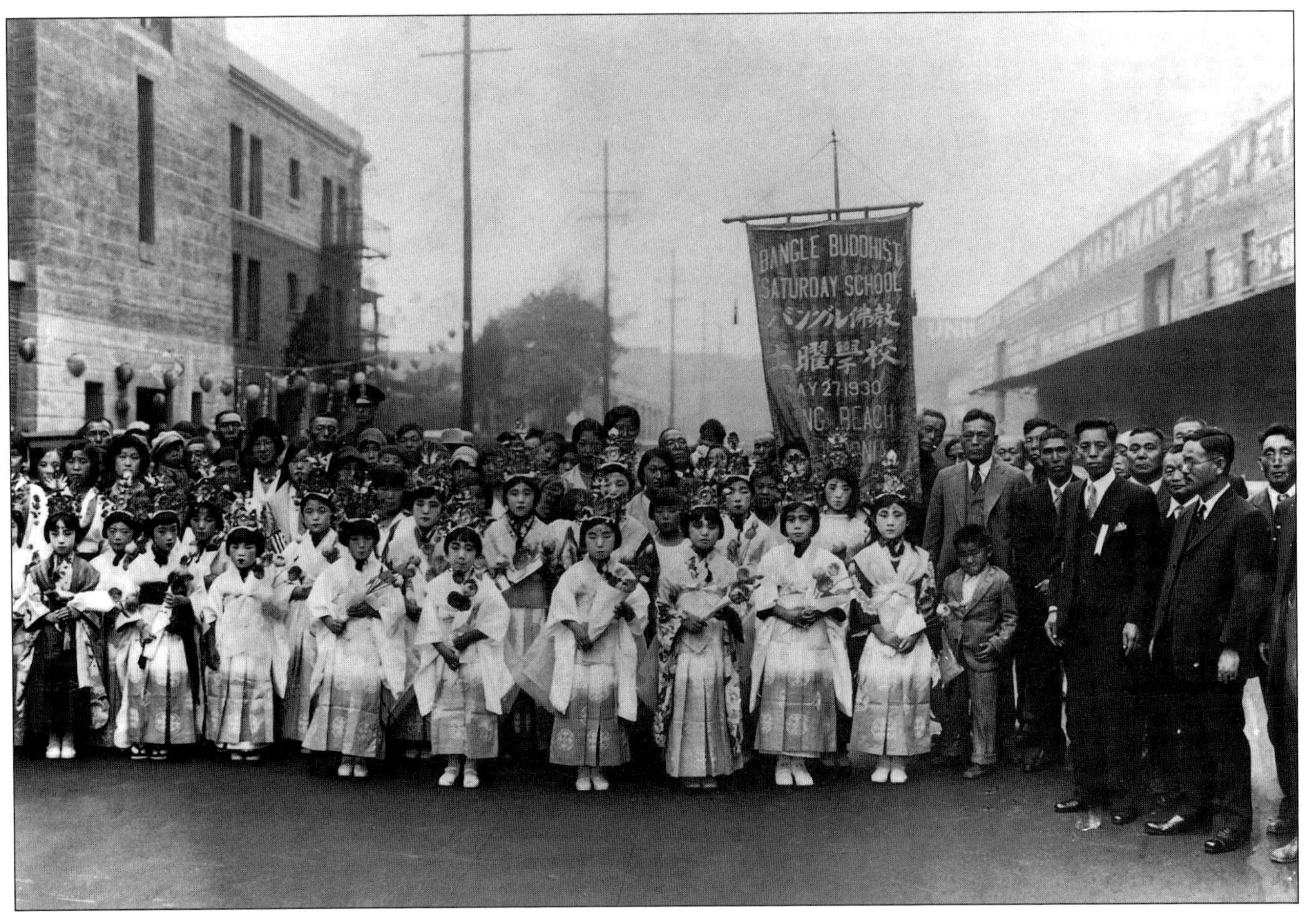

SERVICE TO COMMEMORATE THE ELEVATION OF THE LOS ANGELES HOMPA HONGWANJI BUDDHIST TEMPLE TO BETSUIN STATUS, 1931.

The Los Angeles Temple was the first in the mainland United States to reach this special status, which recognized it as a major temple of this branch of Buddhism.

(Japanese American)

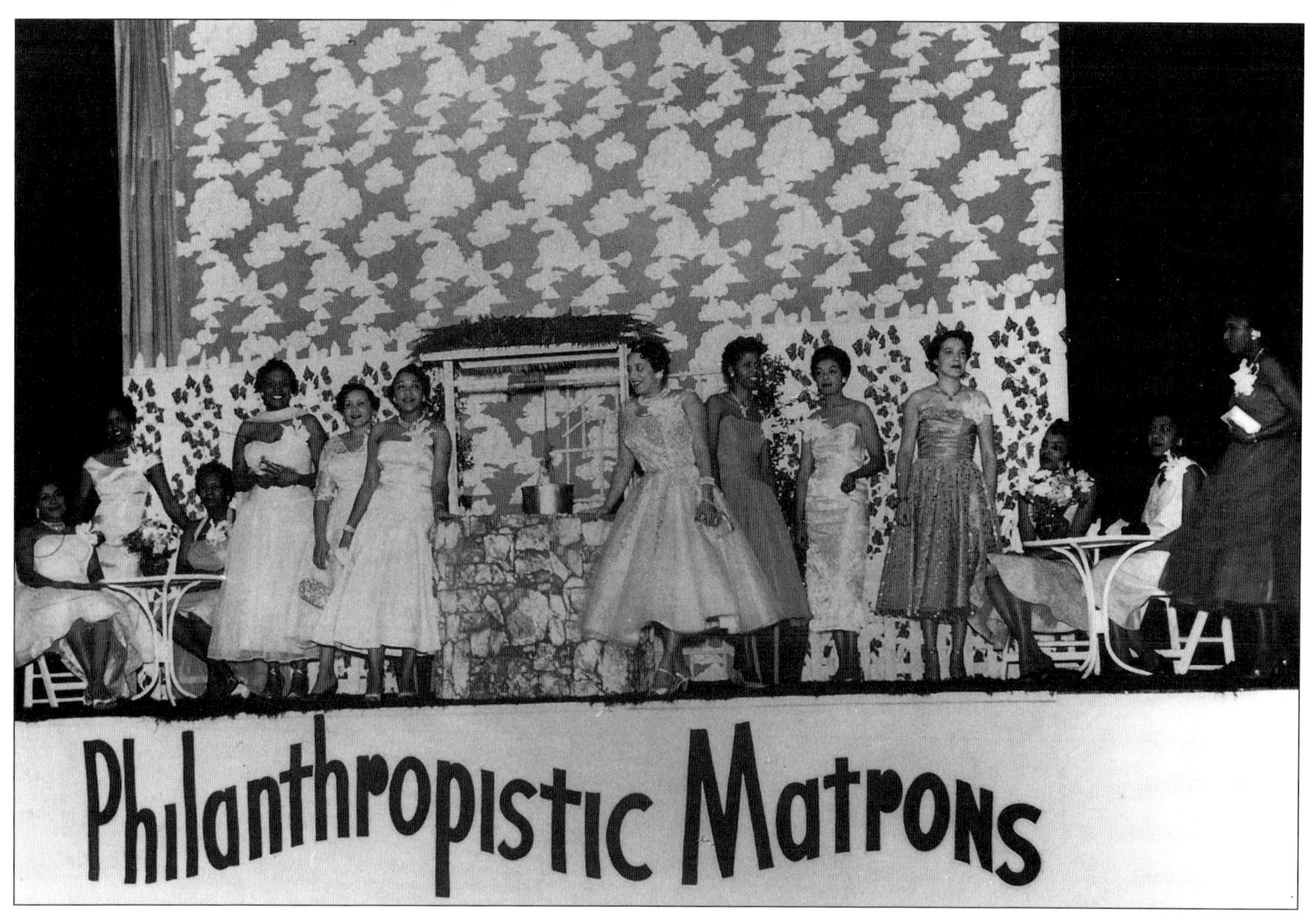

THE PHILANTHROPISTIC MATRONS,

ca. 1955.

(African American)

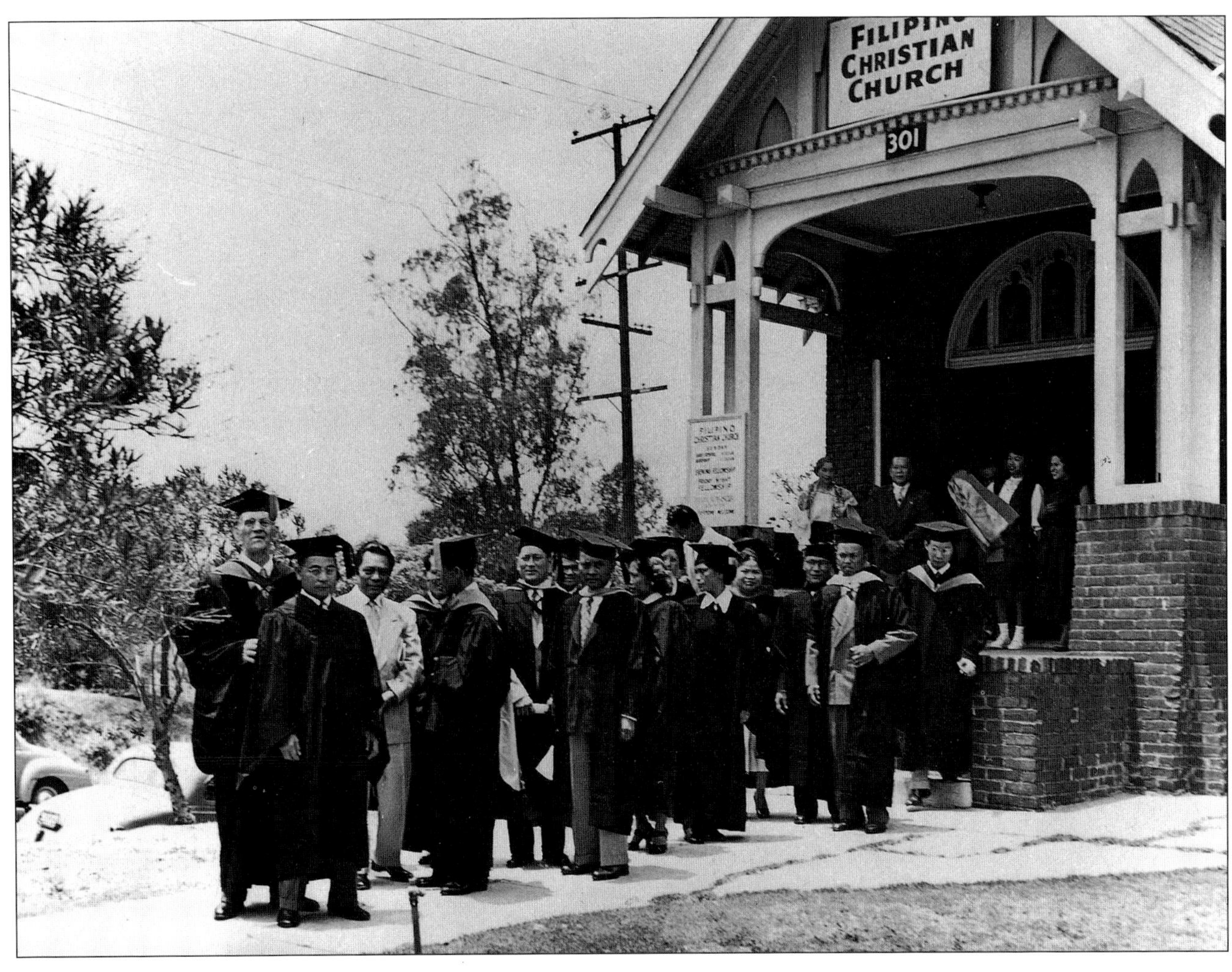

Alumni homecoming and worship at the Filipino Christian Church
on North Union Street in Los Angeles, June 10, 1951.
Discriminated against and forced to band together to worship, often moving from one site to another, earlier Filipino immigrants had dreamed of building this church.
(Filipino American)

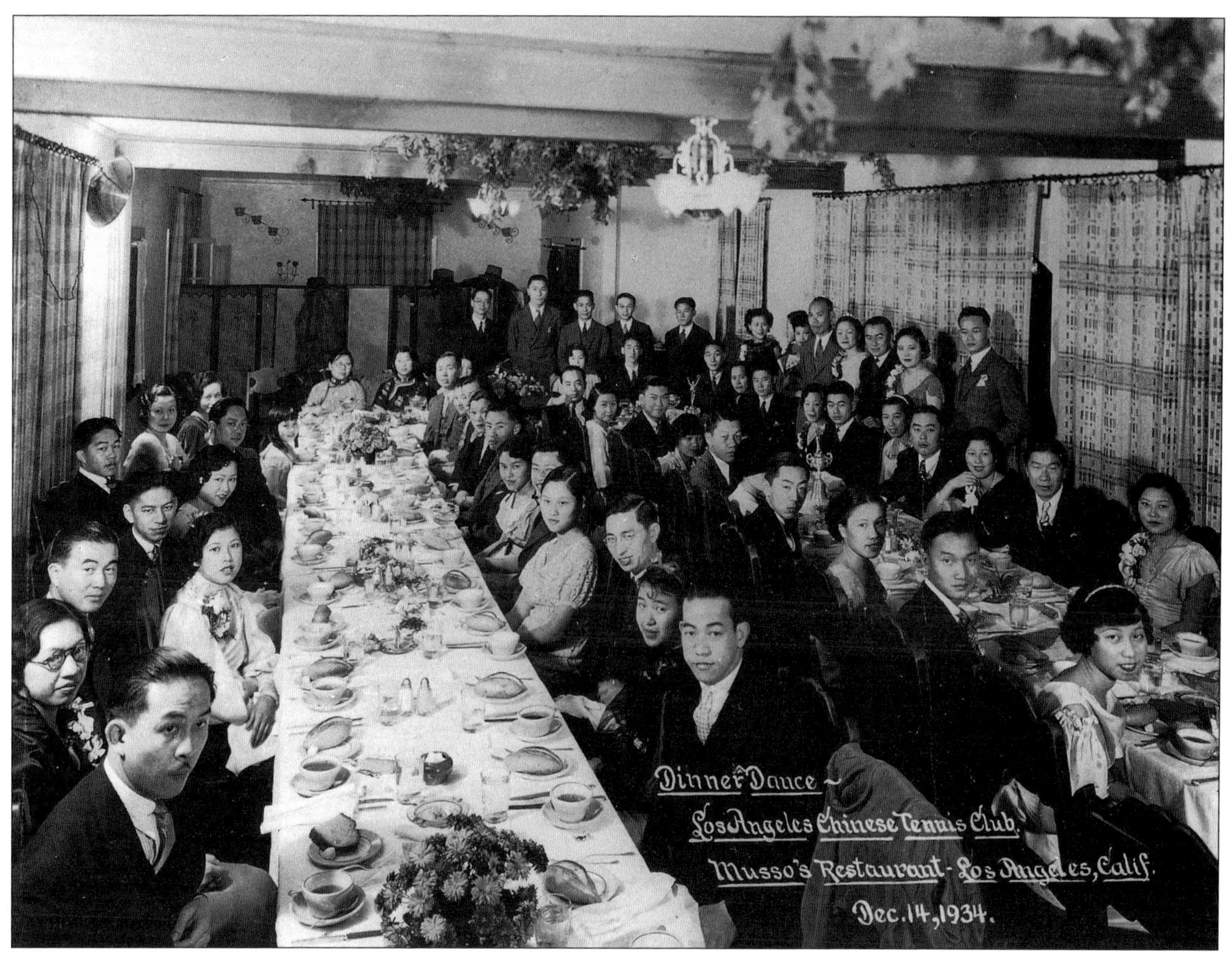

A Los Angeles Chinese Tennis Club dinner dance
held at Musso and Frank's Restaurant, 1934.
(Chinese American)

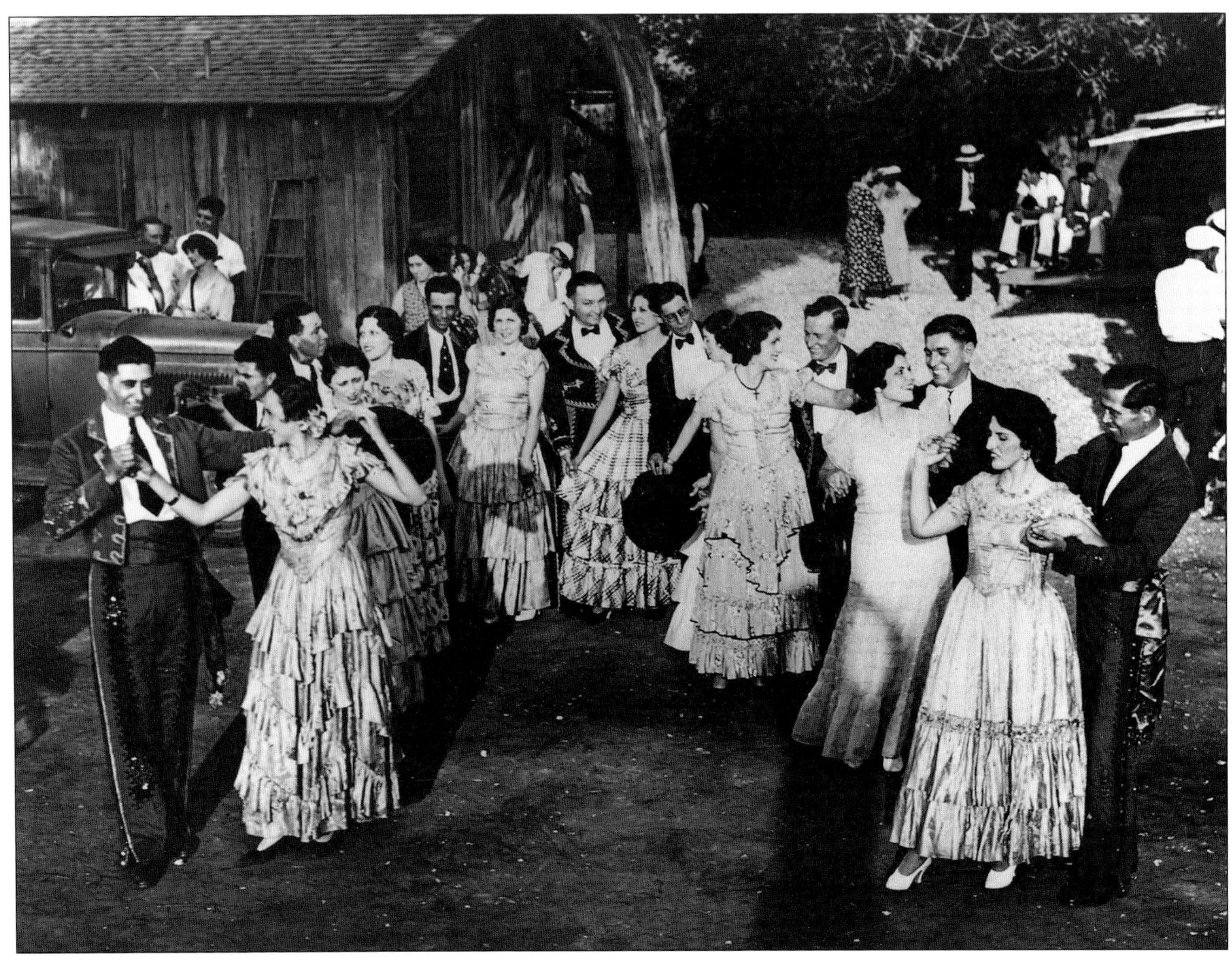

A gathering of the El Recuerdo Club,

a social club which performed Spanish dancing at the Lugo Adobe at Rancho San Antonio in the 1920s. Now the site of Bell Gardens, the rancho was a huge Spanish land grant awarded to pioneer settler Antonio Maria Lugo in the 18th century.

(Mexican American)

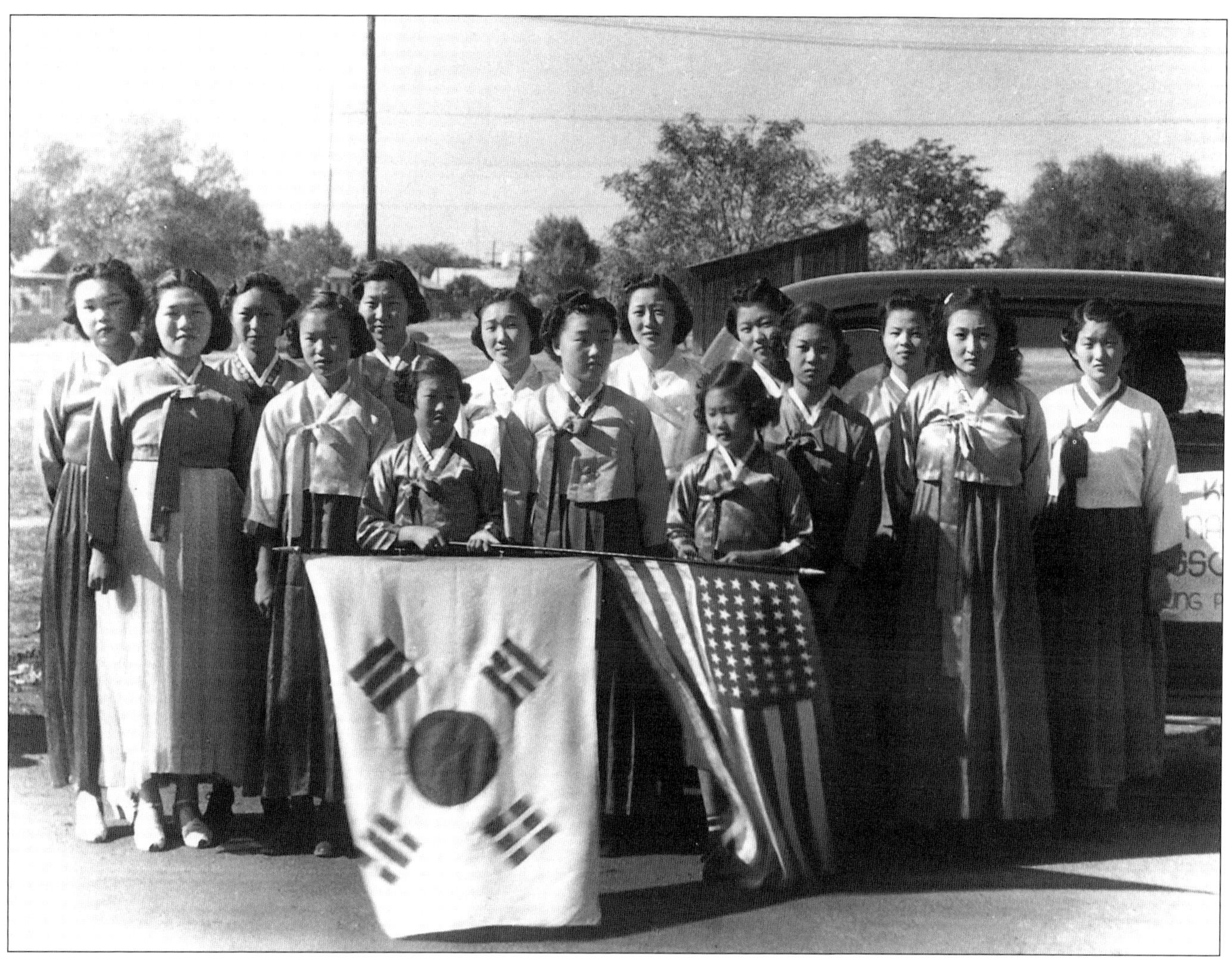

Louise Hahn *(front center)* in the Independence Day program given by the Korean National Association in Dinuba, California, March 1, late 1930s. Early Koreans in America joined together every year on March 1 to celebrate Korea's declaration of independence from Japan, years before Korea actually became independent of Japanese rule.

(Korean American)

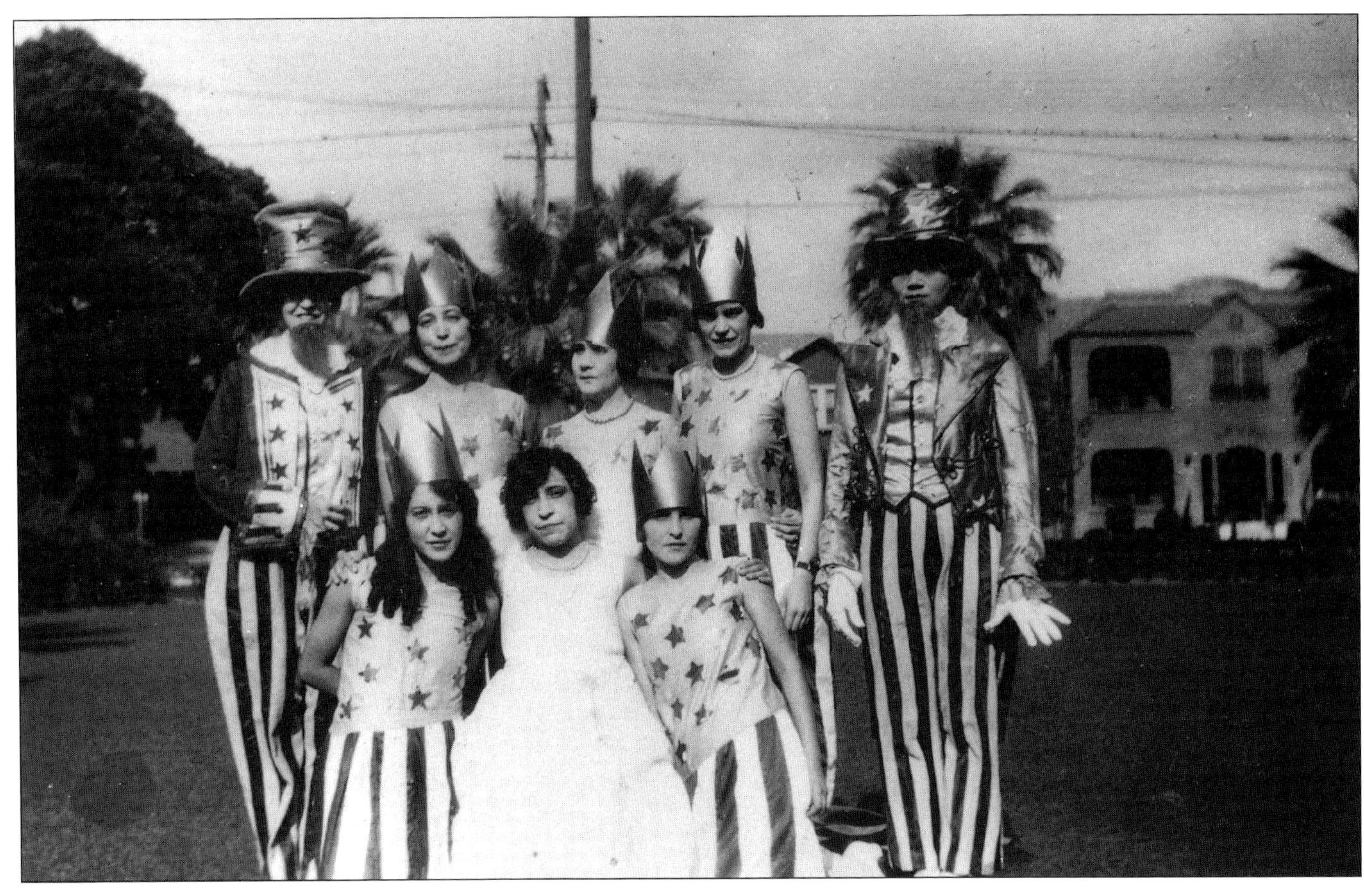

THE INTERNATIONAL INSTITUTE'S FOURTH OF JULY CELEBRATION in Los Angeles, 1923. Founded in 1914 as an outgrowth of the settlement house movement, the International Institute of Los Angeles was one of the earliest organizations assisting the diverse immigrant groups in Boyle Heights.

(Mexican American)

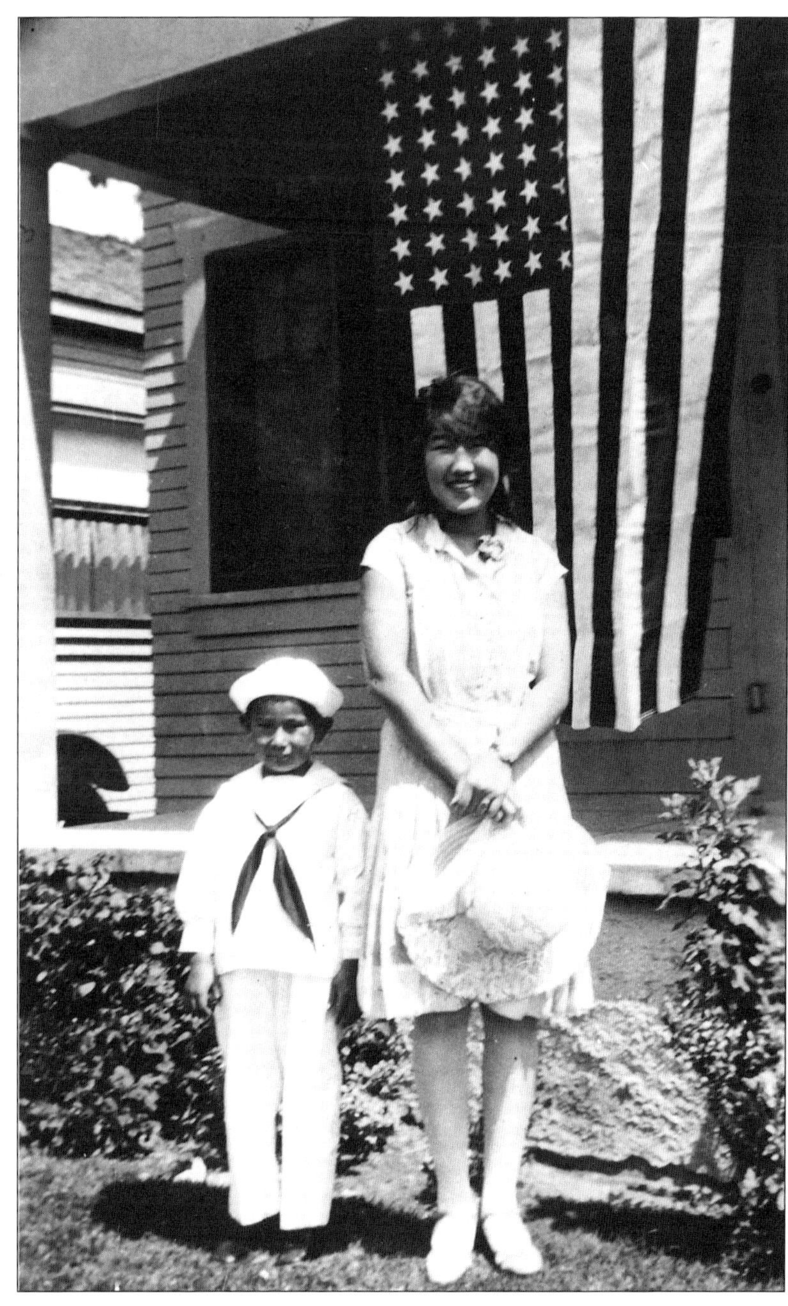

Enhe Hyun *(right)* and friend

celebrating the Fourth of July, 1928.
(Korean American)

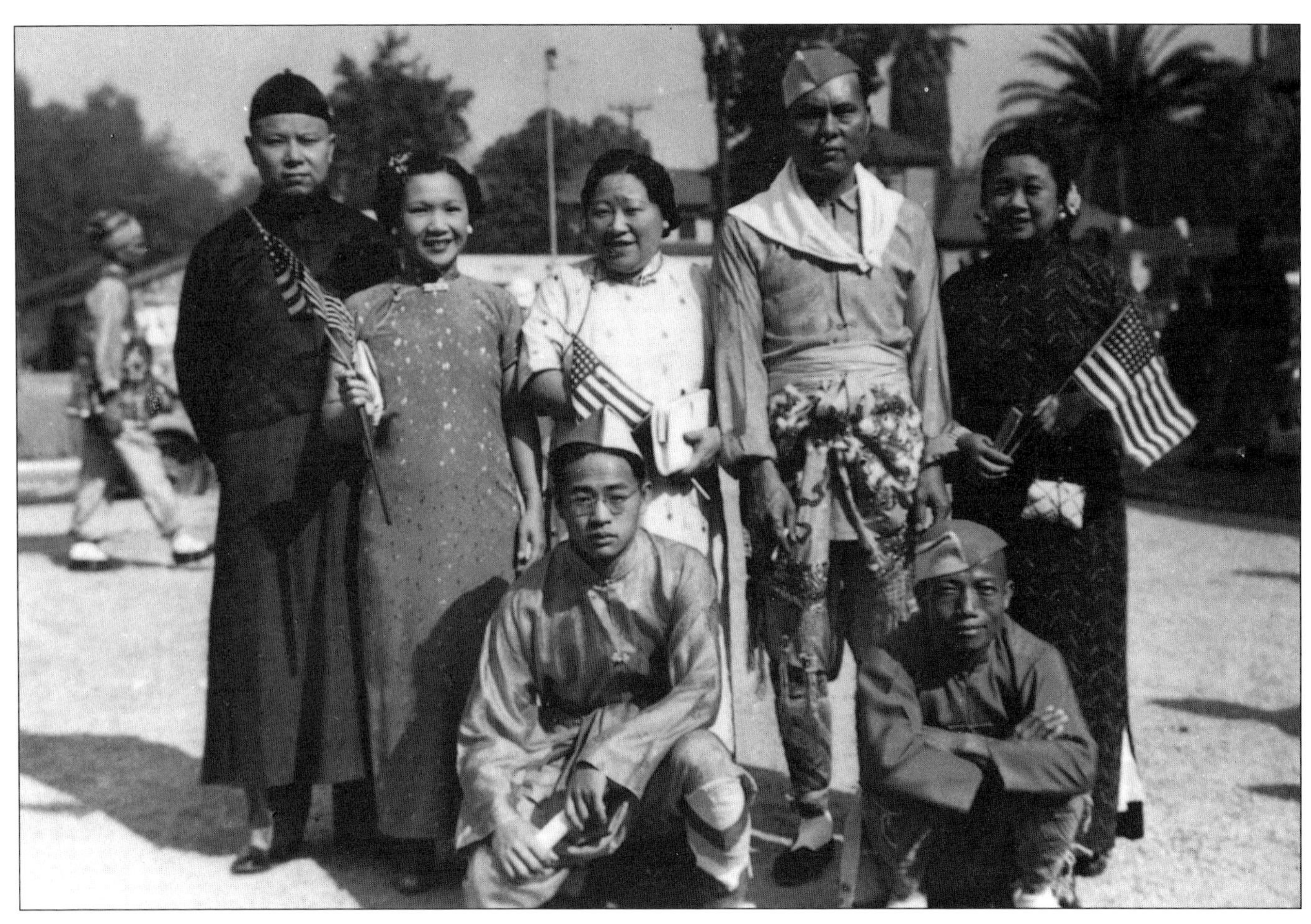

Chinese motion picture extras

pose after a Labor Day parade in Los Angeles, ca. 1934. Eddie Lee and his wife Jennie are in the back row, left. *(Chinese American)*

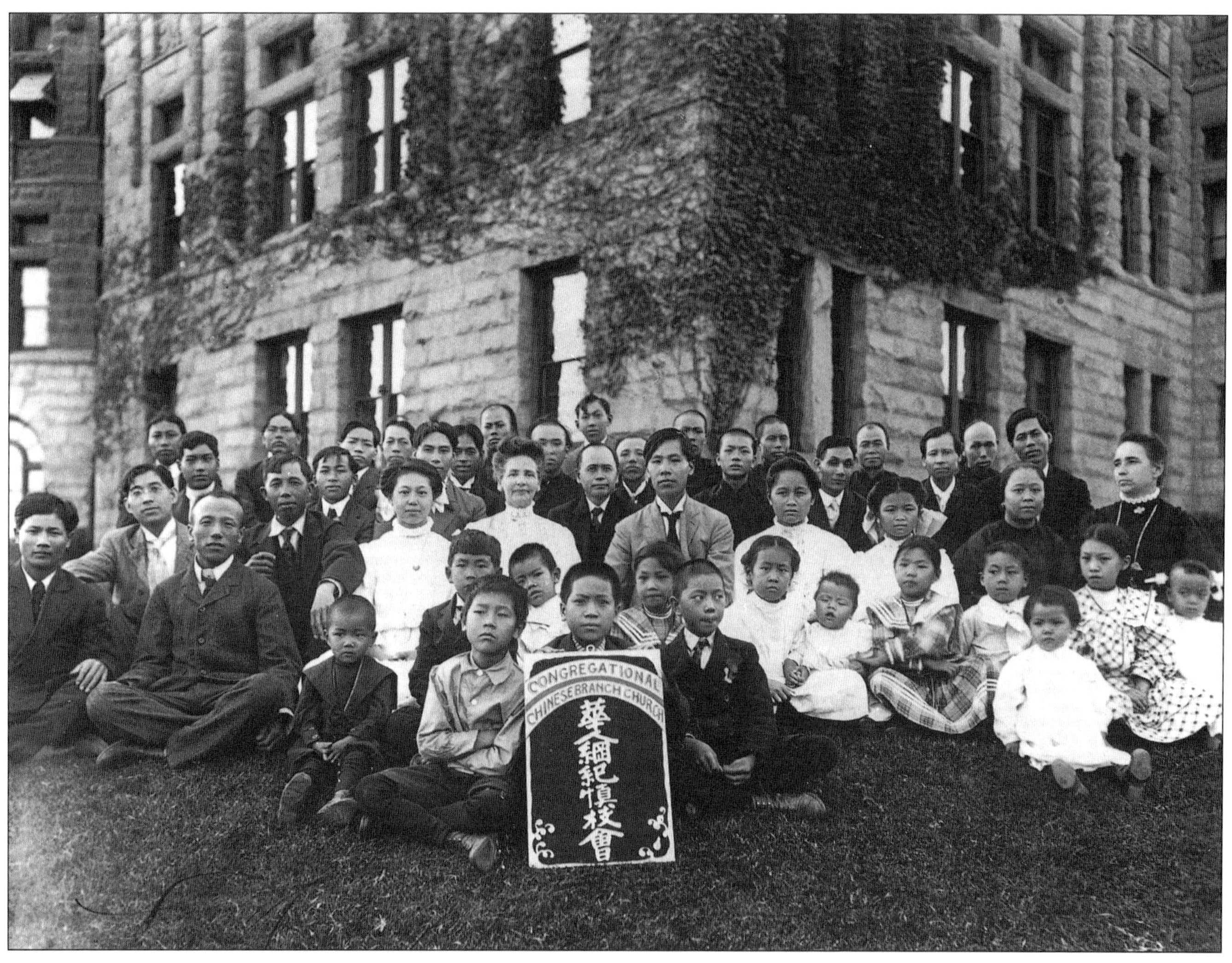

The Congregational Chinese Branch Church

in Los Angeles, 1908.

(Chinese American)

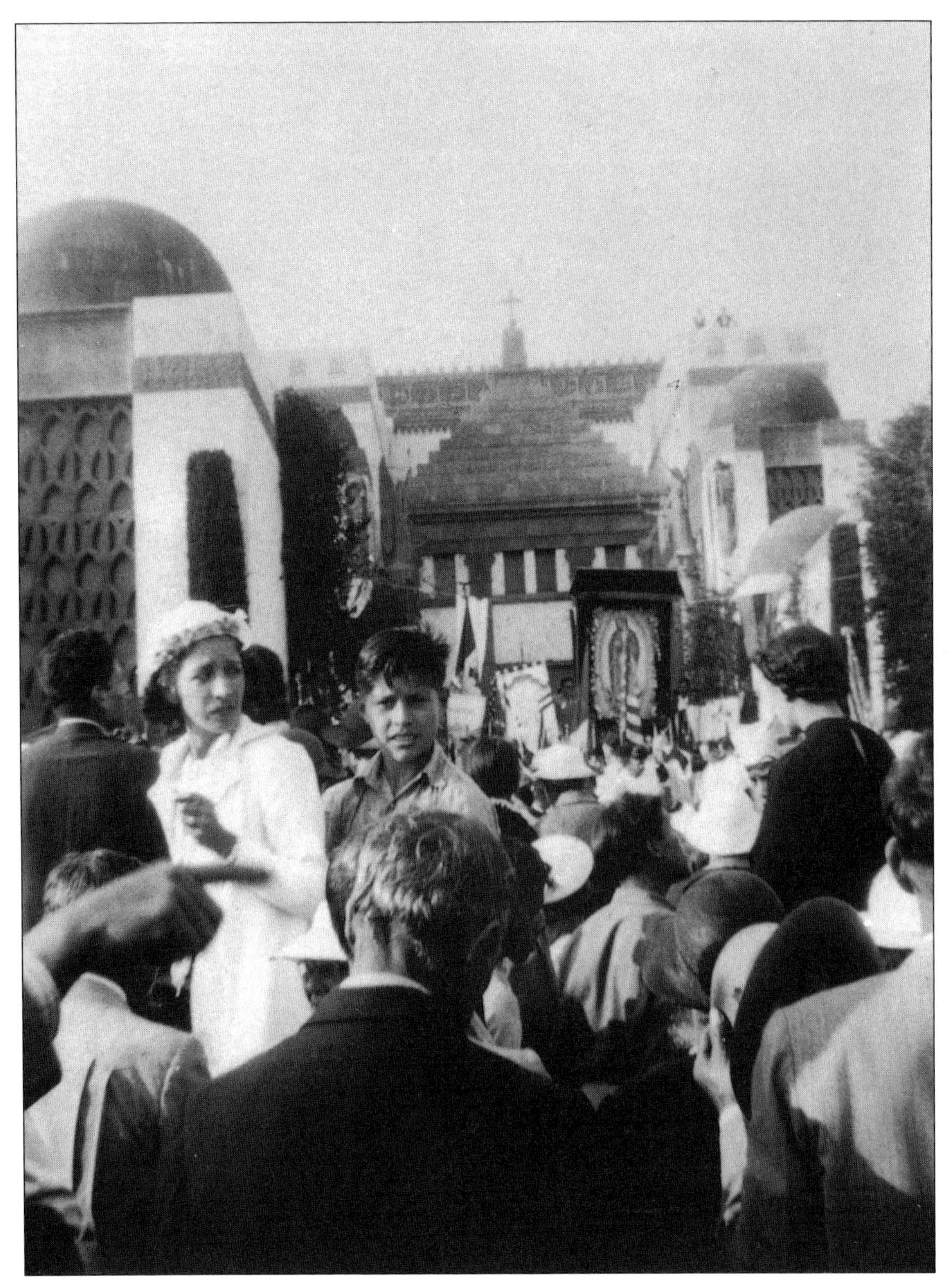

Procession for the Virgen de Guadalupe,
the patron saint of Mexico,
outside a Los Angeles church, December 12, ca. 1930.
(Mexican American)

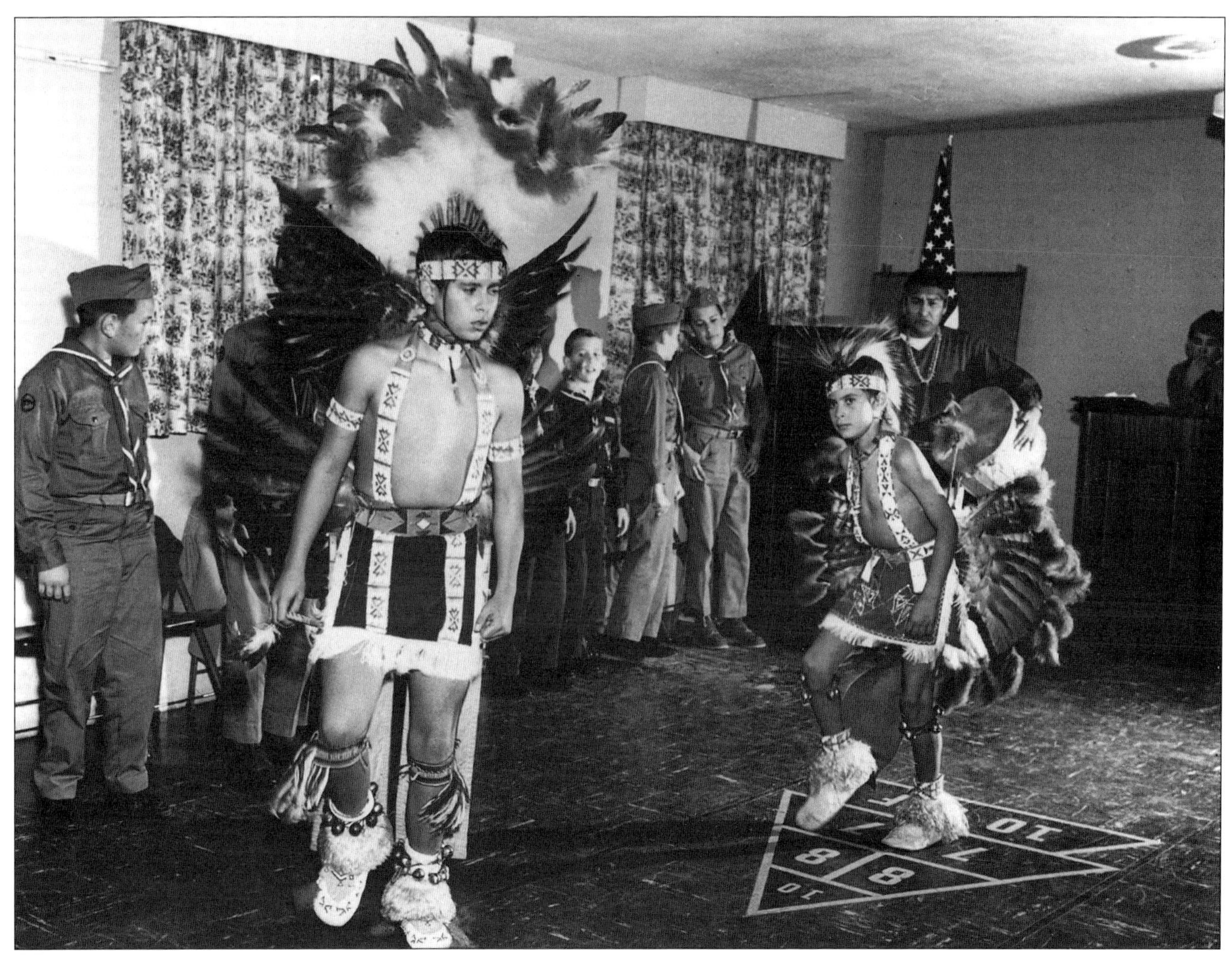

Mike and Dennis Tafoya

dancing to raise funds for the Indian Center in Los Angeles, early 1960s.
(American Indian)

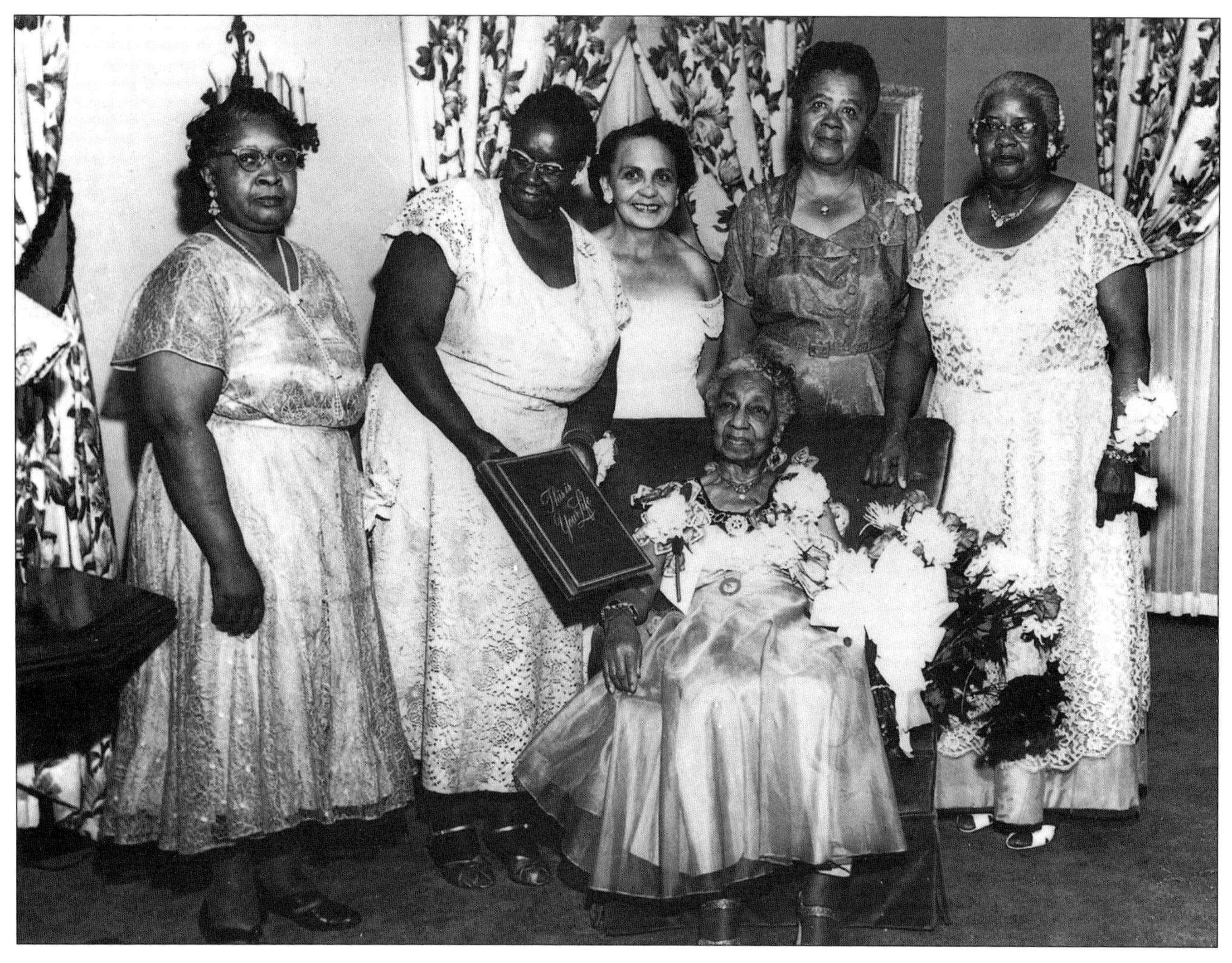

Ella Sarah Thompson White

being honored for her community work in Los Angeles
by the Ladies' Elks group, 1950s.
(African American)

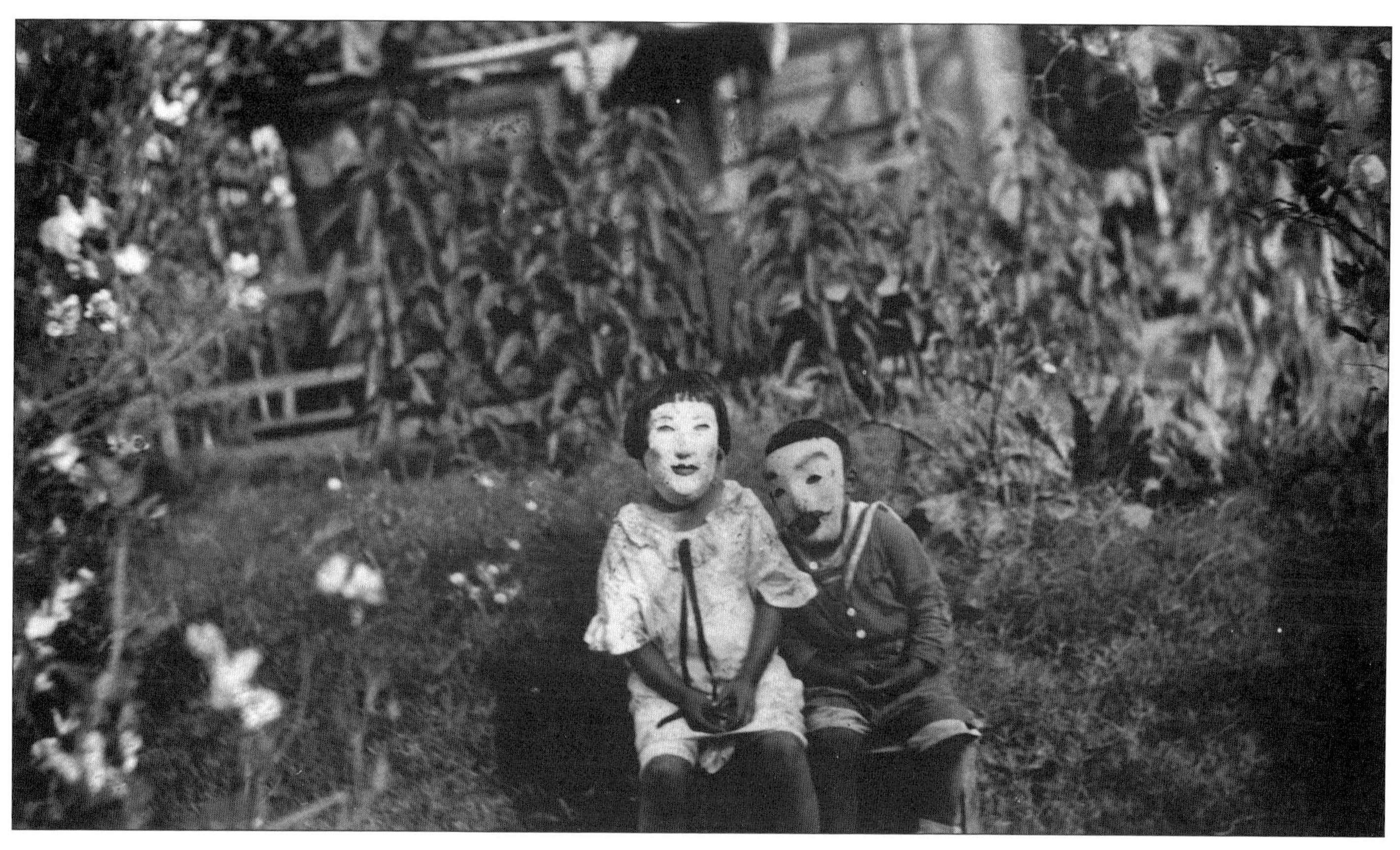

Aiko Kuromi and her brother, Isamu,

in Halloween masks at their home on
Los Feliz Boulevard in Los Angeles, 1925.
(Japanese American)

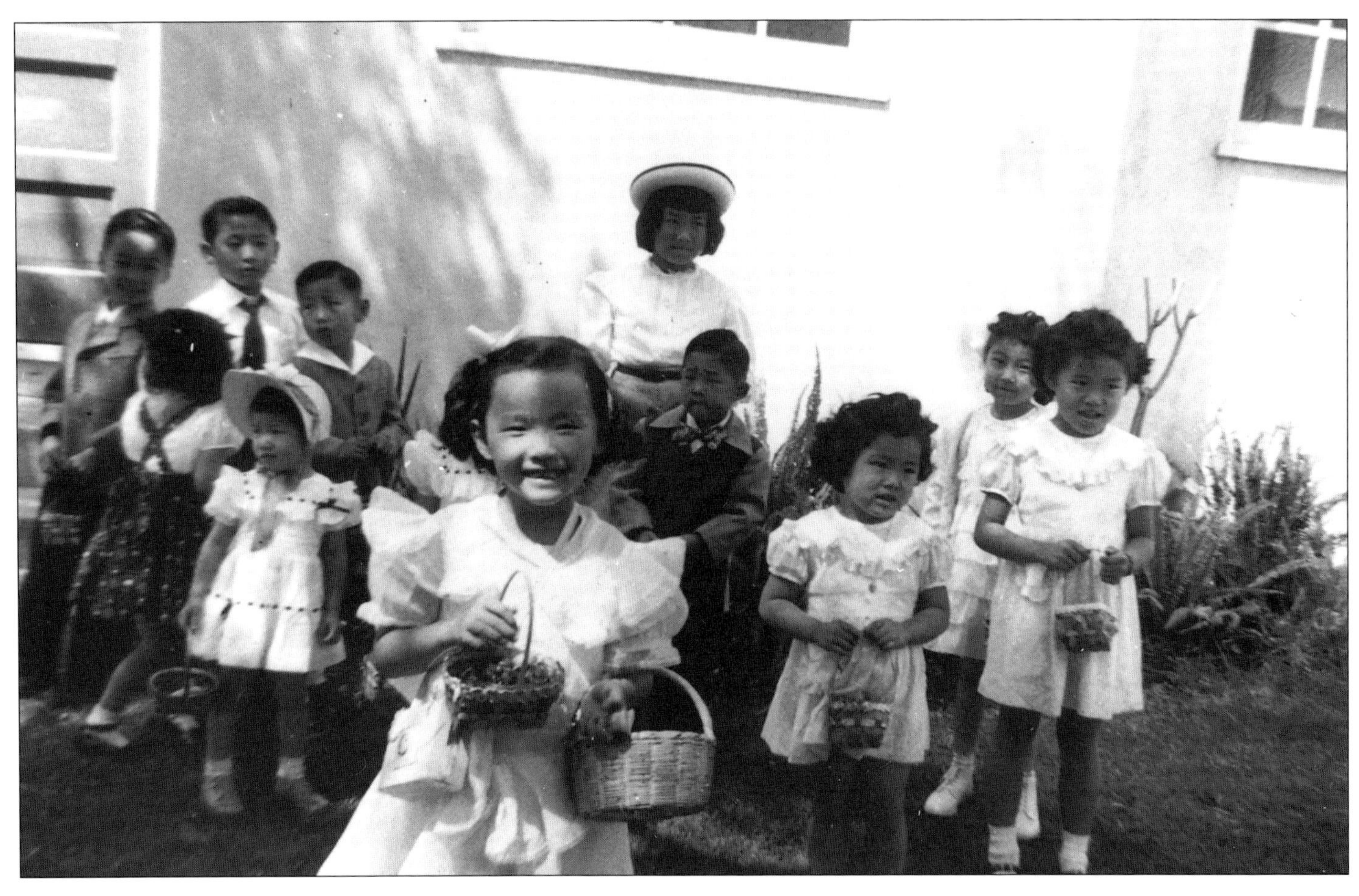

Easter at the Korean Methodist Church

on 29th Street near USC, 1945.

(Korean American)

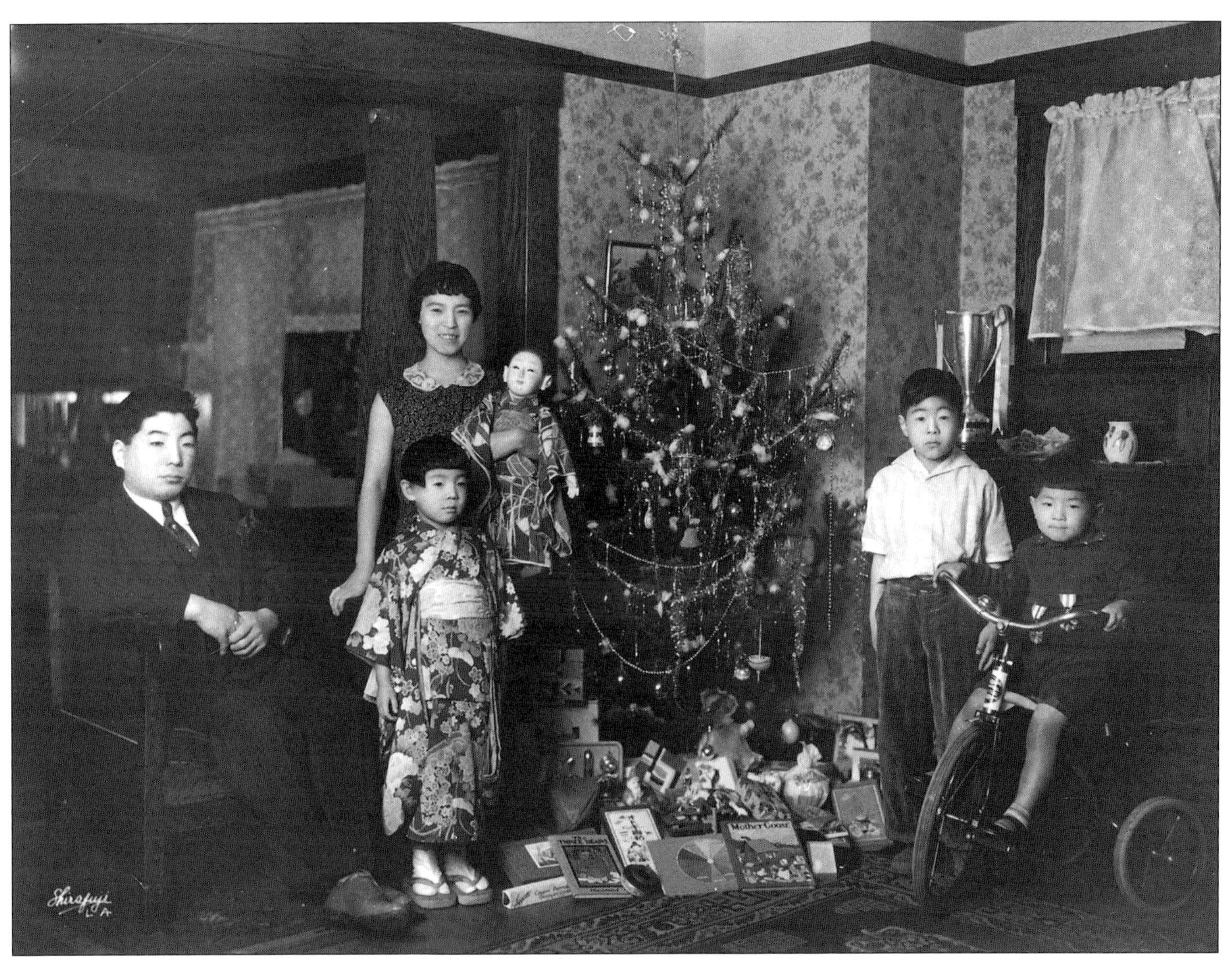

Christmas at the Nagano family's home
on West 30th Street in Los Angeles, in 1930.
(Japanese American)

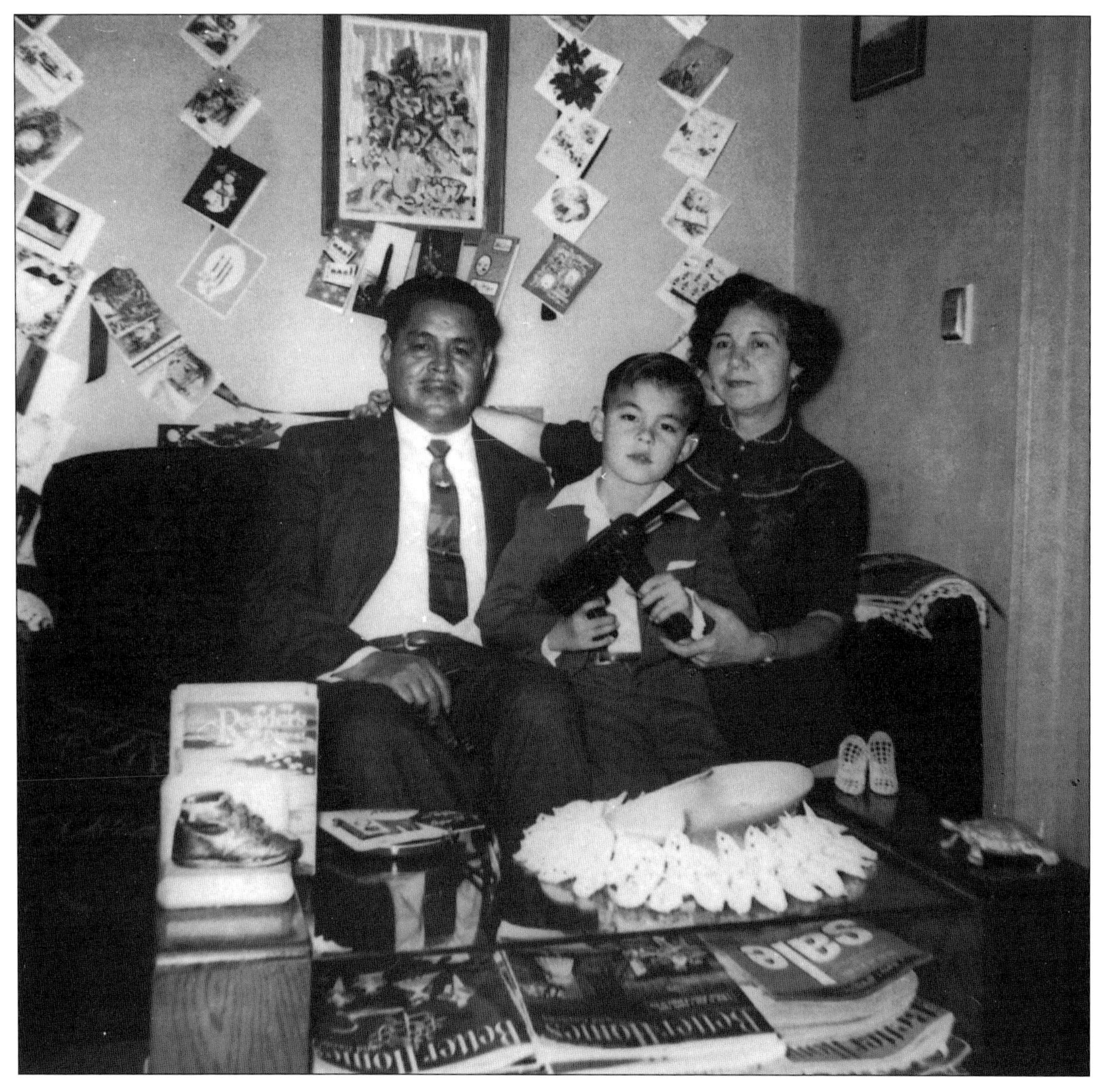

Luis Lucero and his parents

during Christmas.

(Mexican American)

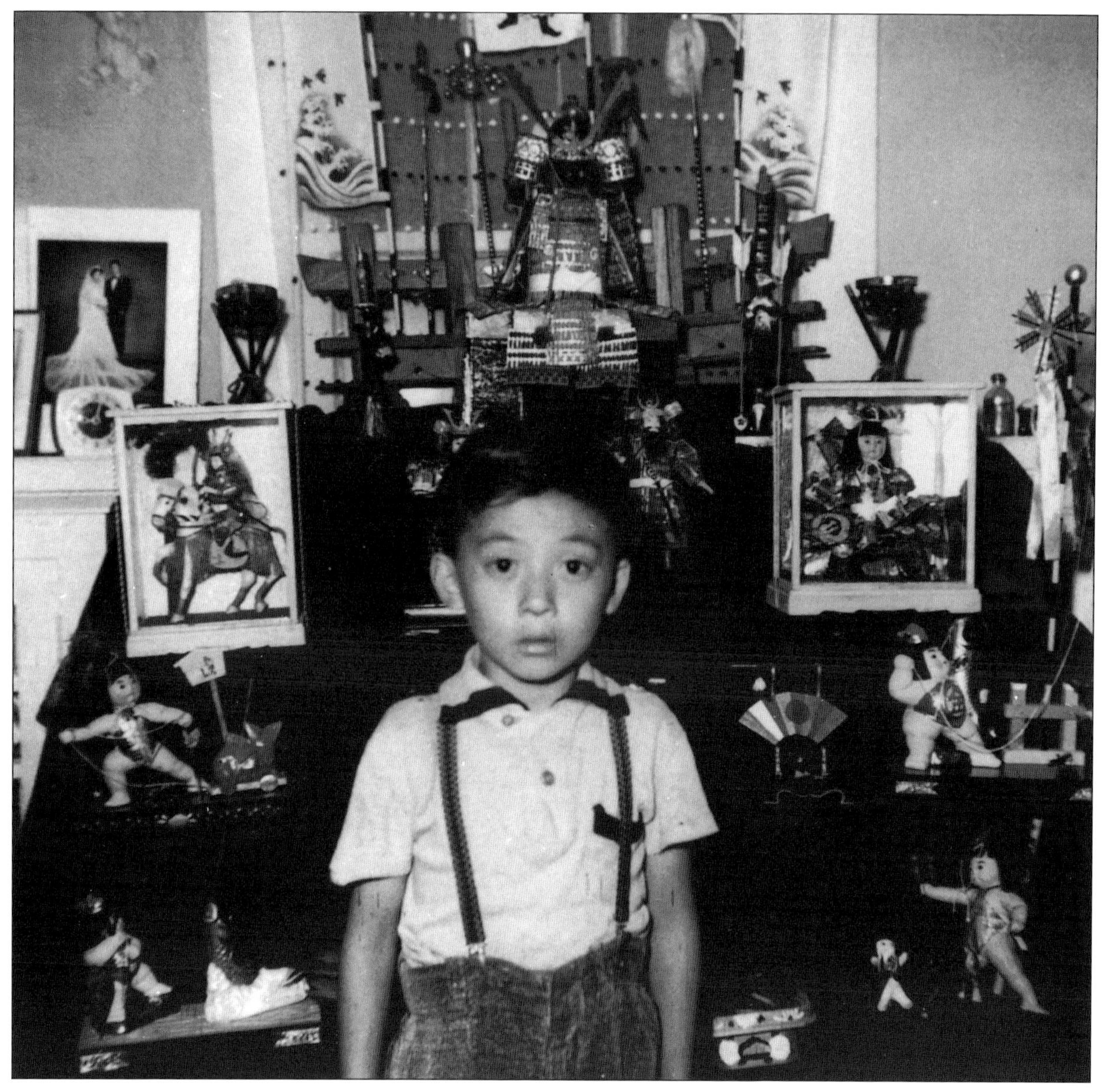

MASAFUMI FUJIMOTO ON MAY 5, 1954,

observing Boys' Day, a traditional Japanese holiday celebrated on the fifth day of the fifth month. Children's Day is the more modern version of this holiday.

(Japanese American)

A "September 16" parade on Brooklyn and Ford Streets in East Los Angeles celebrating Mexico's independence from Spain. Antonio Sandoval is the *charro* on horseback, 1938. *(Mexican American)*

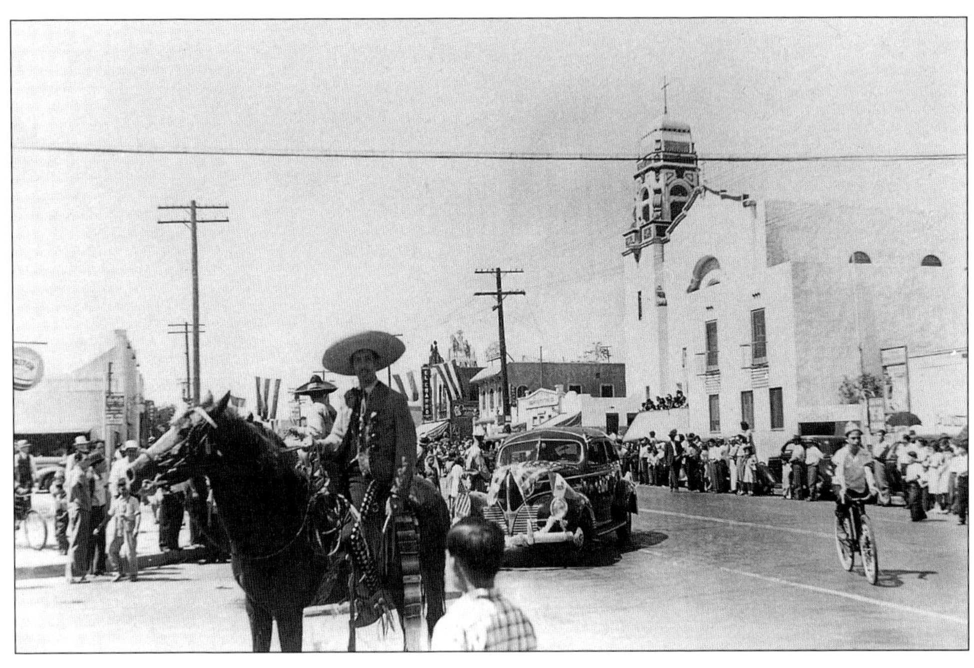

Band member Louis Banuelos *(center, standing)*, with his Los Angeles band, 1927. *(Mexican American)*

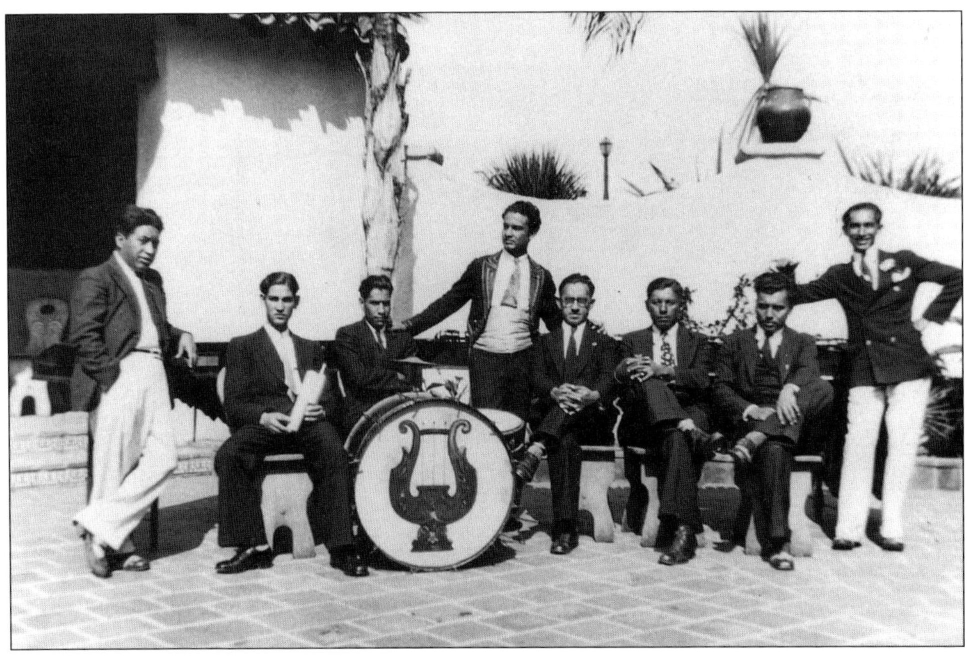

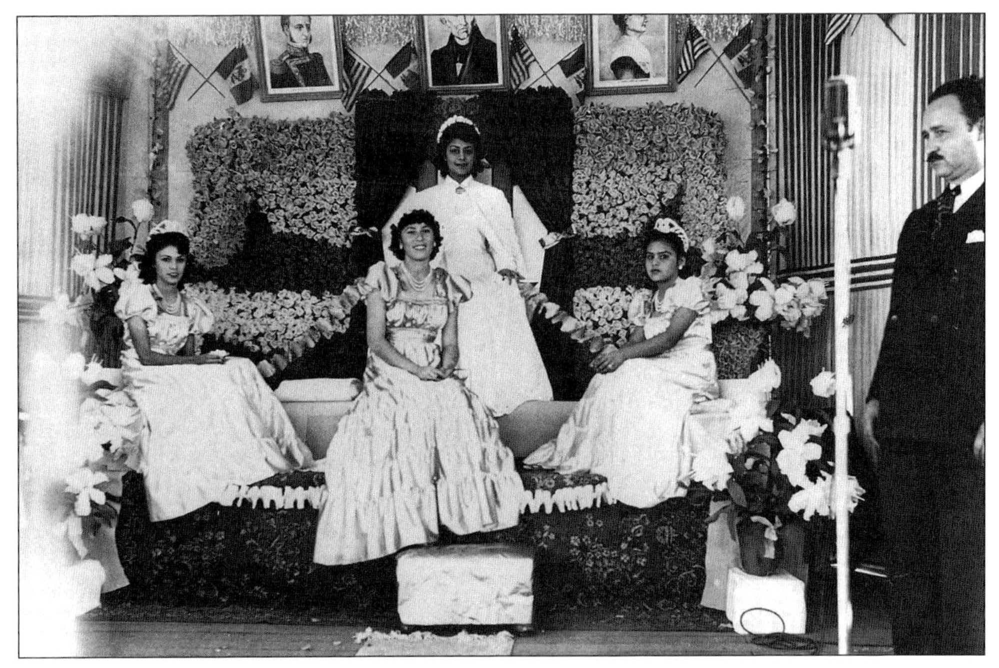

Queen Rosalie Perez and her court from La Sociedad Civica celebrate "September 16" in 1941. *(Mexican American)*

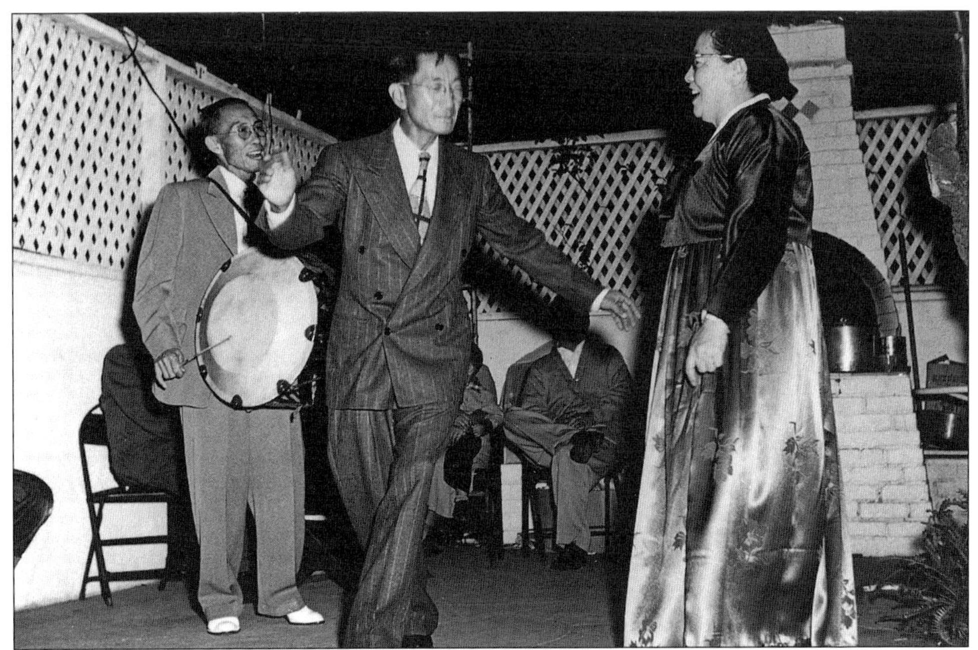

Pil Kwan Kim playing the drums for unidentified dancers in Woonha and Louise Park's backyard in Inglewood, ca. 1950. *(Korean American)*

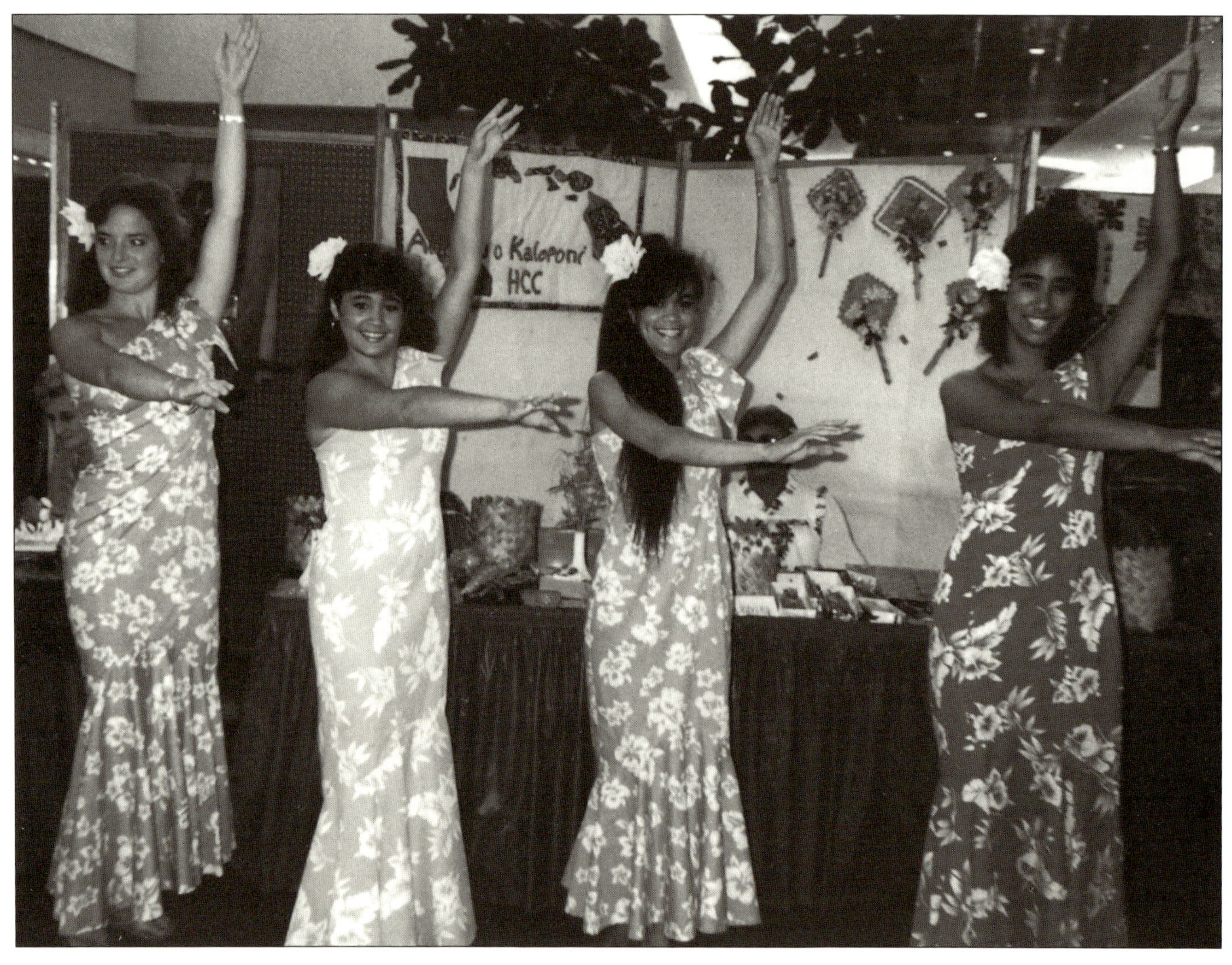

BERNICE JUDD *(left to right)*, CHARLENE YEE,
KANANI FAHILGA-LAUGHLIN AND KEALOHA ARELIANO

perform at a presentation on Hawaiian culture at the Huntington Beach Center, 1987.
(Pacific Islander American/ Hawaiian)

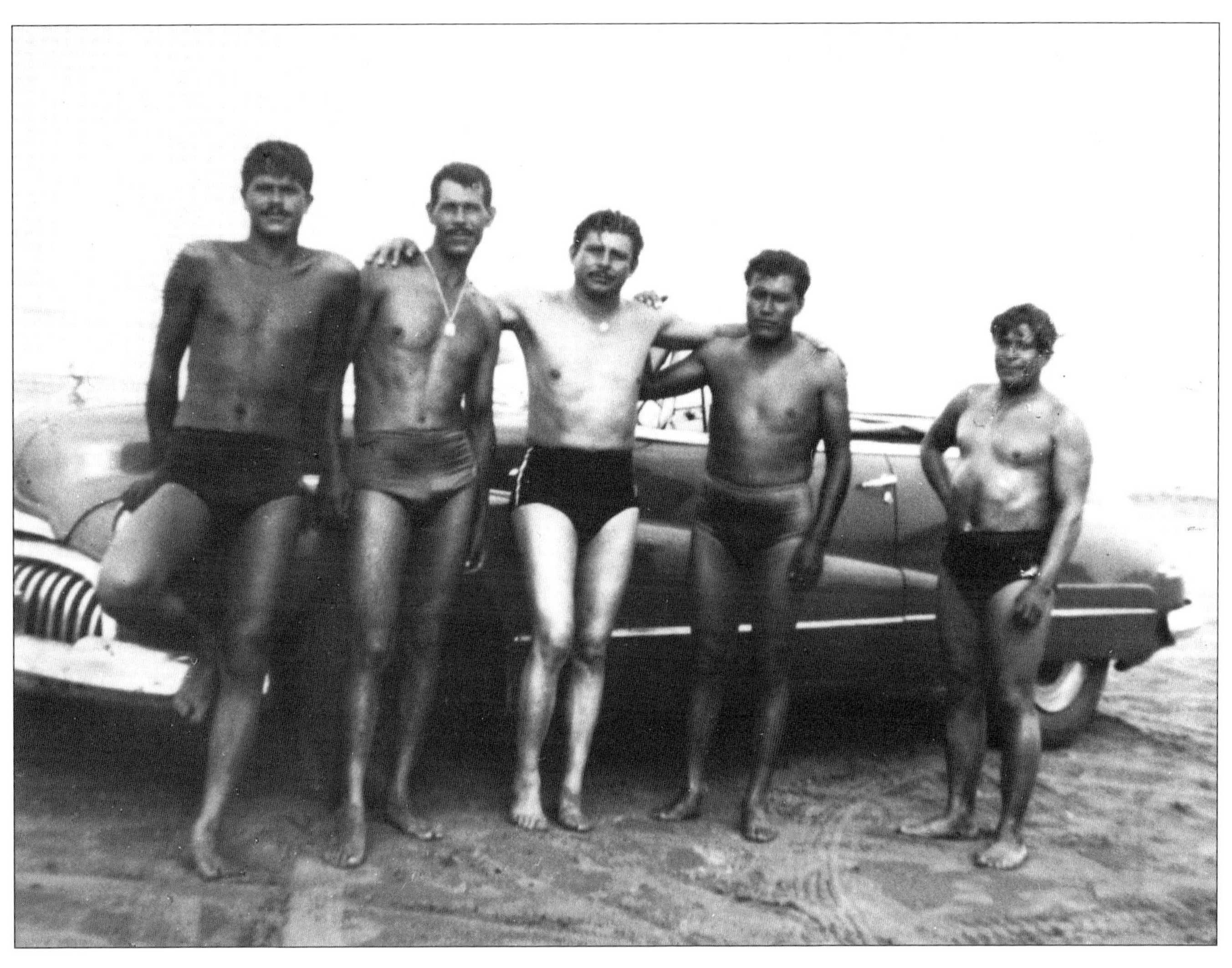

Brothers Rosendo and Vicente Orozco *(from left)*
with friends at Santa Monica Beach, 1951.
(Mexican American)

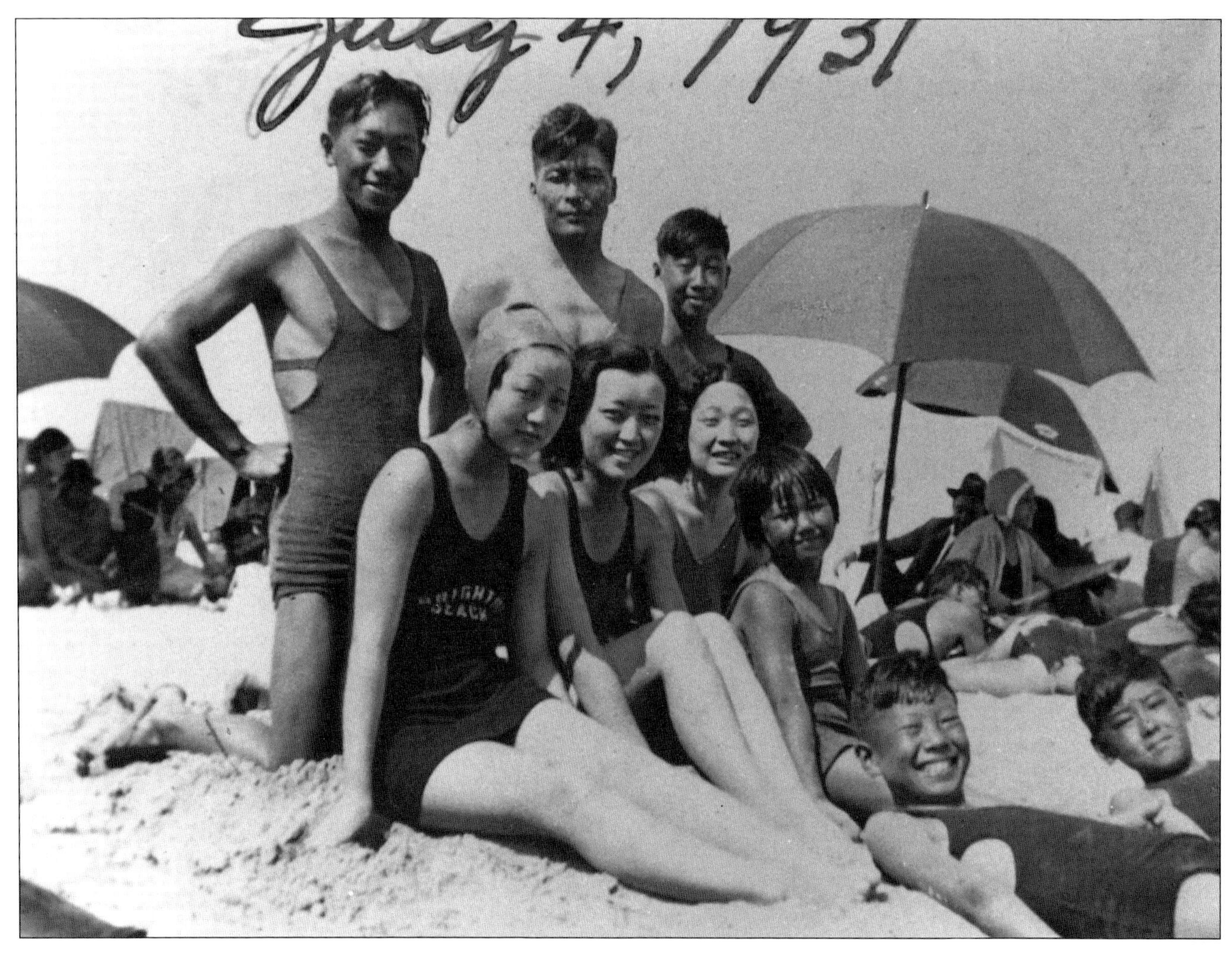

HELEN HONG *(center)*

celebrates the Fourth of July with friends on Venice Beach, 1931.

(Korean American)

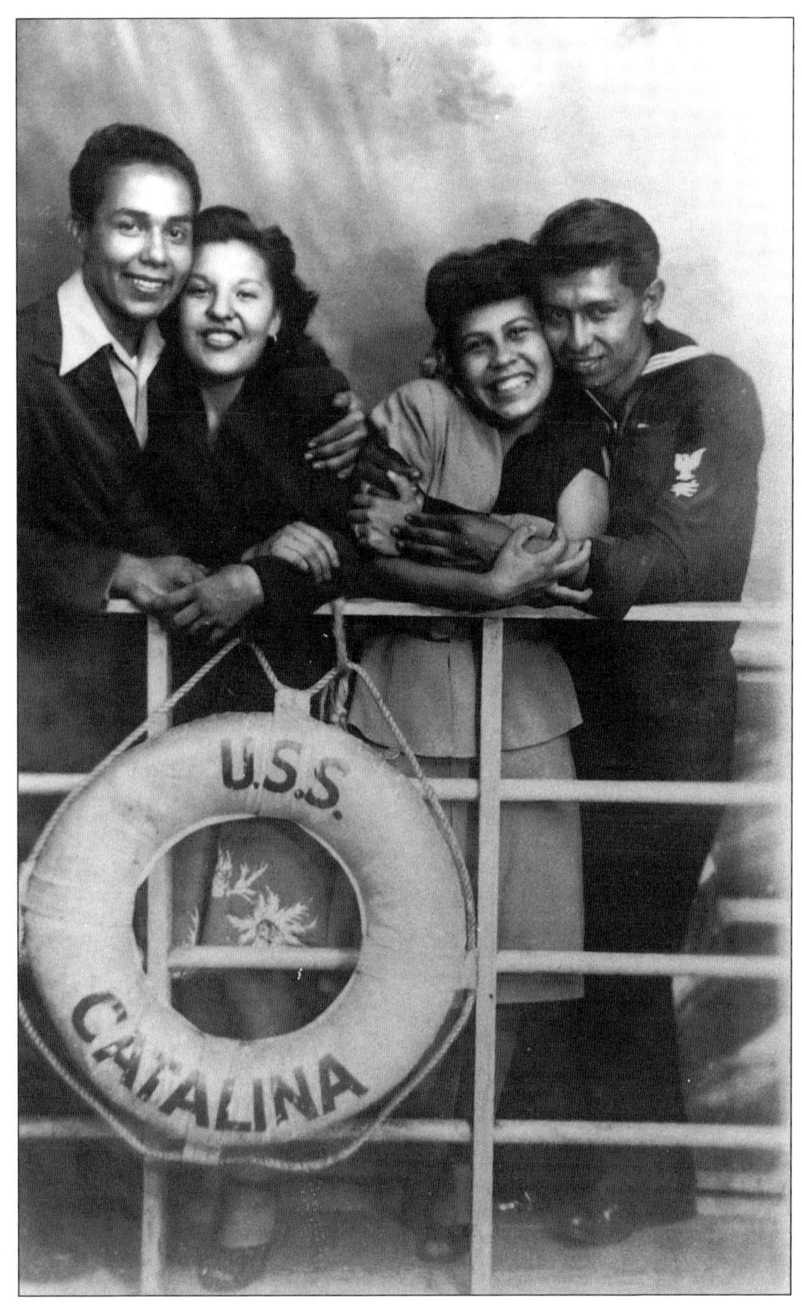

Lupe Moreno *(left)* and friends

photographed for a Catalina Island souvenir, late 1940s.
(Mexican American)

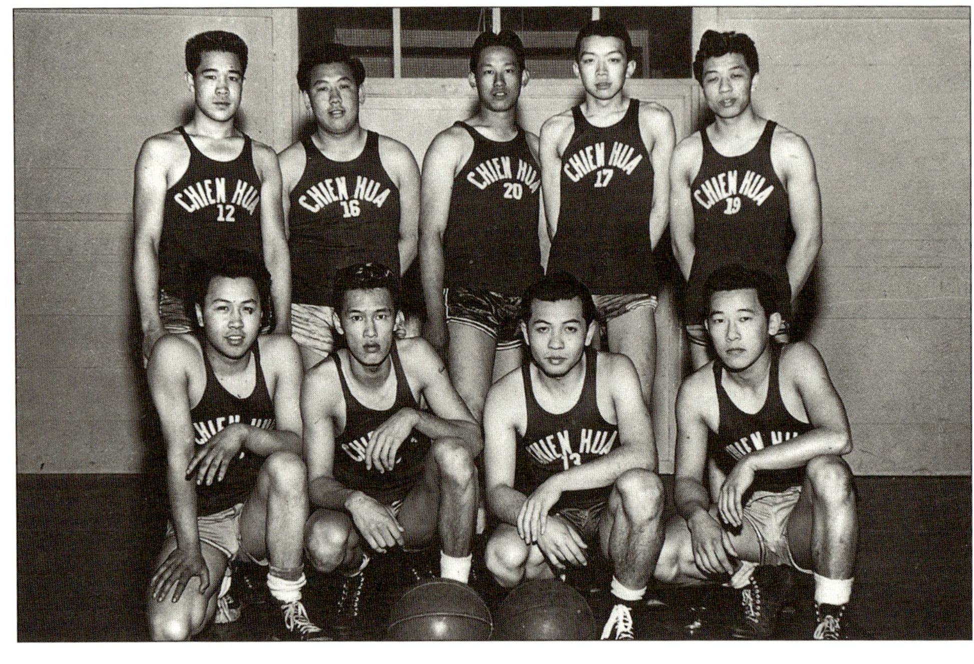

Chien Hua, a basketball club in Los Angeles,

ca. 1940s. This team mostly played other Chinese American teams in California and the Southwest. *(Chinese American)*

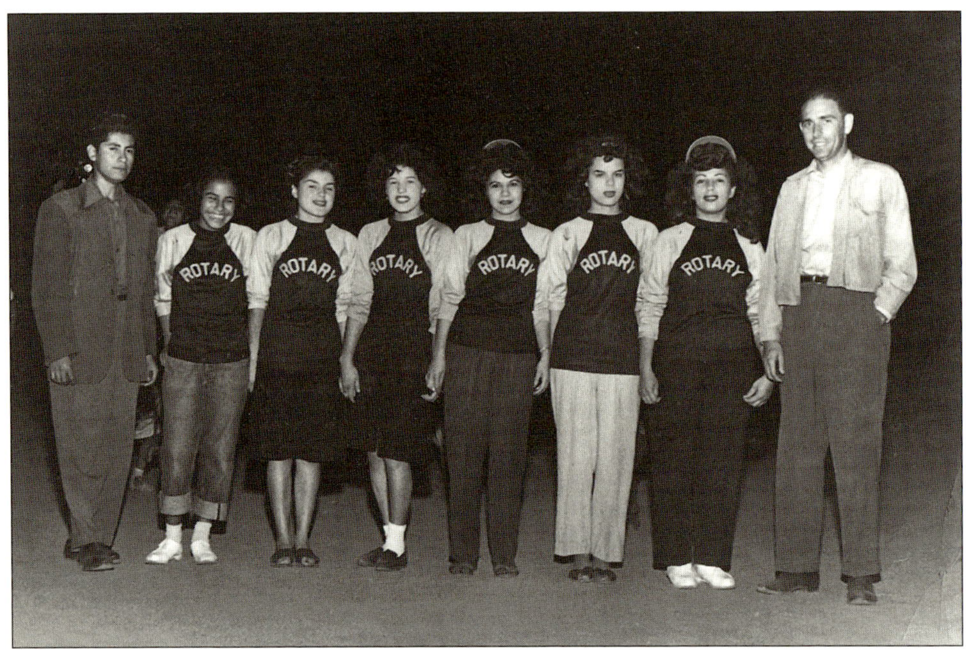

Rotary Club baseball team

at Las Palmas Park in San Fernando, 1943. *(Mexican American)*

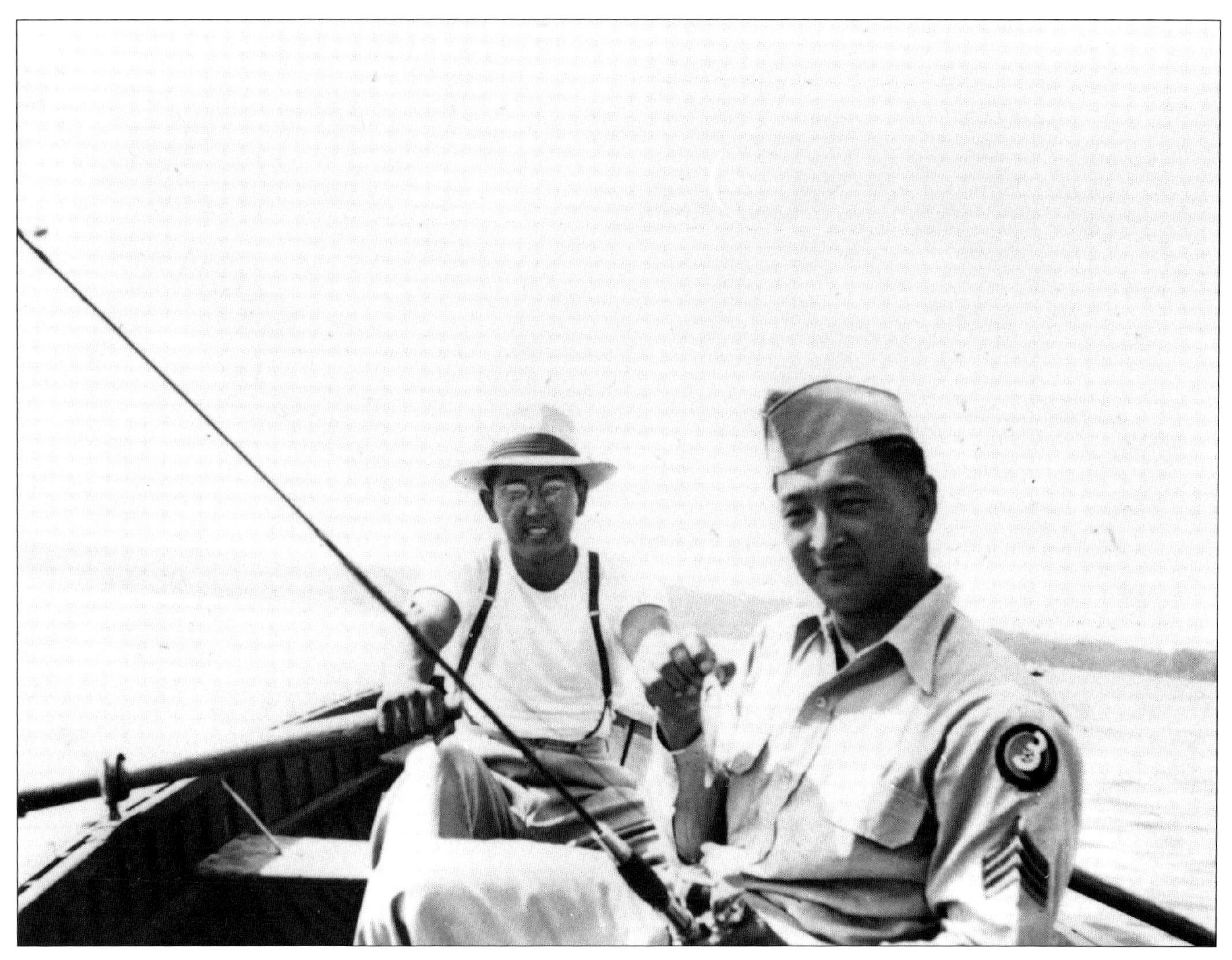

Arthur T. Ito of Los Angeles *(right)* fishing with his brother, Thomas,
in Minneapolis, Minnesota, summer of 1943. Arthur was on leave before his next assignment.
(Japanese American)

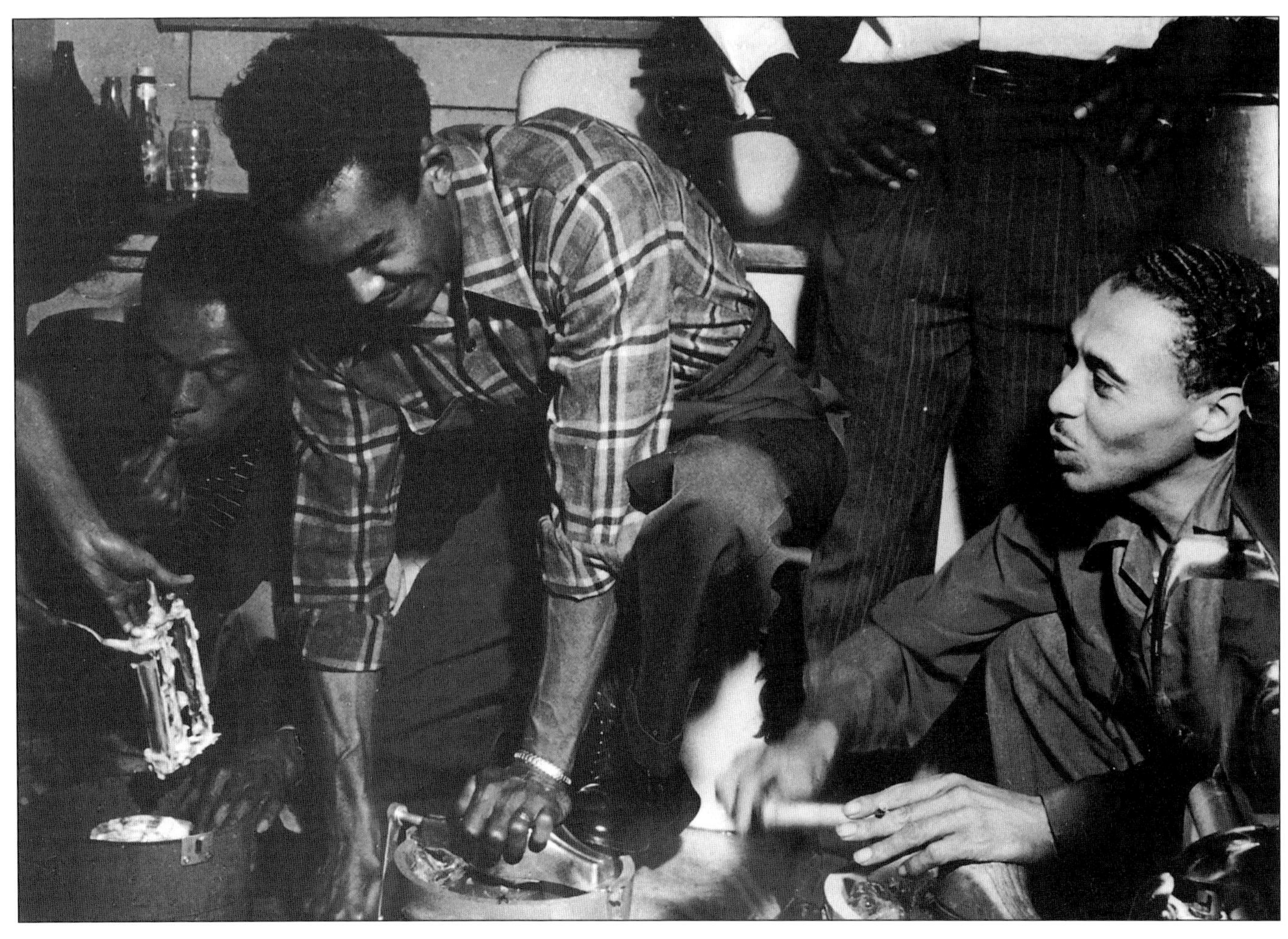

William Knox *(right)*

making ice cream for Amelia Lightner's birthday party on East 43rd Street in Los Angeles, late 1940s. *(African American)*

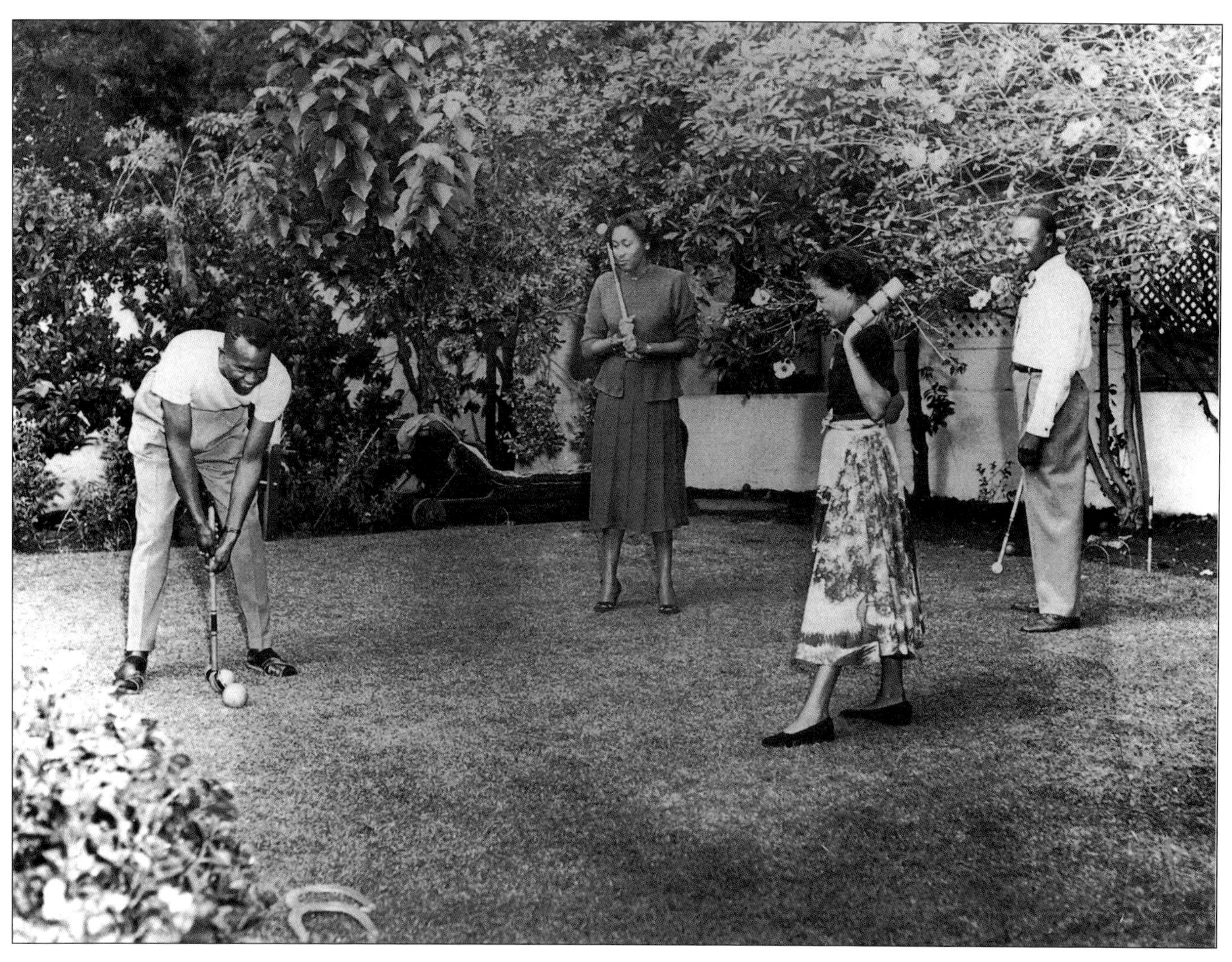

CLOTHILDE WOODARD *(second from right)* AND HER HUSBAND *(left)*

with friends at their home on Franklin Avenue, ca. 1940.

(African American)

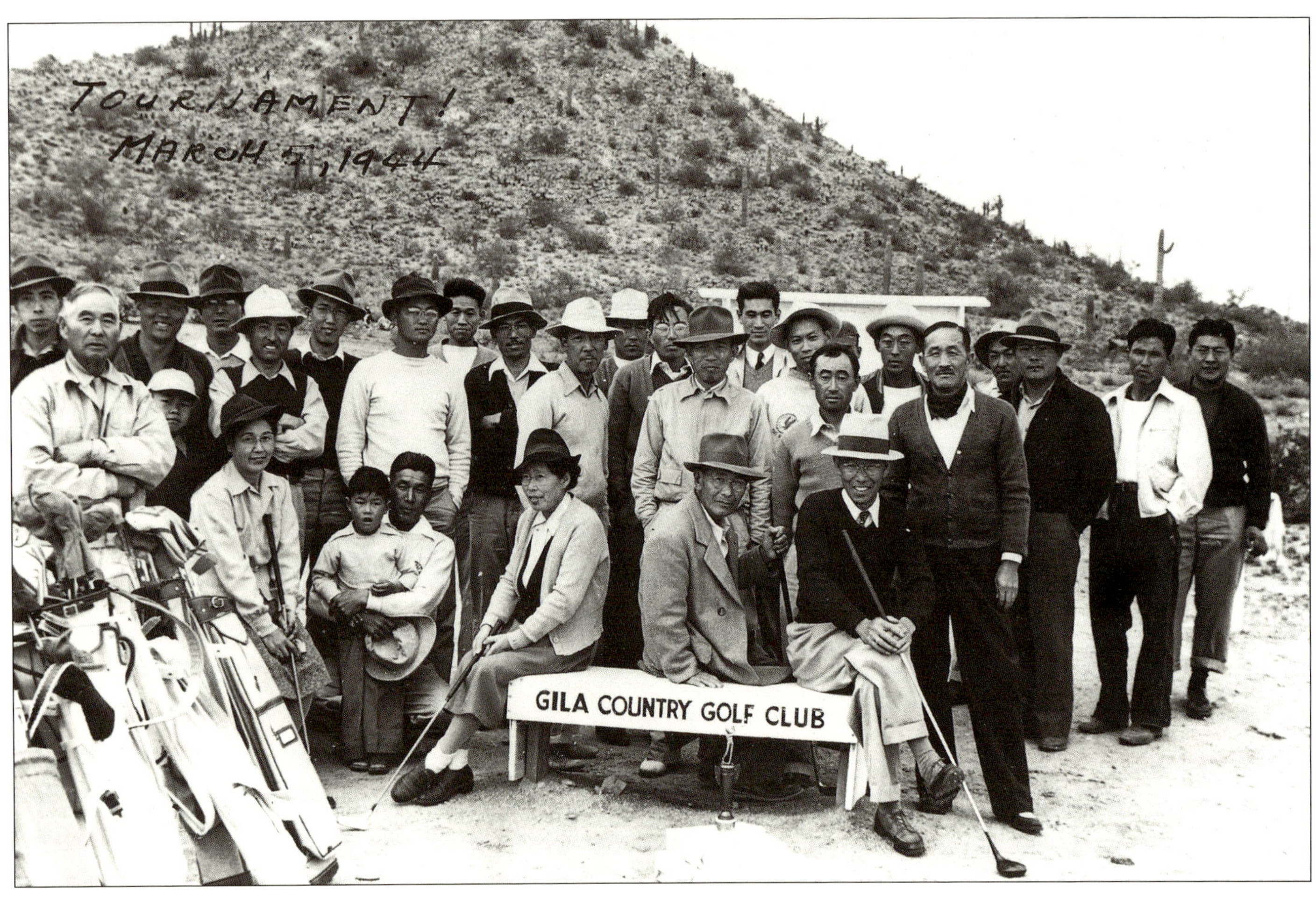

A golf tournament at the Gila Internment Camp, Arizona, March 5, 1944.

In spite of their forced internment in the barren desert during World War II, Japanese Americans did what they could to maintain their spirits and their sense of humor.

(Japanese American)

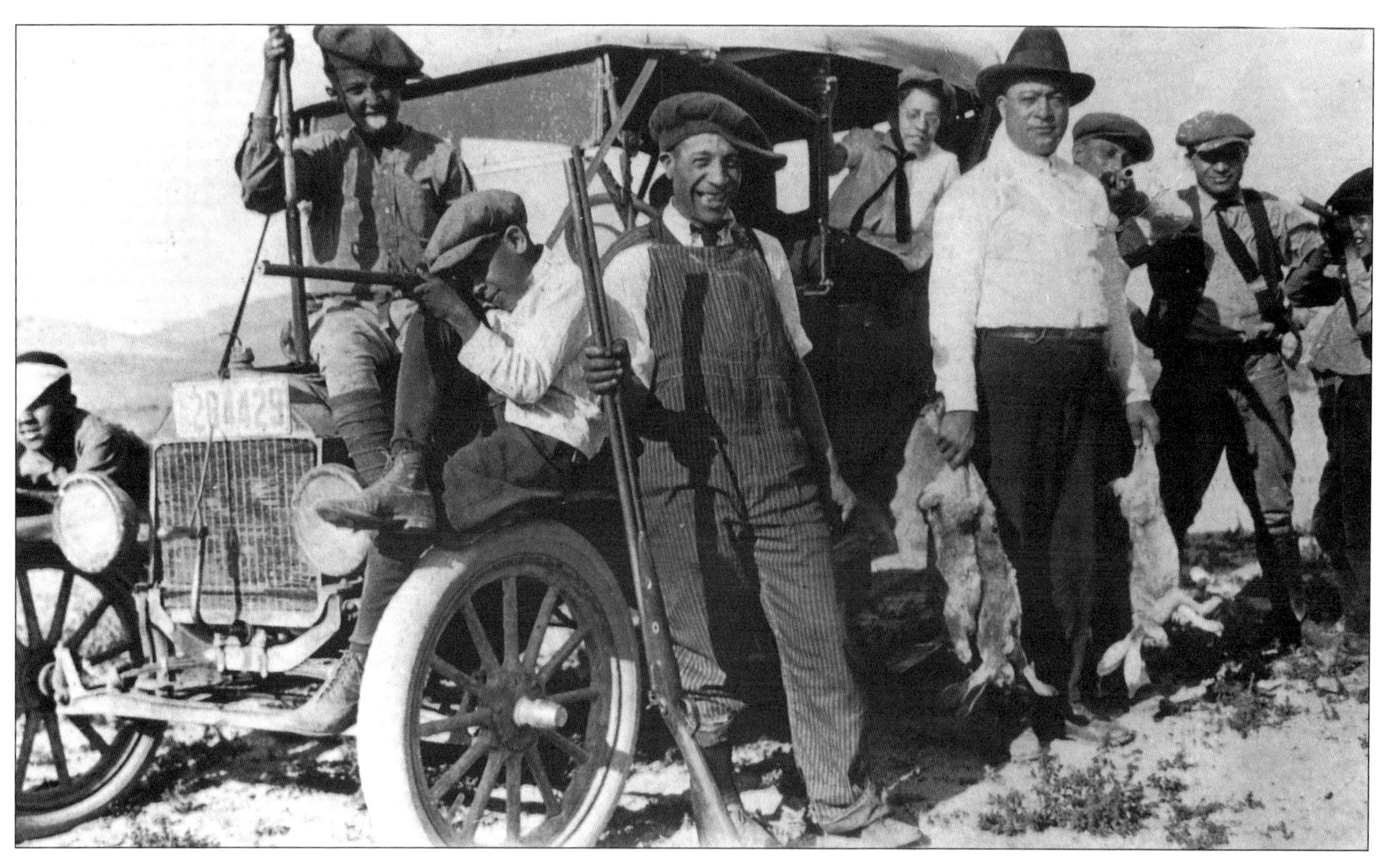

HUNTING RABBITS

in Rosamond, California, 1922.
(African American)

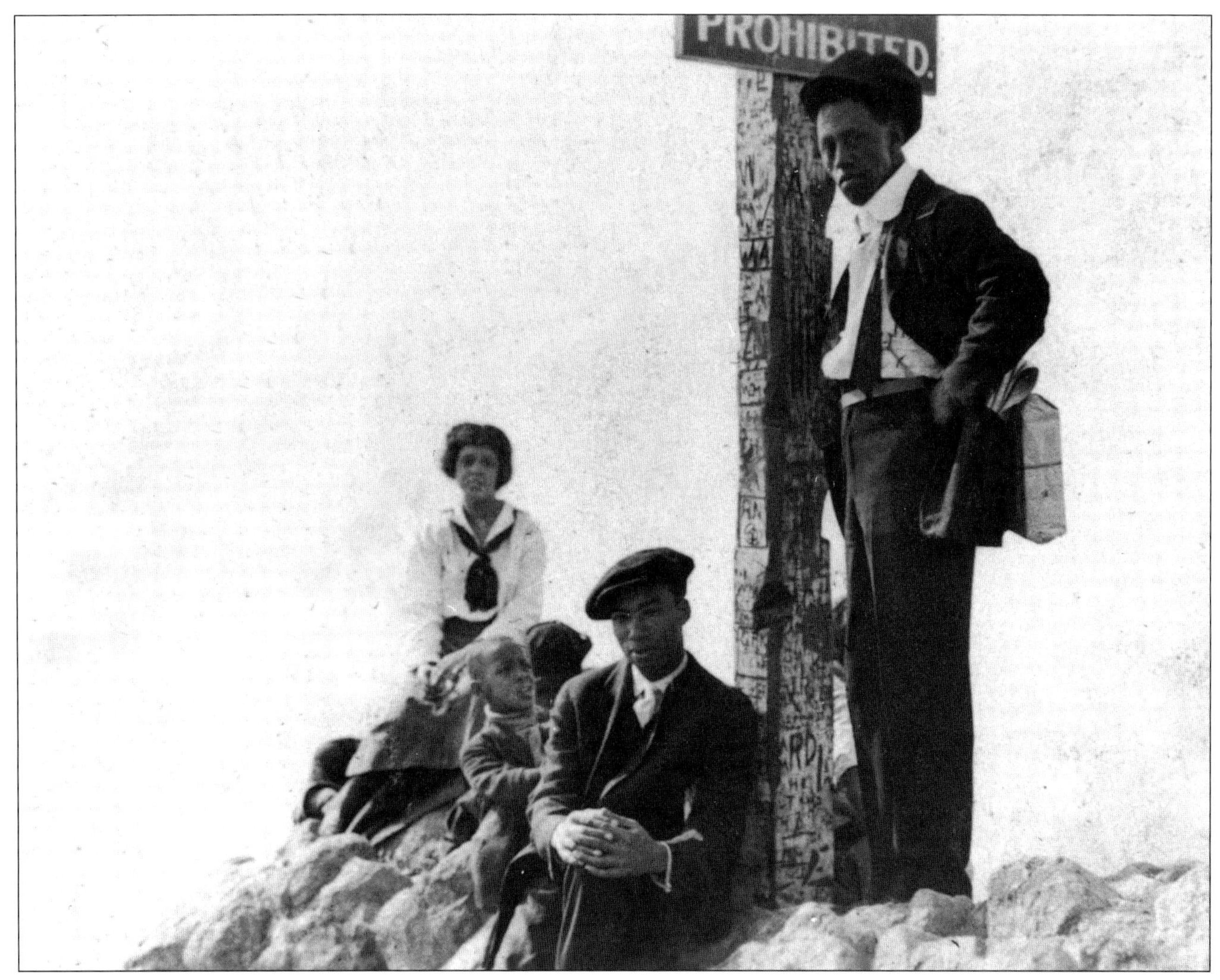

The boundary between the segregated sections of Santa Monica beach.

Beaches and swimming pools in Southern California were segregated by local ordinances in the 1920s and 1930s. De facto segregation continued long after these ordinances were challenged and repealed.

(African American)

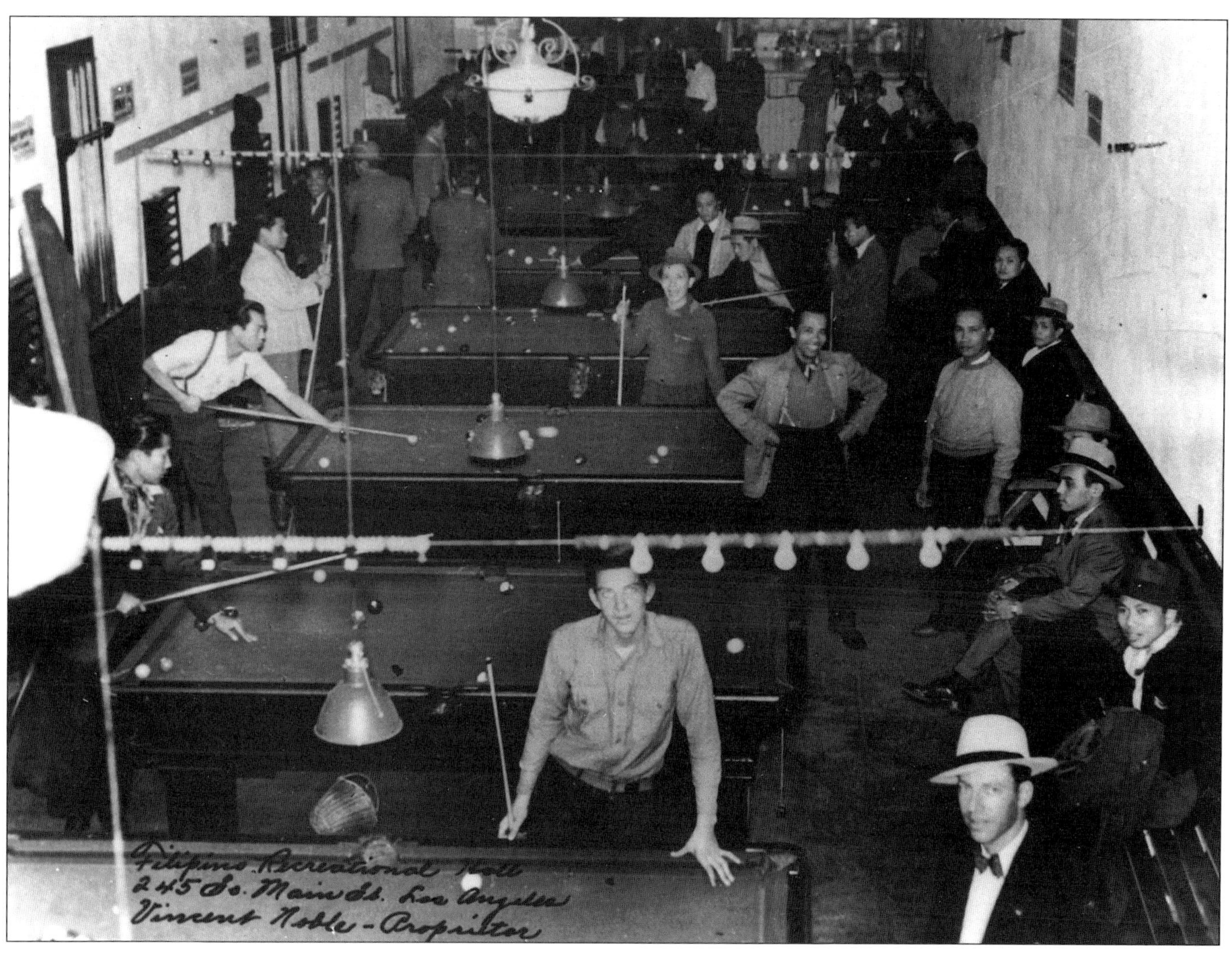

FILIPINO RECREATIONAL HALL

at 255 South Main Street in Los Angeles, with owner Vicente Noble *(center right with arms at waist)* early 1940s. *(Filipino American)*

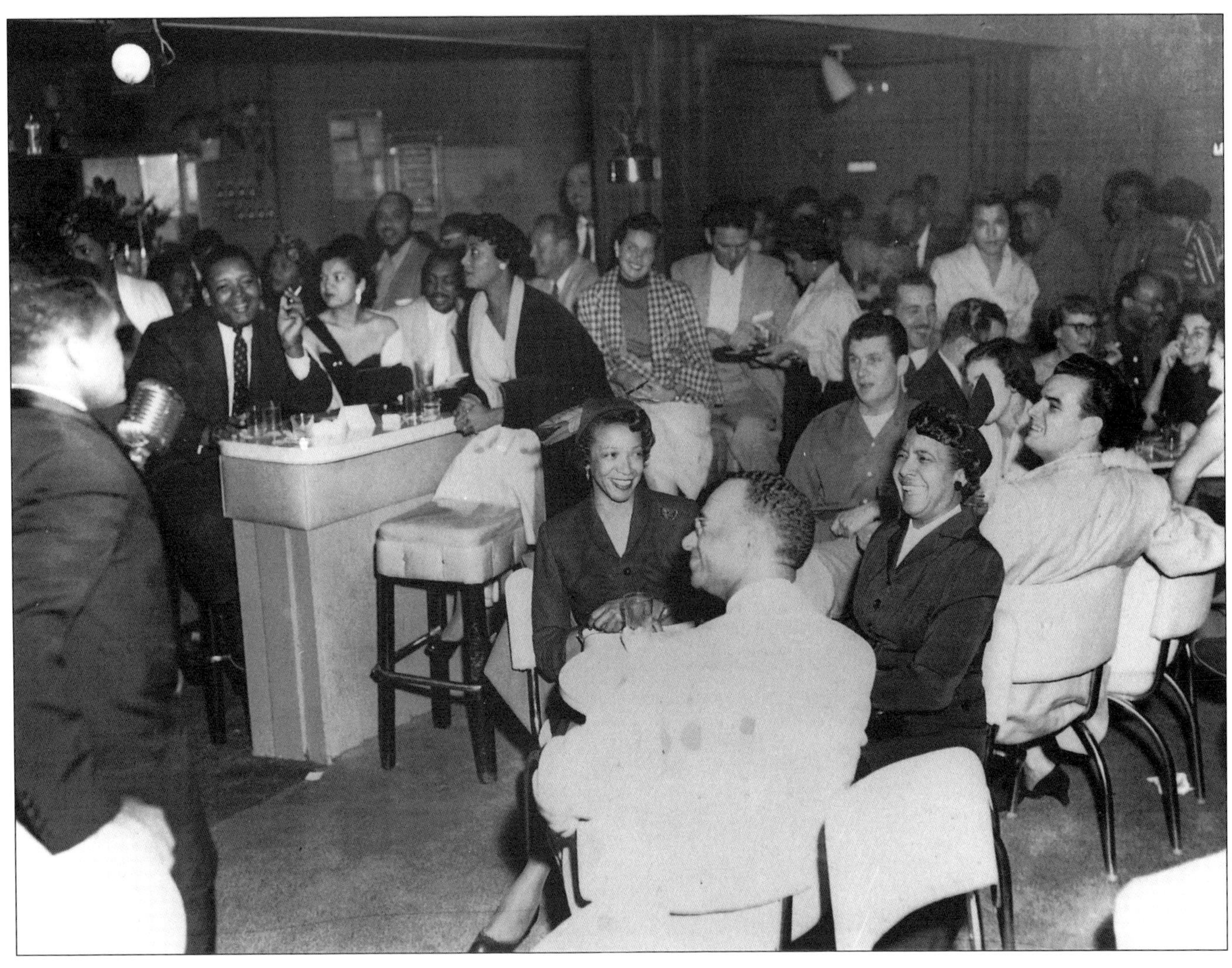

Slappy White performing

at Joe Adams' Club Pigalle on Figueroa Street in Los Angeles, ca. 1950.
(African American)

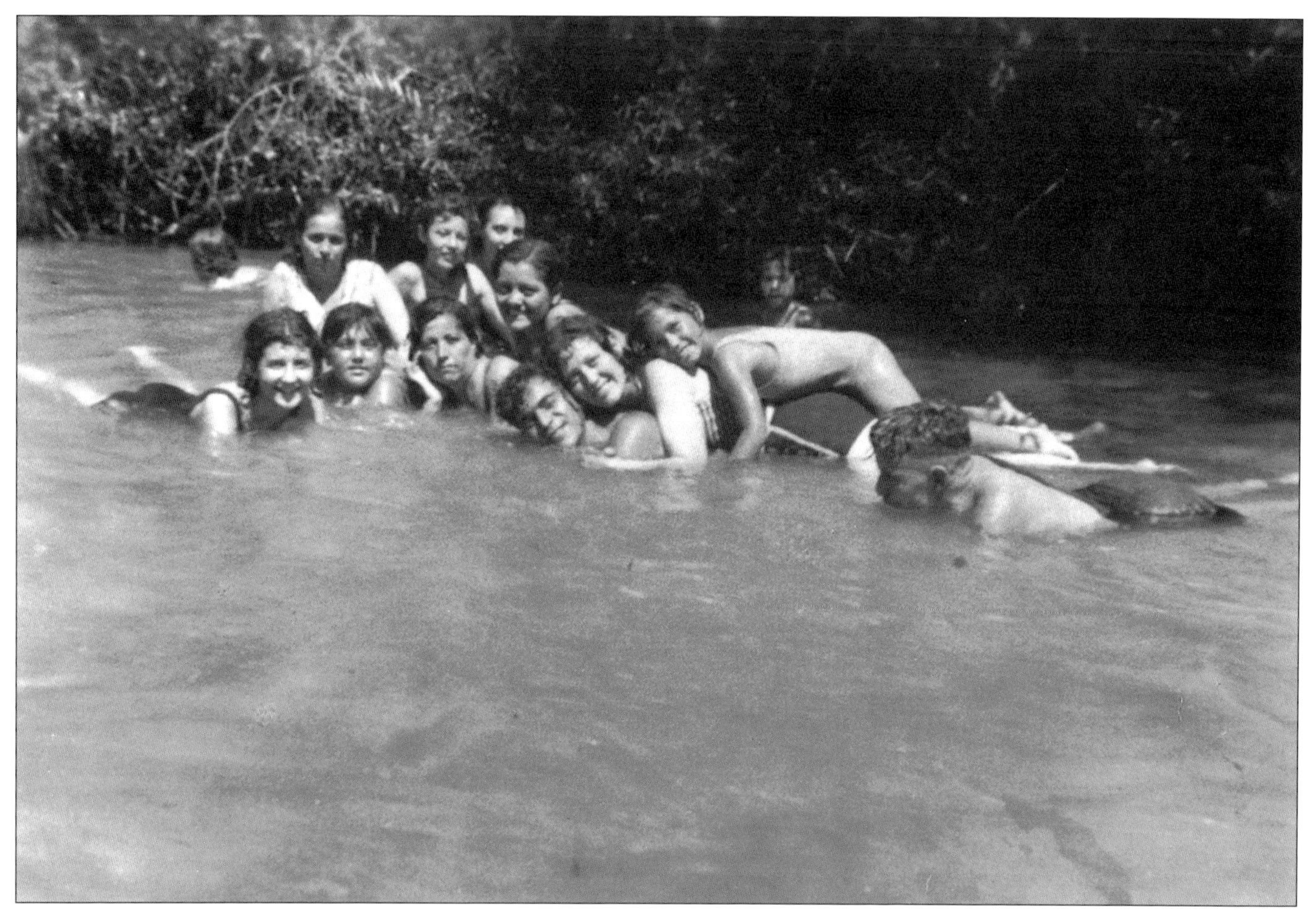

THE CASTRO FAMILY AND FRIENDS

on a summer day at the Santa Ana River, 1934.
(Mexican American)

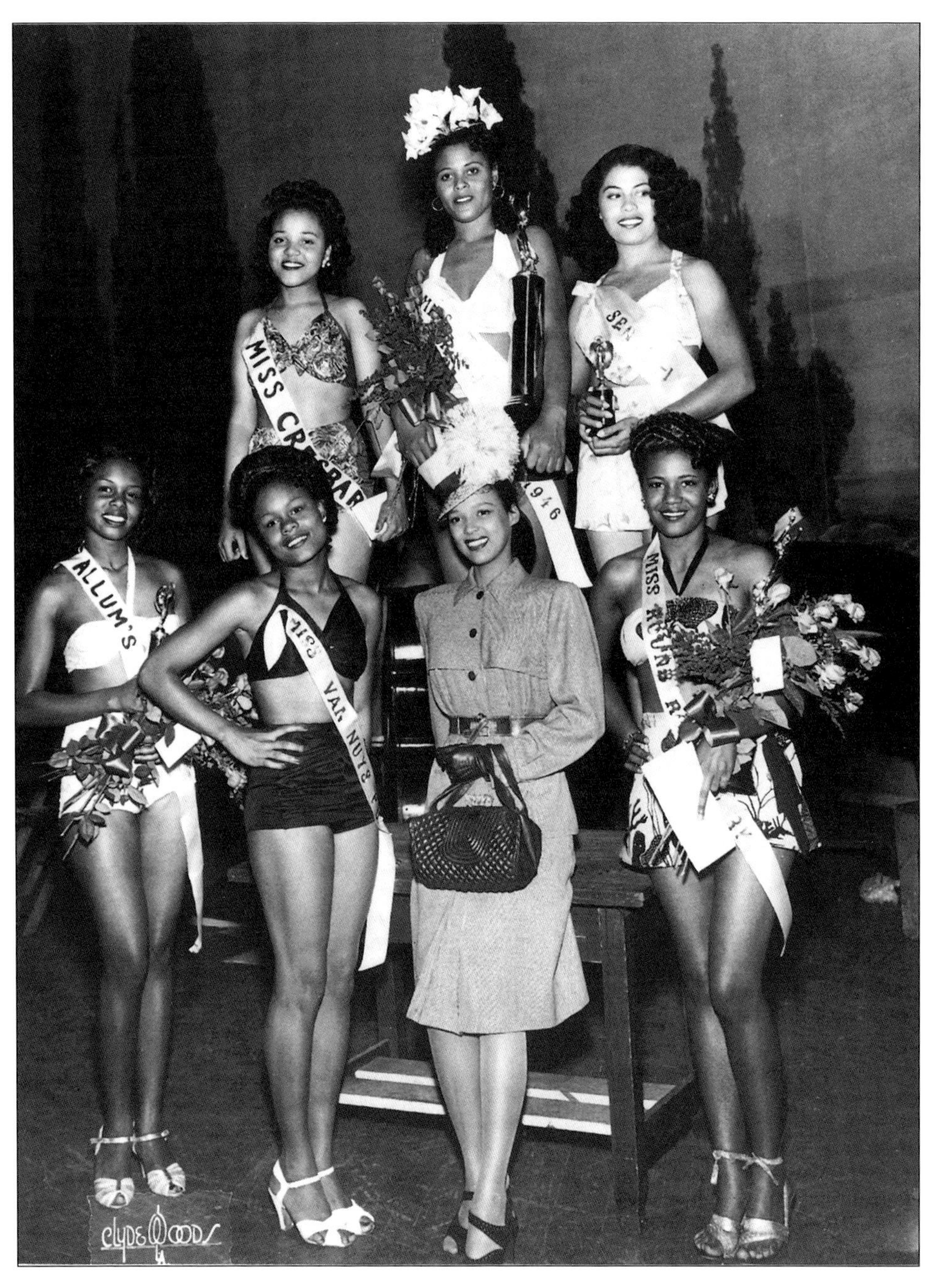

Beauty contest winners with actress Dorothy Dandridge *(first row, third from left)*, photographed by Clyde Woods in Los Angeles, 1946.
(African American)

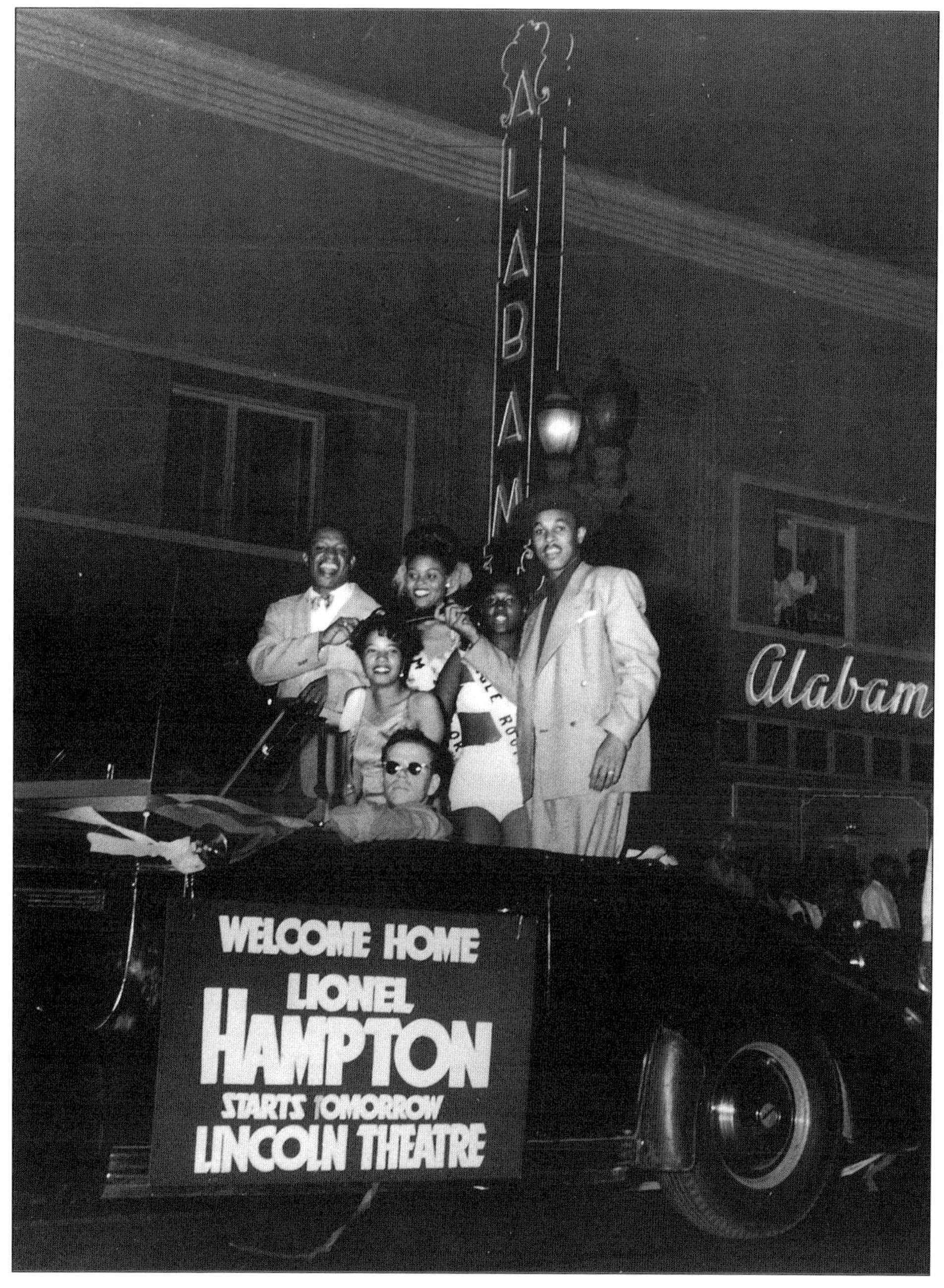

THE CLUB ALABAM

on Central Avenue, a busy thoroughfare of African American businesses, jazz nightclubs, and homes ranging from the modest to the stately, early 1950s.
(African American)

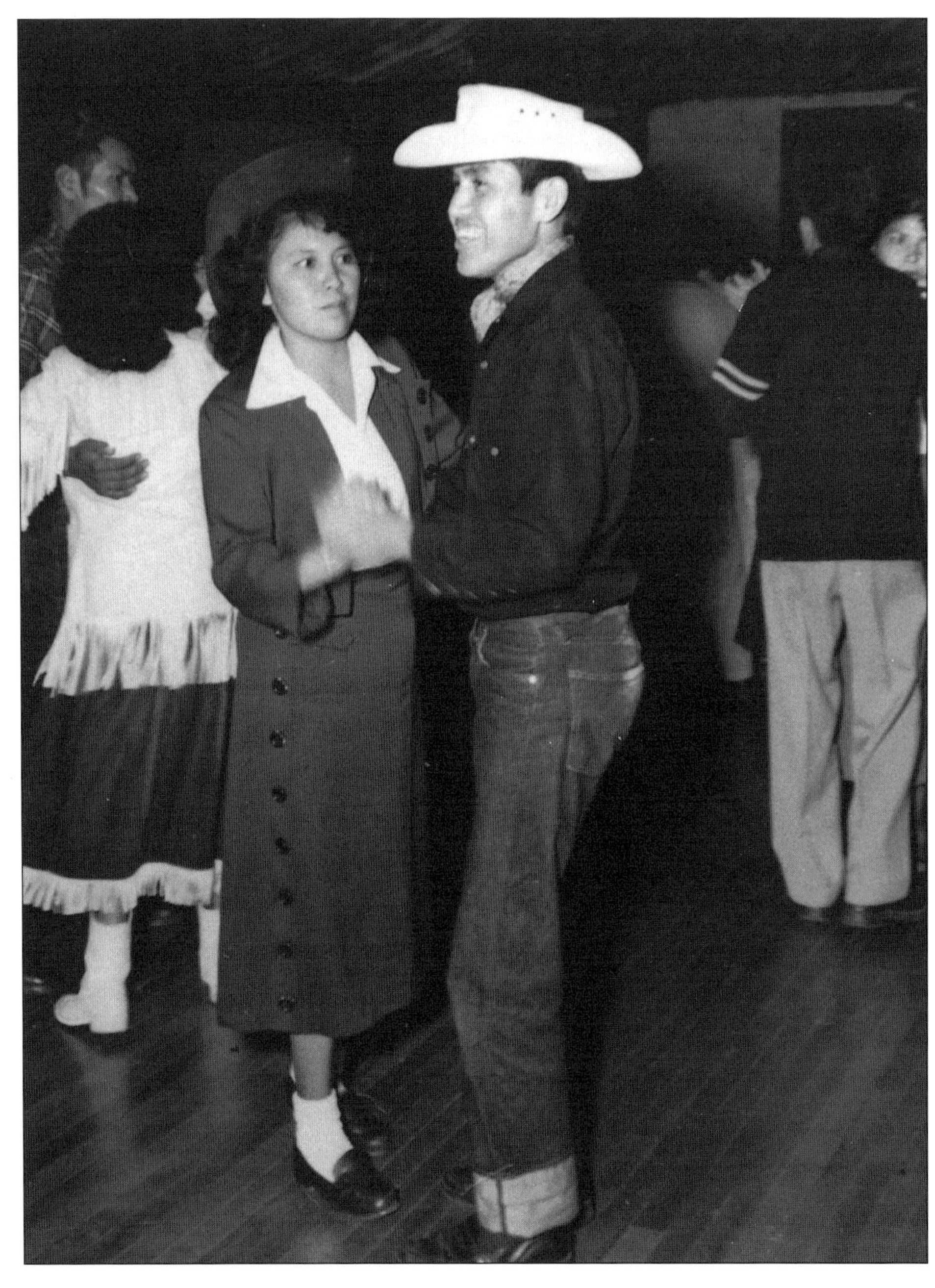

Students at the Sherman Institute,
an American Indian boarding school in Riverside, ca. 1960s.
(American Indian)

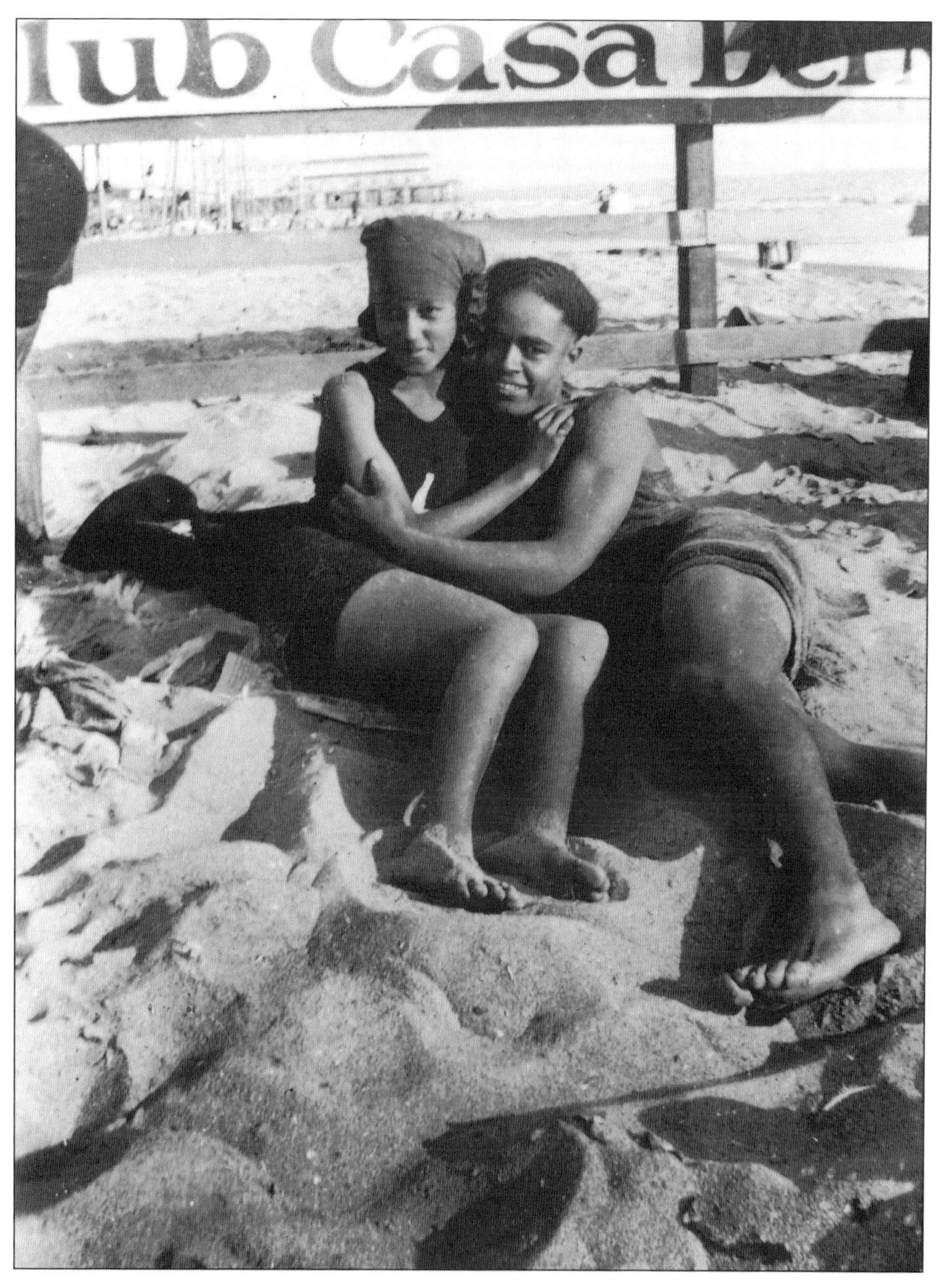

Arthur Lewis and Verna Deckard

at Santa Monica Beach in the segregated section, August 2, 1924.
They married later that month.
(African American)

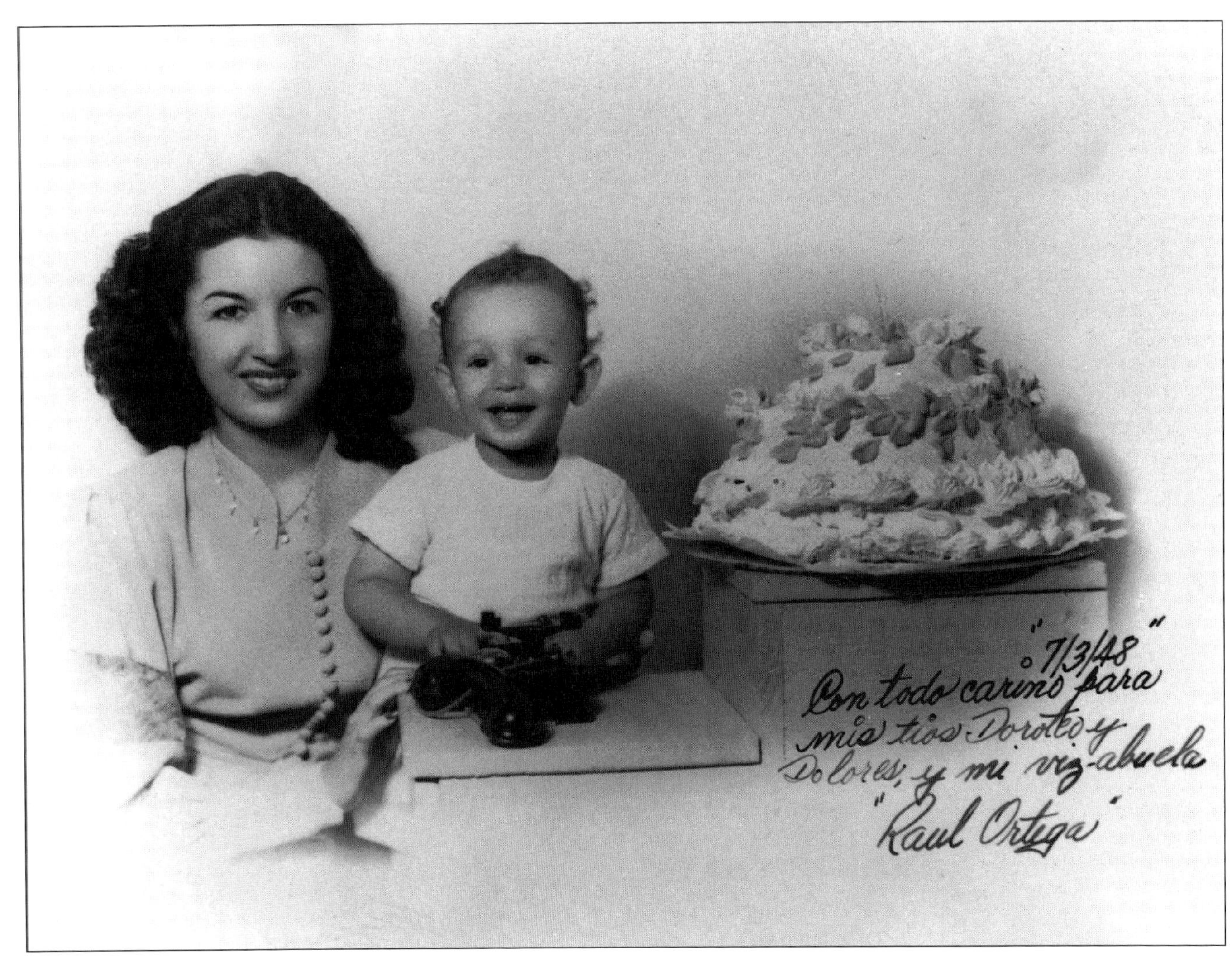

Stella Anaya Ortega and Raul Ortega

on his first birthday, July 3, 1948.

(Mexican American)

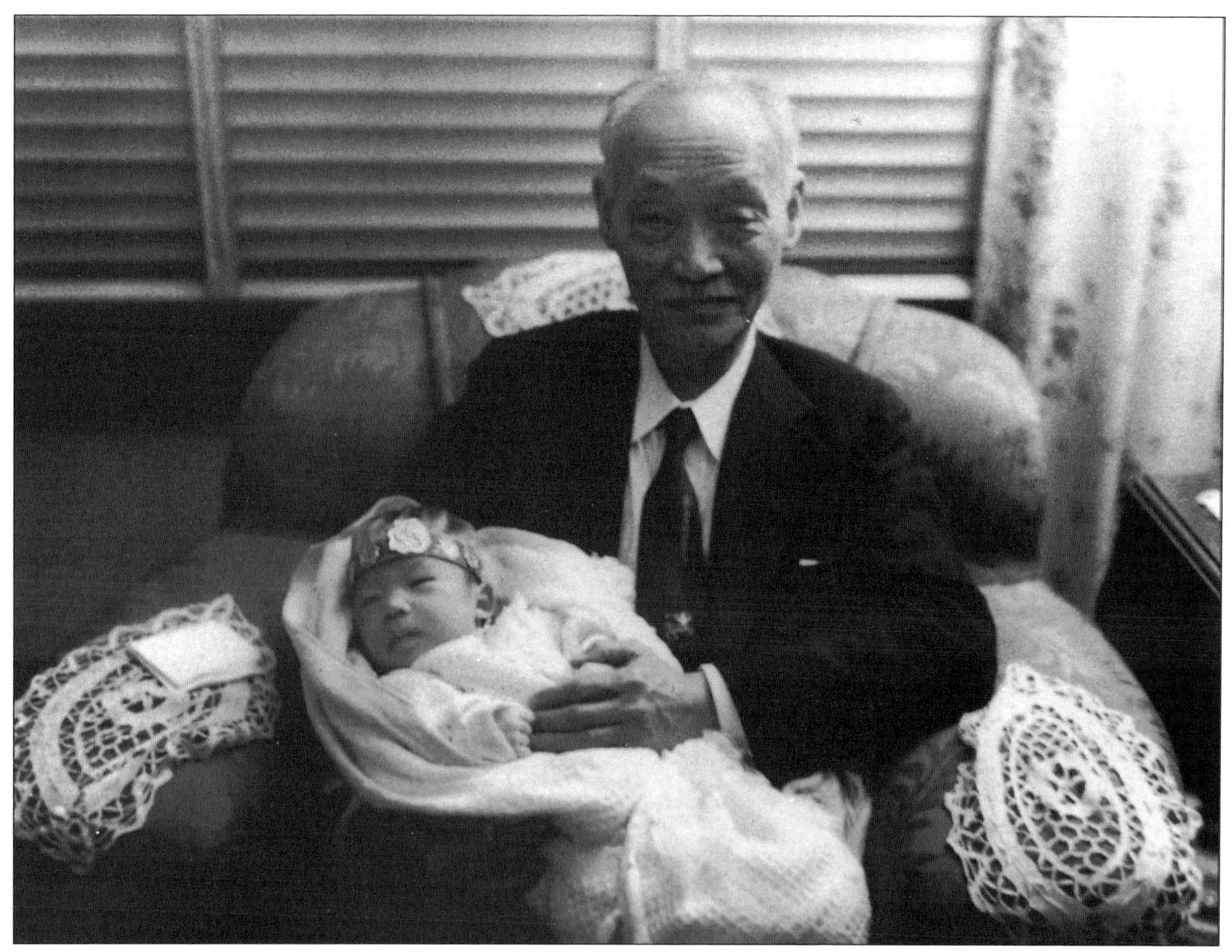

TOM CHONG HOLDING HIS GRANDNEPHEW, DEAN BRIAN TOM,

at the traditional celebration of the child's first month of life, 52nd Street and Broadway in Los Angeles, 1956. Tom is their family name: as an older Chinese immigrant with a Chinese given name, Tom Chong put his family name first, according to Chinese custom, but the baby, with his American given name, has his family name last.

(Chinese American)

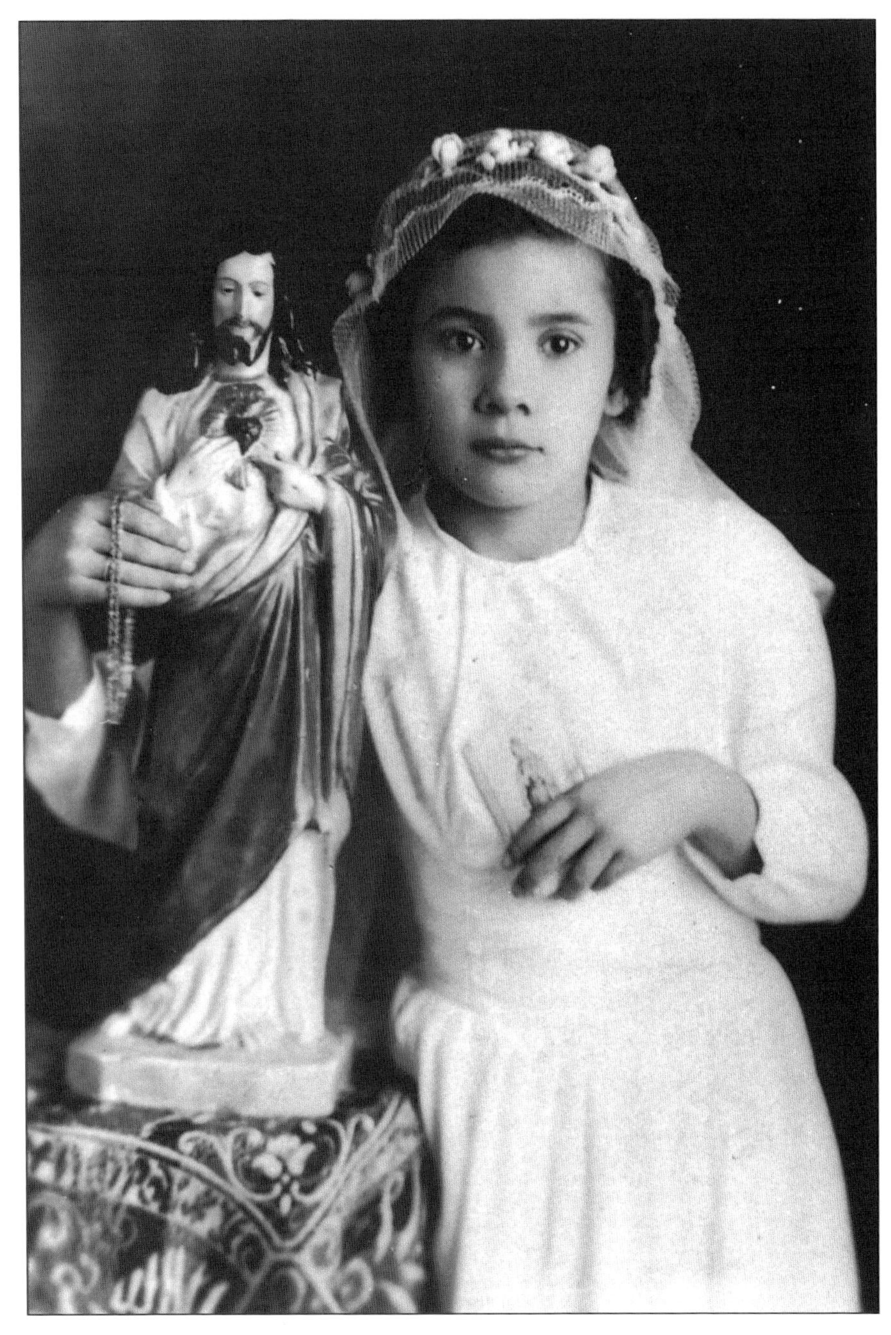

Helen Soto's first communion,

1944.
(Mexican American)

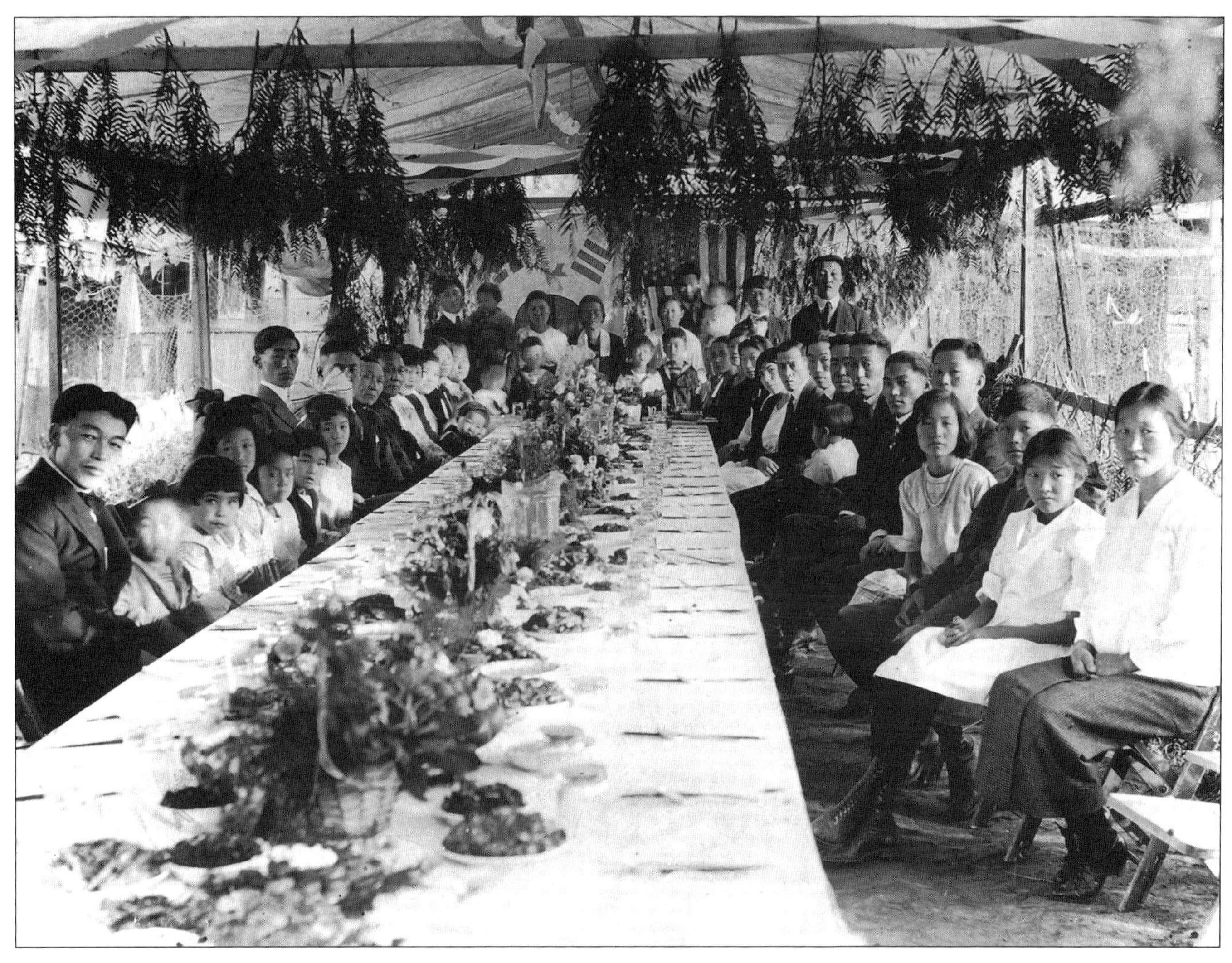

BIRTHDAY PARTY FOR SHANG SOON PARK

in Riverside, 1925.
(Korean American)

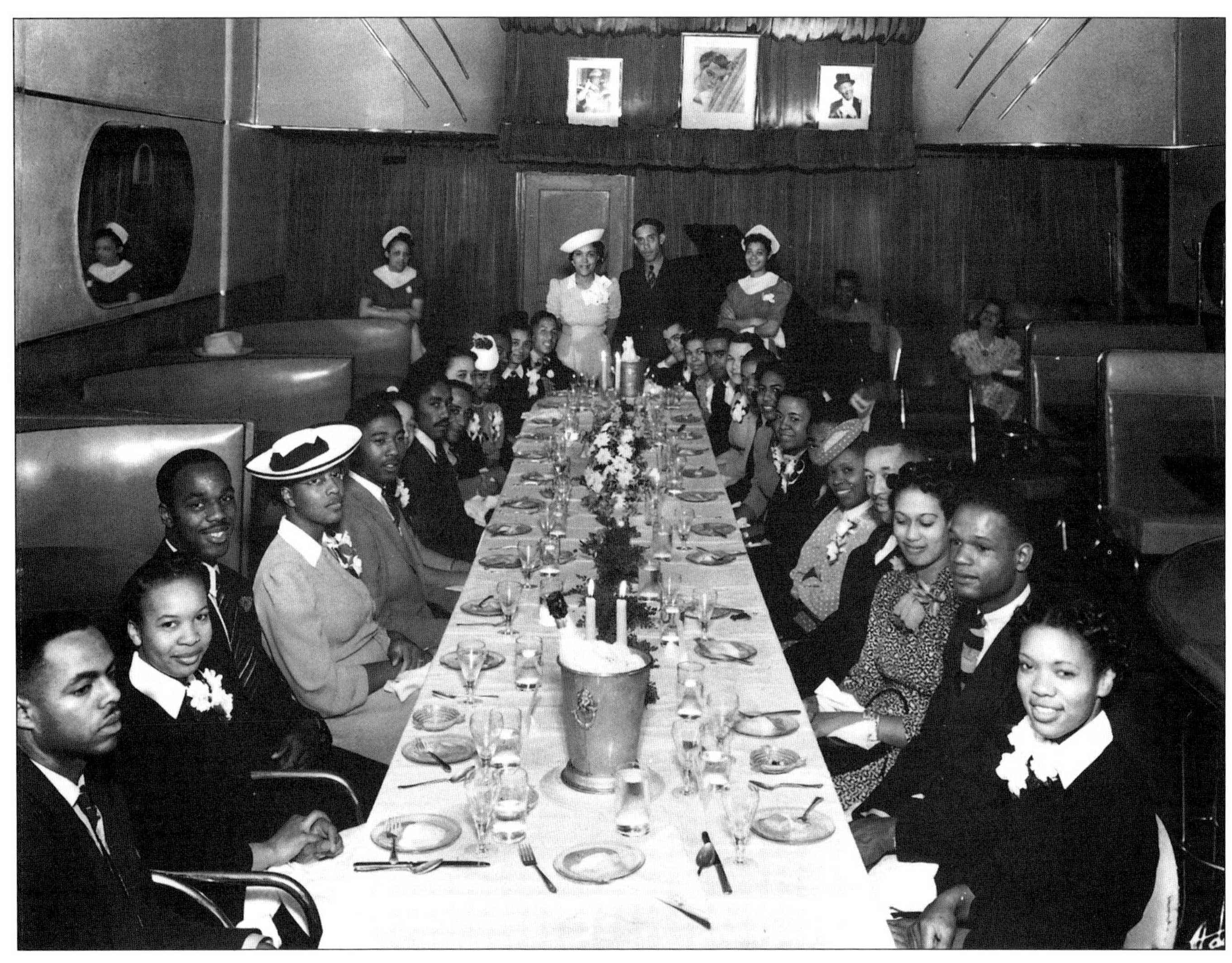

Nursing school graduation dinner

with Ruth Davis *(right side, third from front)* at the Me Mo Club at 42nd and Central 1940.
(African American)

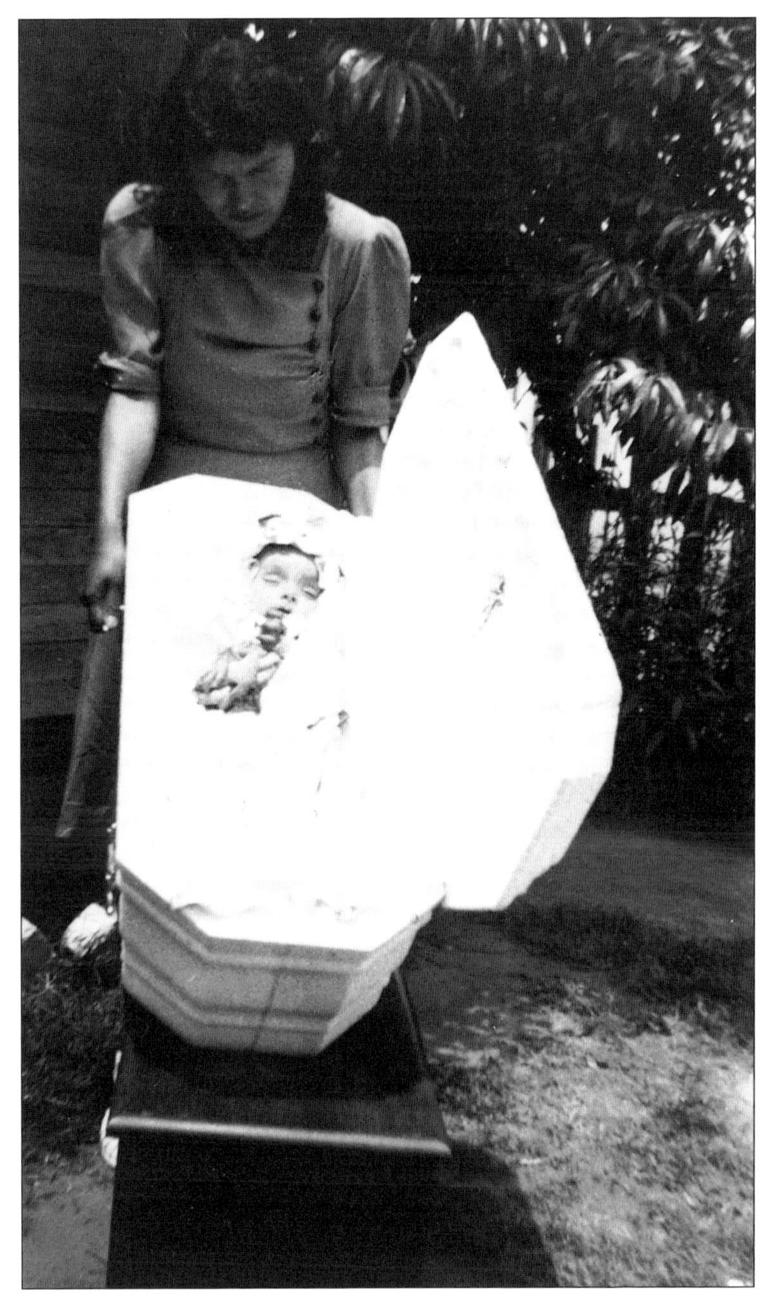

Felicita Viera

beside her deceased daughter, Rosemary, in Pico Rivera, ca. 1940.
(Mexican American)

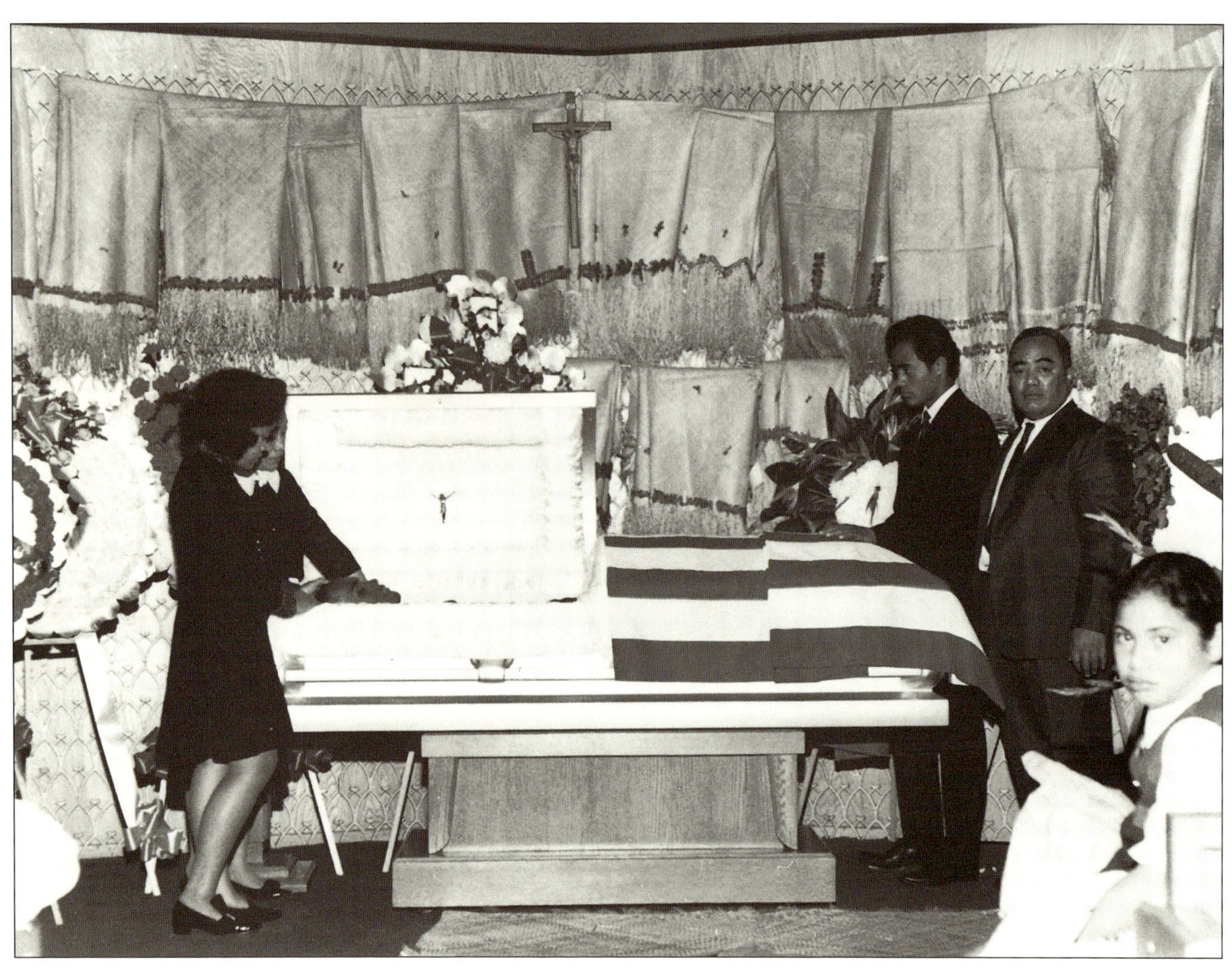

Pulu Momoli's funeral in 1969.

In the background, on the wall, are the traditional Samoanfine mats. These mats are used for both weddings and funerals and symbolize the social class of this family.

(Pacific Islander American/ Samoan)

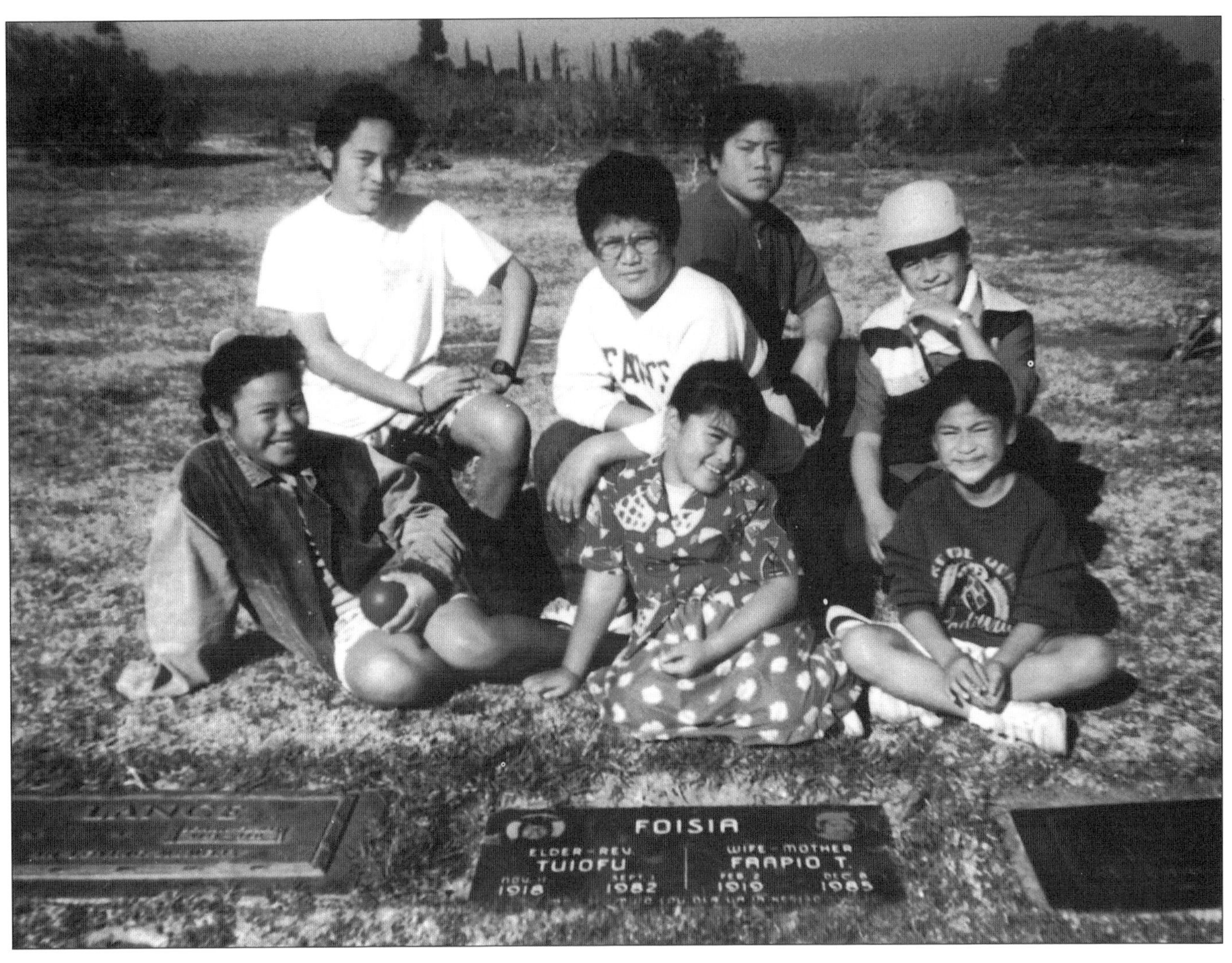

THE FOISIAS

at the family grave site at Greenhills Memorial Park in San Pedro, 1986.

(Pacific Islander American/ Samoan)

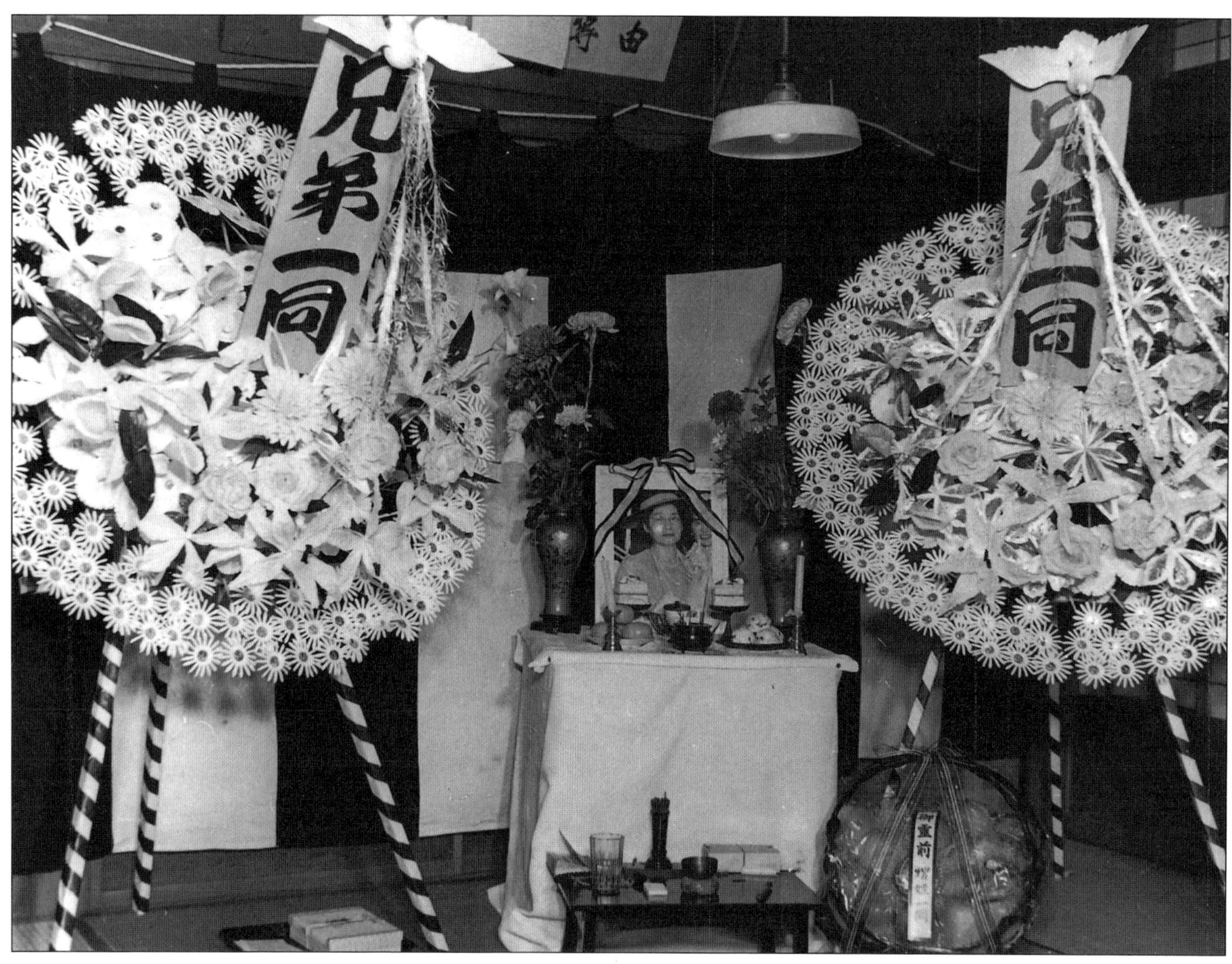

MEMORIAL SERVICE FOR OSAKI TAHARA IN JAPAN, 1957.

She was an issei, a first generation Japanese immigrant, who came to California in the 1910s. When she died, her funeral was held at the Gardena Buddhist Church, and she was buried in San Pedro, but her brothers, who had stayed in Japan, also held a memorial service for her, and sent this photo back to her family in California.

(Japanese American)

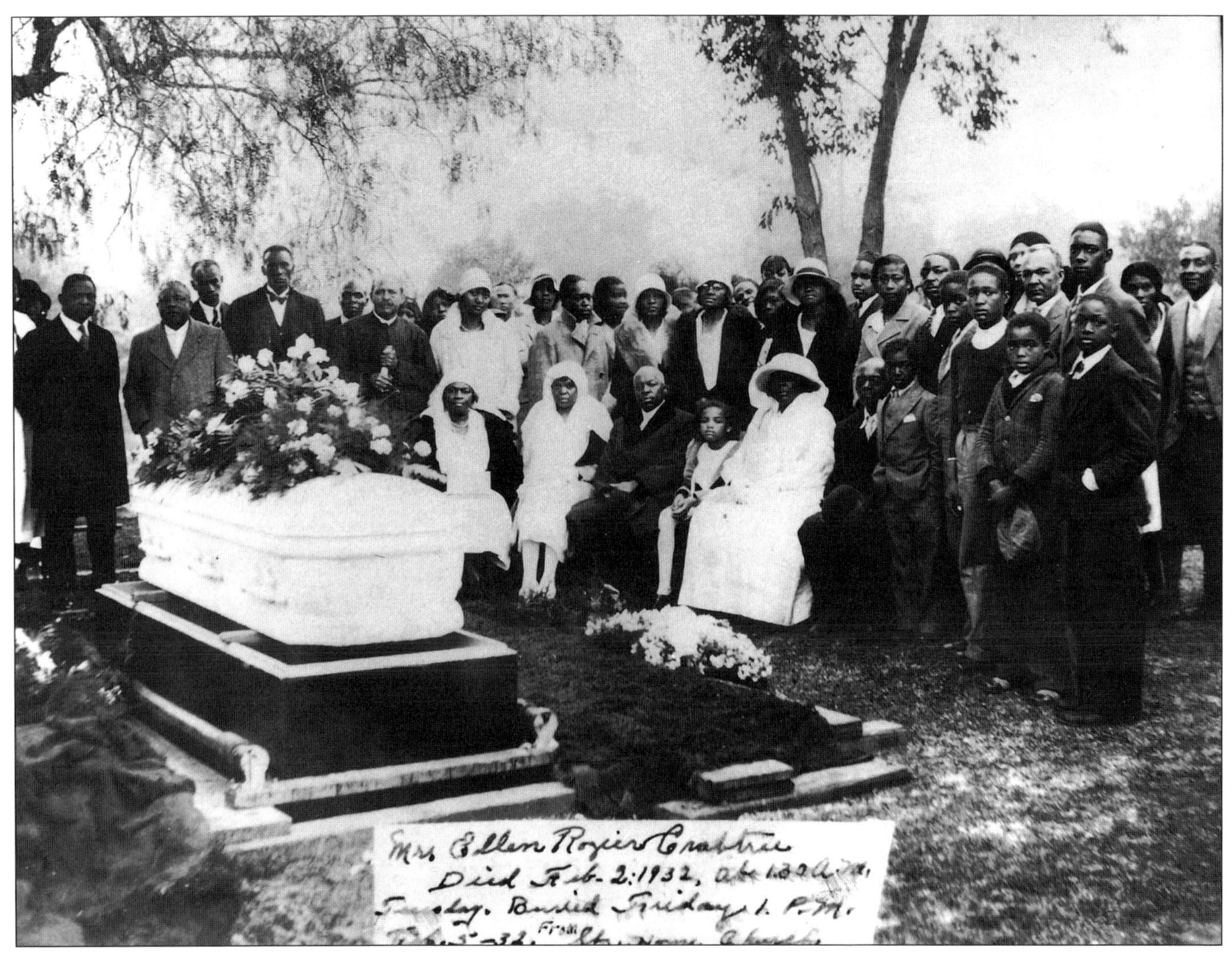

THE FUNERAL OF MRS. ELLEN ROZIER CRABTREE,

February 5th, 1932.

(African American)

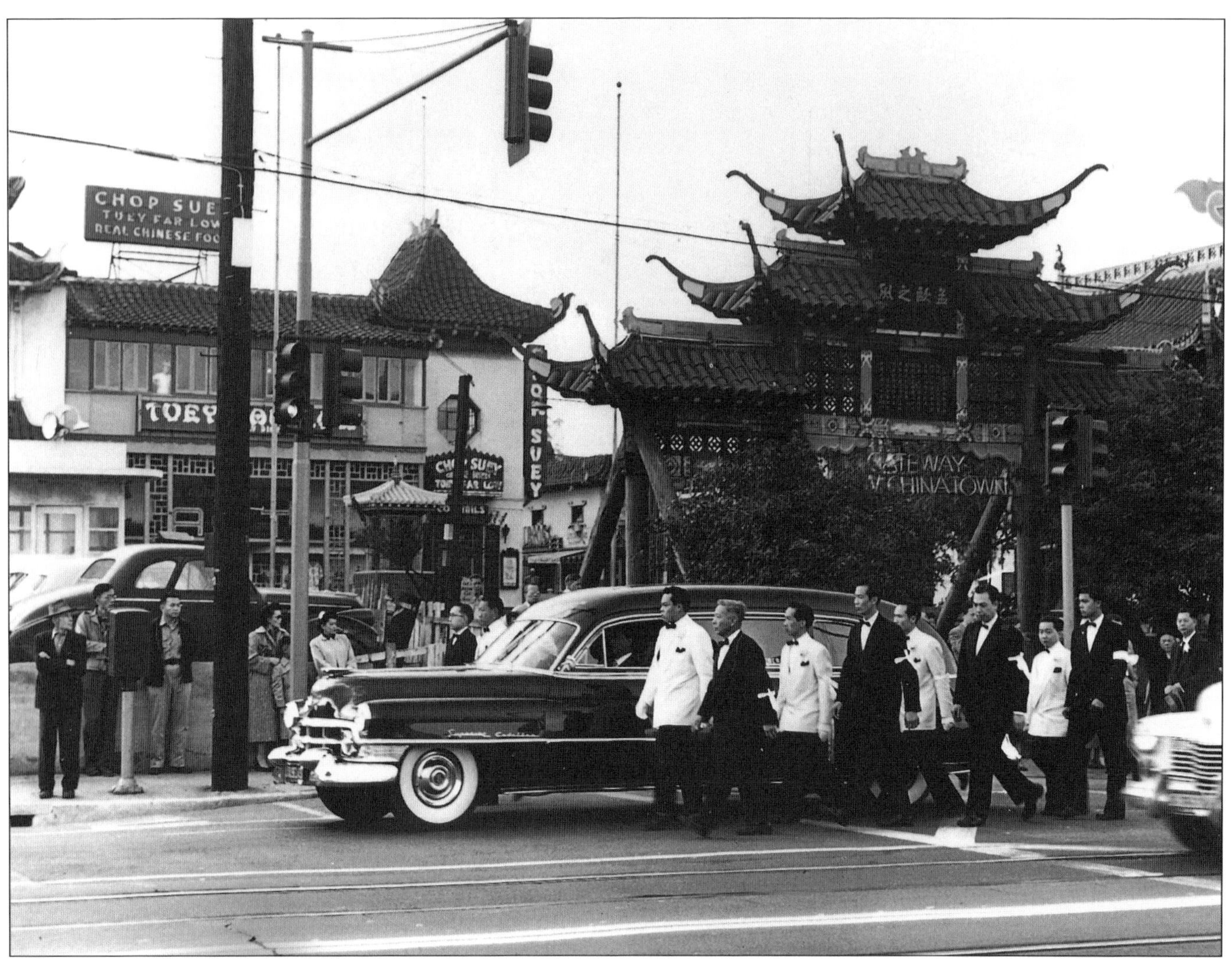

Funeral procession

on North Broadway in Chinatown for Edith Jung's grandfather, 1953.

(Chinese American)

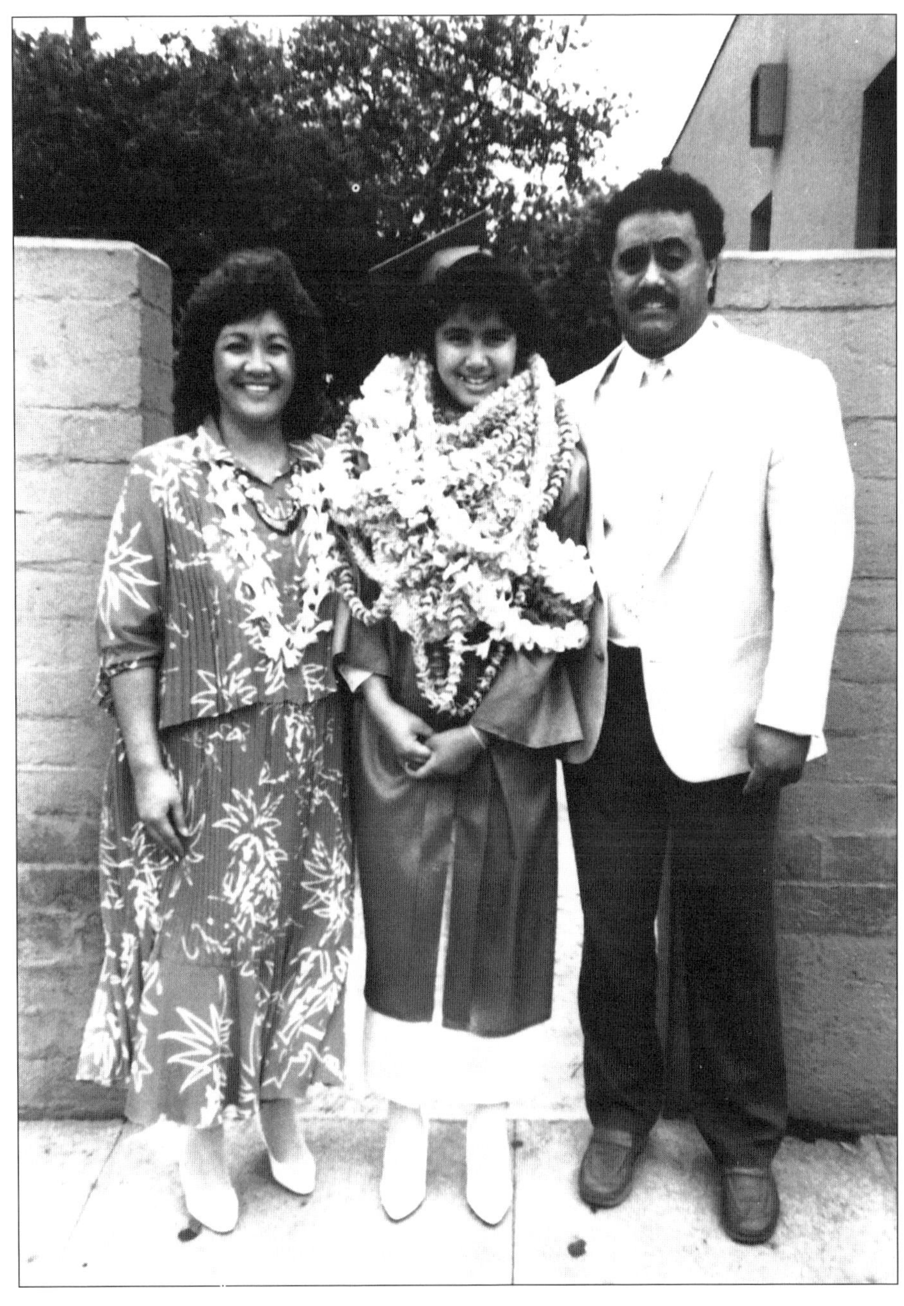

Jackie, Janny, and Sai Momoli at Janny's graduation

from St. Anthony High School in Long Beach, 1987.

(Pacific Islander American/ Samoan)

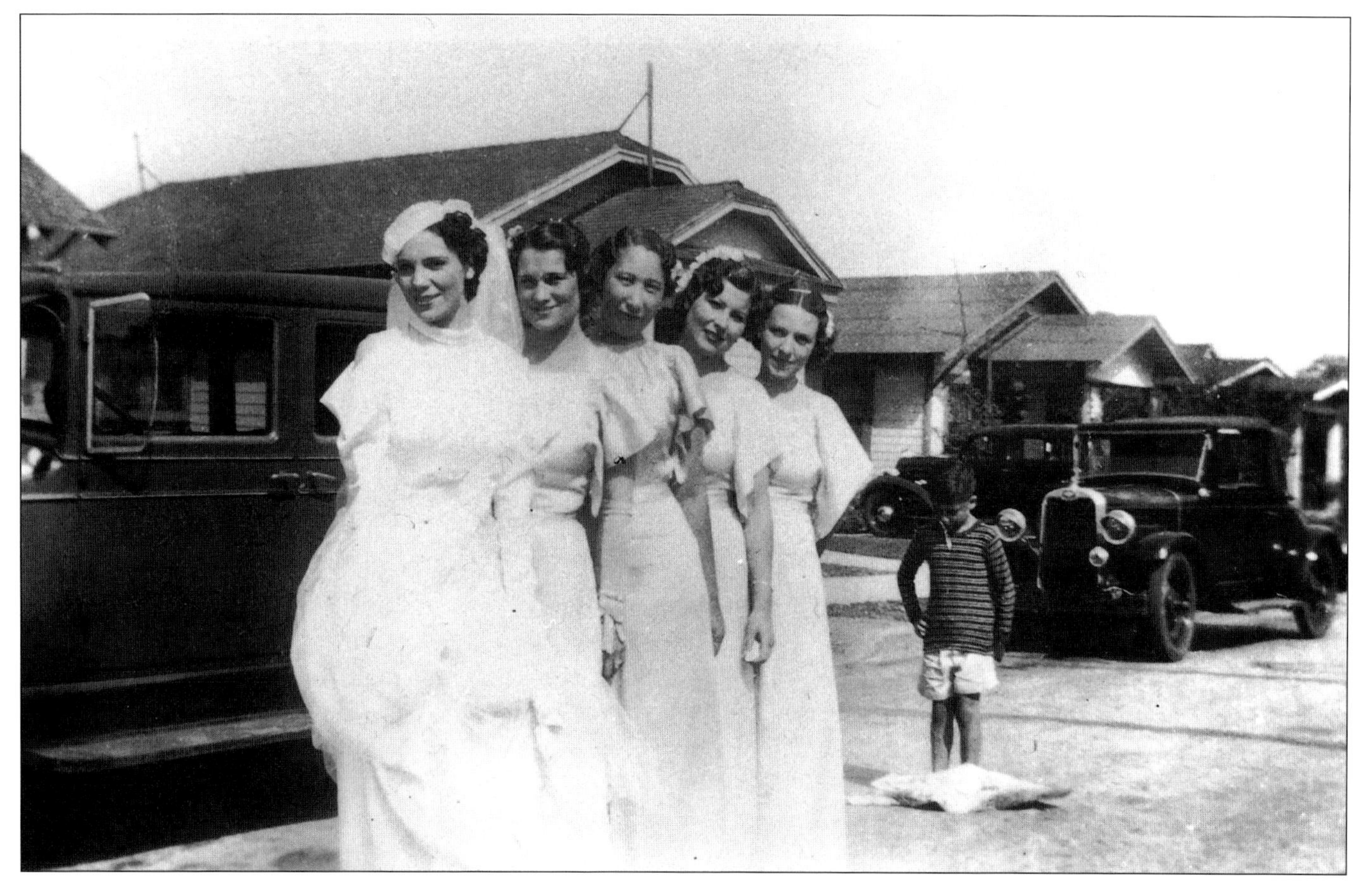

Adaline Vega and her bridesmaids

on the day of her wedding to Joe Vega, on Judson Street in Boyle Heights, ca. 1930s.
(Mexican American)

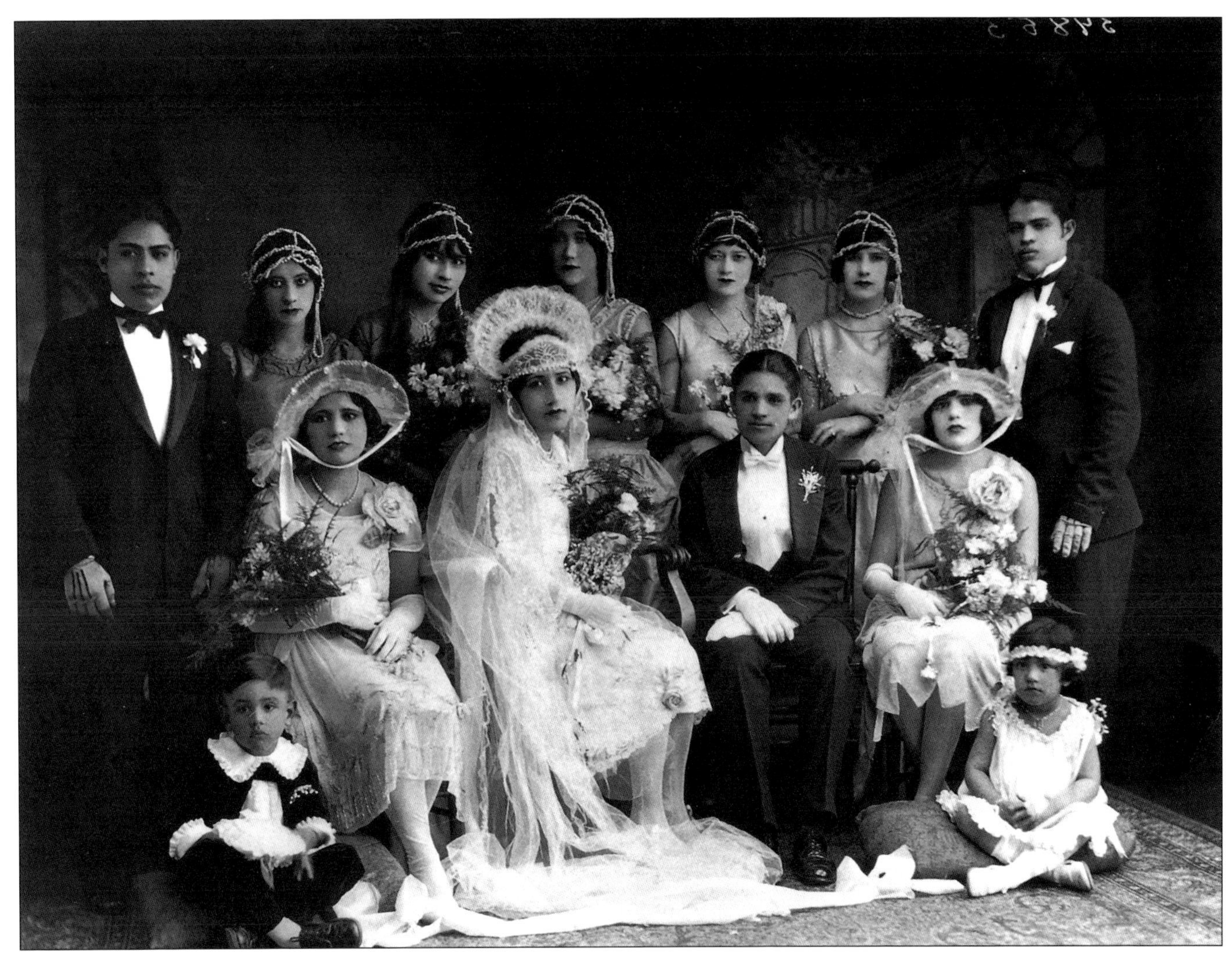

Wedding portrait

of cousins of Roberta Chavez *(not pictured)* in Los Angeles, ca. 1920s.
(Mexican American)

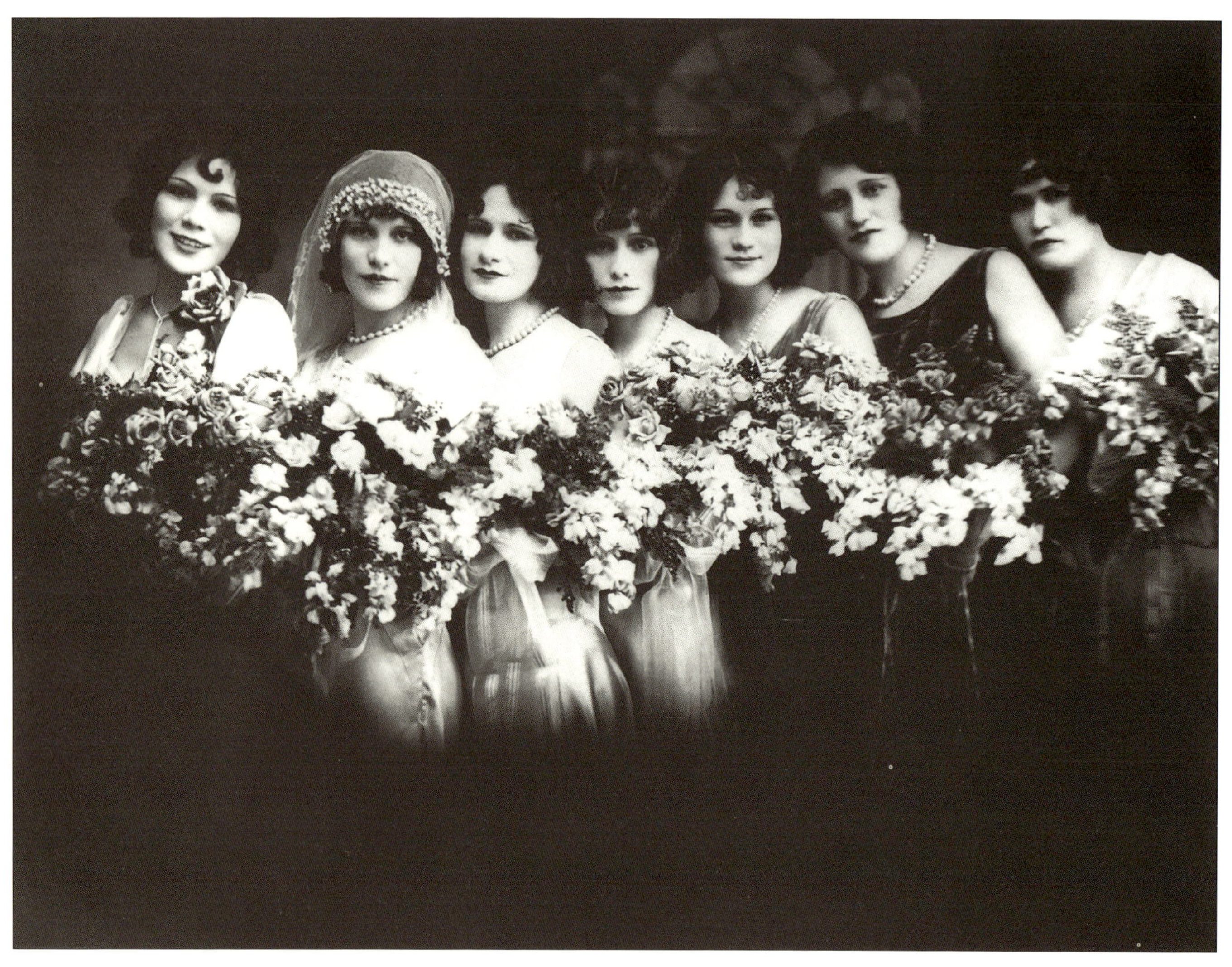

The Arciniega sisters

photographed at the wedding of Henrietta Arciniega
and Edward Turbay in Boyle Heights, September 4, 1931.
(Mexican American)

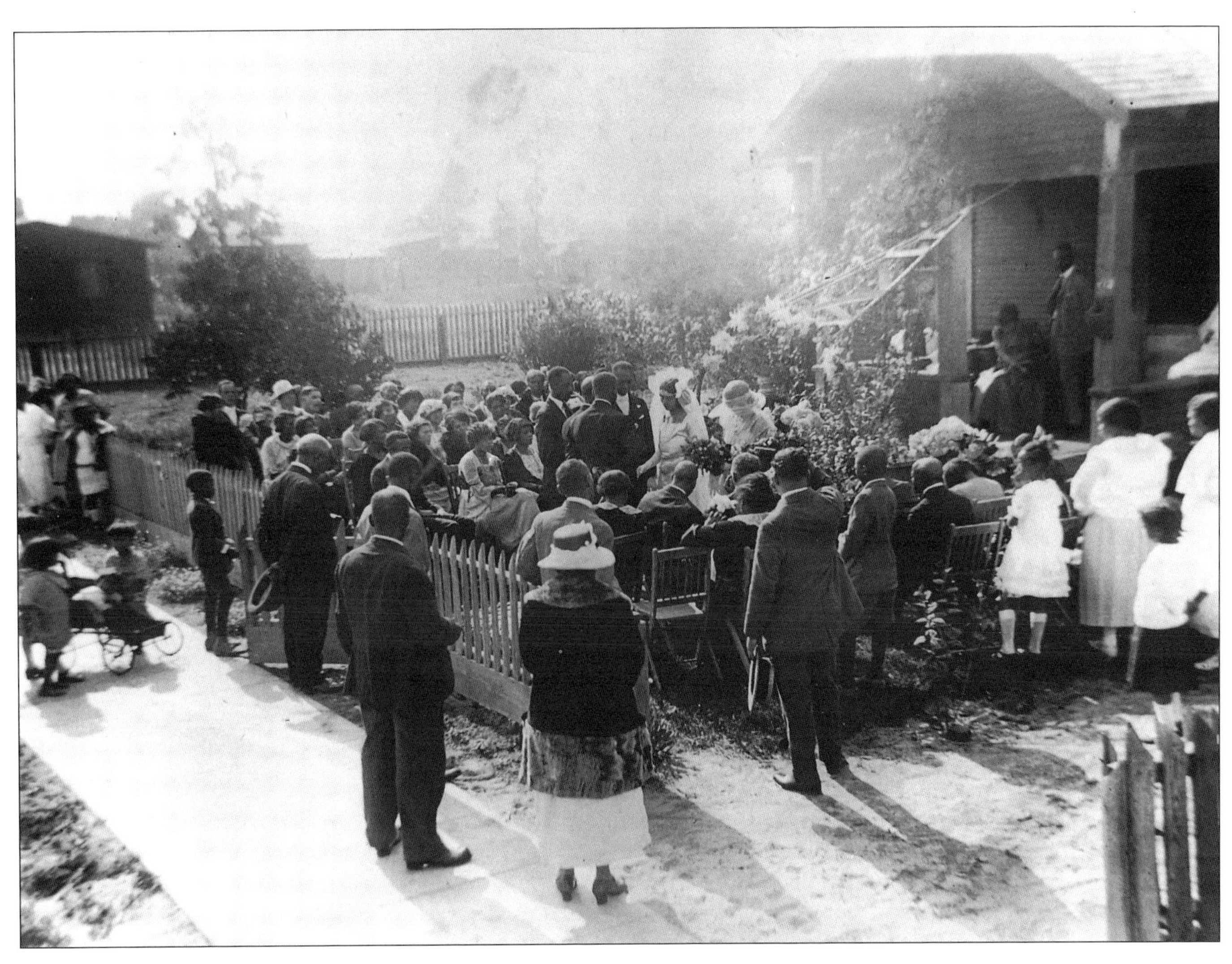

The wedding of John and Helen Cummings

in the groom's front yard on 111th Street in Watts, ca. 1920.
(African American)

Timeline of L.A. Ethnic History

This timeline presents an outline of important trends in the history of Los Angeles' major ethnic communities from the 1880s until the 1960s, when changes in laws and policies opened the way for significant new waves of immigration. This is the period covered by the first phase of the "Shades of L.A." project, which form the basis of this book. As explained in the introduction, later phases of the project are dealing with newer immigrants and more recent history.

In using this timeline, you can follow the grid horizontally to trace changes over time in the history of Los Angeles and its specific ethnic groups, or you can read the grid vertically in order to relate what is happening to different groups during the same period. For example, after looking at photos of African Americans at segregated beaches (pages 92 and 99), you can refer to the timeline and place those photos in the context of both the vibrancy of L.A.'s black community and the wide variety of discrimination against all ethnic groups in the city, which intensified in the 1920s.

Please note that the population figures, which are based on U.S. Census returns for Los Angeles County, should be taken only as rough estimates, particularly because ethnic populations were generally undercounted. It may also be interesting to note, especially for those unfamiliar with L.A. geography, that most of the specific places in this timeline and book are located east and south of downtown Los Angeles, in the traditionally ethnic areas of the city.

	1880
L.A. History	L.A.'s First Boom • railroads act as catalyst for growth, especially as the first direct transcontinental railroad to L.A. opens in 1886 • promoters tout L.A. climate to farmers, tourists, and health seekers • older economic base of agriculture expands
L.A. County Population	• 1880: 30,000 including area that became part of Orange County in 1889
Laws & Restrictions on Immigration and Ethnic Relations	• 1880–1948: state antimiscegenation laws limit marriage of whites and non-whites, including "Negroes and Mongolians" • 1882 Federal Chinese Exclusion Act restricts Chinese immigration
Mexican Immigrants, Mexican Americans	L.A.'s First Barrio • Mexicans settle in the Plaza area, near the original pueblo • increasing discrimination against Mexicans as Anglo American population rapidly increases and gains power and Mexican population drops below 50% • decline of the Californio families, descendants of the older Mexican leadership born in California when it was a province of Mexico • rise of Spanish-language press and social and political clubs
African Americans	African American Migration • blacks, migrating from Southern United States, are drawn by relatively high employment and good social conditions
Asian Immigrants, Asian Americans	L.A.'s First Chinatown • mostly male Chinese settle on east side of Plaza area • jobs in railroad work, farm labor, as servants, in small stores • fraternal and economic organizations form • increasing hostility toward Chinese, culminating in the end of Chinese immigration
American Indians	American Indians, Local and National • very few from local tribes (e.g., Gabrieleno, Chumash) remain in L.A. area due to high mortality rates from disease and poor working and living conditions • small scattered tribes persist throughout California • elsewhere in the U.S., Indian removal policies beginning in the 1810s forced tribes to move from their homelands to reservations and Indian territory • nationally, policies in the 1880s begin promoting the breaking up of reservations and tribal culture by replacing communal ownership with private property allotments

1890	1900	1910
CONTINUED GROWTH • population and economy of L.A. still growing, but at slower rate than in 1880s • rise of citrus industry • discovery of oil, which stimulates manufacturing	L.A. BECOMES A CITY • rise of the middle class and Progressive reform • large streetcar system set up • growth of early suburbs • rates of home ownership among all groups higher than in most other places in United States	SETTING THE STAGE FOR FURTHER GROWTH • 1913 water arrives via Owens Valley Aqueduct, overcoming the limits of local water supply • L.A.'s man-made harbor and Panama Canal open • World War I has little direct impact on California, especially compared to World War II
1890: 100,000	1900: 170,000	1910: 500,000
• state legislatures in the American South impose strict codes of racial segregation, contributing to black migration to other parts of the United States, including California	• 1905: state antimiscegenation laws strengthened • 1907–1908: federal legislation and the Gentlemen's Agreement end the immigration of Japanese laborers	• 1913: California alien land law prohibits "aliens ineligible to citizenship," meaning Japanese and other Asian immigrants, from owning land in the state
TRANSITION FOR L.A.'S MEXICANS • continuation of the patterns of the 1880s • Anglo American society begins to romanticize L.A.'s past as "Spanish," downplaying the importance of Mexicans	NEW PERIOD OF EXPANSION • Plaza area increasingly crowded, initiating movement to east of downtown, Boyle Heights • jobs in railroad work and farm labor • poor conditions for most	INCREASING IMMIGRATION • dramatic increase in population, due to Mexico's poor economy and upheavals of the Mexican Revolution • rise in segregation and racial tension
EMERGENCE OF NEIGHBORHOODS • blacks begin to settle in several neighborhoods, including downtown east of Main and other scattered areas • rising social organizations, newspapers, and churches	CONTINUED GROWTH • expansion into new areas south and east of downtown, Boyle Heights, and other scattered areas • many laborers and some businessmen • cases of housing discrimination and prejudice from local stores and businesses	L.A.'S BLACK COMMUNITY FLOURISHES • further expansion south of downtown on Central Avenue and in Watts • growth of social and political organizations • leisure at Bruce's Beach and in Santa Monica
JAPANESE POPULATION INCREASES • Japanese replace Chinese labor supply, which is now excluded from immigration • jobs in farm labor (later more as tenants and owners), gardening, fishing	MORE IMMIGRATION • more Japanese immigrants, especially before 1907 • migration from San Francisco after the earthquake • settling in Little Tokyo, Boyle Heights, Terminal Island, and some outlying areas • very small but politically influential group of Koreans move to L.A.	CONTINUED GROWTH • continued immigration of some Japanese, especially women, but no laborers • Japanese immigrant neighborhoods become more established • L.A.'s small Korean community organizes for Korean independence after annexation by Japan in 1910
NATIONAL POLICY VS. INDIAN CULTURE • for most American Indians, U.S. government attempts to break up reservations and tribes continue • in California, federal reservations are being formed for the first time • boarding schools and day schools established off reservations, beginning in the 1870s and 1880s, work to acculturate American Indian youth to American society	GOVERNMENT POLICY CONTINUES • Sherman Institute, a boarding school, established in Riverside, California, as part of the trend encouraging the acculturation of American Indian youth	

	1920	1930
L.A. History	Another Boom • rise in automobile ownership and consumer culture • growth of movie industry, aircraft manufacturing, oil production, and tourism	Great Depression • conditions in L.A. bad, but better than elsewhere in the country • continued migration from rest of U.S. • greatly decreased immigration • New Deal government programs provide jobs • 1932 Olympics in L.A. attract worldwide attention • union organizing increases
L.A. County Population	1920: 940,000	1930: 2,210,000
Laws & Restrictions on Immigration and Ethnic Relations	• 1924 Federal Immigration Act restricts Asian and European immigration, but has little effect on the continued immigration from Mexico • local restrictive housing covenants against non-whites increasing • segregation of beaches, pools, and social organizations	• 1934: national limits on Filipino immigration • restrictions from the 1920s continue
Mexican Immigrants, Mexican Americans	Rise of the Eastside Communities • vibrant communities emerge east of downtown—Boyle Heights, Lincoln Heights, and Belvedere—with active social organizations and churches • new communities are mostly Mexicans, but other ethnic groups, including European immigrants, mix in • Plaza area still important Mexican center • 1920: less than 100,000 of Mexican ancestry	Repatriation • deportation of Mexicans, including many U.S.-born citizens • 1930: 170,000 of Mexican ancestry
African Americans	Good Times and Bad Times • rise of Central Avenue • growth of black middle class, businesses, jazz nightclubs, social and political organizations • rise in racial discrimination—KKK becomes more active, blacks confined to smaller areas • 1920: 20,000 African Americans	Hard Times • rising unemployment and protest • "Don't Spend Your Money Where You Can't Work" campaign • 1930: 50,000 African Americans
Asian Immigrants, Asian Americans	Fewer Japanese, More Filipinos • end of Japanese immigration to the United States in 1924 • rise in immigration of Filipinos who come as U.S. nationals, especially for farm work • 1920: 20,000 of Asian ancestry—more than 80% are of Japanese ancestry	Rise of a New Generation • emergence of 2nd-generation Asian Americans, especially Japanese American nisei • few new immigrants to the United States, due to legal restrictions and poor economic conditions • 1930: 40,000 of Asian ancestry—percentage of those with Japanese ancestry slowly declining
American Indians	American Indians in L.A. Area • still very few Indians from local tribes • little migration to L.A. from other parts of U.S. • Sherman Institute in nearby Riverside County has 750 American Indian students from at least 15 tribes and 7 states • 1920: 300 American Indians in L.A. County	Indian New Deal • new government programs, including social relief and educational reform • increased recognition of tribes • 1930: 1000 American Indians

1940	1950	1960
World War II & Post-War Boom • many wartime jobs in L.A.—on military bases and in war industries, especially aircraft and ship building • labor shortage—more jobs for women and ethnics • huge post-war migration from rest of U.S., including those who spent time in California during military service	**Post-War Boom Continues** • rise of new suburbs and freeways • rise of TV and tourism—Disneyland opens • increased population due both to migration and to baby boom • Cold War intensifies	**Continued Growth and the Vietnam War** • increased defense and aerospace spending • social protest
1940: 2,790,000	1950: 4,150,000	1960: 6,040,000
• 1942: Federal Executive Order 9066 interns Japanese immigrants and Japanese Americans on West Coast • 1942: Federal Executive Order 8802 prohibits discriminatory hiring in defense industries • 1943–46: national restrictions on Chinese and Filipino immigration eased • 1948-53: restrictive housing covenants overruled by U.S. Supreme Court • 1948: state antimiscegenation laws declared unconstitutional	• 1952: Japanese naturalization and small Asian immigration quota allowed • state alien land laws invalidated	• 1964: Federal Civil Rights Act bans discrimination on the basis of race, color, creed, gender, or national origin • 1965: federal legislation ends quotas based on national origin and opens way for increased immigration from non-European countries, as well as from Europe • 1968: Federal Open Housing Act prohibits housing discrimination
Rise of a New Generation • emergence of second-generation Mexican Americans • Zoot Suit riots, with conflicts between Mexican American youth and Anglo servicemen • most Mexican Americans remain in East L.A. area, with some moving farther east • 1940: 190,000 of Mexican ancestry	**East L.A. Barrio** • Mexican Americans increasingly segregated from other ethnic groups, as well as from whites • Mexican American neighborhoods divided by freeway construction and disrupted by urban development • 1950: 290,000 of Mexican ancestry	**More Immigrants and More Activists** • increasing immigration from Mexico and Central America • increasing political involvement, especially among U.S.-born Mexican Americans, some in political offices, some in Chicano movement • 1960: 580,000 of Mexican ancestry
Next Big Wave of Migration • dramatic increase in black population, due to wartime and post-war jobs • Central Avenue jazz scene thrives and business district continues • 1940: 80,000 African Americans	**Crowding and Protest** • Civil Rights movement begins throughout U.S. • large African American population increasingly crowded into old neighborhoods through de facto segregation • 1950: 220,000 African Americans	**Crowding and Protest Continues** • 1965 Watts Rebellion erupts in South Central L.A. • increasing political protest, including Black Power militance as well as more main-stream political action • 1960: 460,000 African Americans
Asian American Experiences during World War II • West Coast Japanese Americans forced into internment camps, yet some serve in U.S. military • status improves among Asian Americans whose mother countries are U.S. allies—Chinese, Koreans, and Filipinos • 1940: 50,000 of Asian ancestry	**Stability and Transition** • limited number of immigrants, including war brides • small Pacific Islander immigration from Samoa, Tonga, Guam, and Hawaii to L.A. begins • movement to the suburbs by post-internment Japanese Americans and other Asian Americans • 1950: 50,000 of Asian ancestry—those of Japanese ancestry decline from 85% in 1920 to 65% by the late 1950s	**New Wave of Asian Immigration** • new Asian immigration allowed after 1965 changes in federal law, drawing primarily Chinese and Koreans, and later, Vietnamese and Southeast Asians • 1960: 120,000 of Asian ancestry
Beginning of Movement from Reservations • American Indians from around the U.S. begin leaving reservations for military service and wartime jobs, some migrating to L.A. area • 1940: 1400 American Indians	**Urban Relocation** • government programs subsidizing relocation of American Indians from reservations to cities • American Indians also drawn by the more general economic pull of post-war jobs • 1950: 1700 American Indians	**American Indian Activism** • movement toward self-determination, which promotes strengthened tribal authority and tribal culture • rise of political activism and Red Power protests • 1960: 8000 American Indians